Doing Honest Work in College

Chicago Guides to Academic Life

Doing Honest Work in College

HOW TO PREPARE CITATIONS,

AVOID PLAGIARISM, AND ACHIEVE

REAL ACADEMIC SUCCESS

Third Edition

Charles Lipson

The University of Chicago Press CHICAGO AND LONDON

The University of Chicago Press, Chicago 60637
The University of Chicago Press, Ltd., London
© 2004, 2008, 2018 by Charles Lipson
Published 2018
Printed in the United States of America

27 26 25 24 23 22 21 20 19 18   1 2 3 4 5

ISBN-13: 978-0-226-43074-4 (paper)
ISBN-13: 978-0-226-43088-1 (e-book)
DOI: https://doi.org/10.7208/chicago/[9780226430881].001.0001

Library of Congress Cataloging-in-Publication Data

Names: Lipson, Charles, author.
Title: Doing honest work in college : how to prepare citations, avoid
    plagiarism, and achieve real academic success / Charles Lipson.
Other titles: Chicago guides to academic life.
Description: Third edition. | Chicago ; London : The University of
    Chicago Press, 2018. | Series: Chicago guides to academic life | Includes
    bibliographical references and index.
Identifiers: LCCN 2018021878 | ISBN 9780226430744 (pbk. : alk. paper) |
    ISBN 9780226430881 (e-book)
Subjects: LCSH: Bibliographical citations. | Plagiarism. | Research—Study
    and teaching.
Classification: LCC PN171.F56 L56 2018 | DDC 808.02/7—dc23
LC record available at https://lccn.loc.gov/2018021878

♾ This paper meets the requirements of ANSI/NISO Z39.48–1992
(Permanence of Paper).

To the memory of

Dorothy Kohn Lipson

and Harry M. Lipson Jr.

Models of integrity

Google search: "free ethics paper"

8,630,000 results, ironically

—Search on November 18, 2017

CONTENTS

. . . .

Academic Honesty
. . . .

THE THREE PRINCIPLES
OF ACADEMIC HONESTY

• • • • • • • • • • • • • •

Academic honesty boils down to three simple but powerful principles:

- When you say you did the work yourself, you actually did it.
- When you rely on someone else's work, you cite it. When you use their words, you quote them openly and accurately, and you cite them too.
- When you present research materials, you present them fairly and truthfully. That's true whether the research involves data, documents, or the writings of other scholars.

These are bedrock principles, easy to remember and follow. They apply to all your classes, labs, papers, and exams. They cover everything from English papers to chemistry experiments, from computer codes to architectural drawings. They apply to everyone in the university, from first-year students to professors. They're not just principles for students. They're principles for academic honesty across the entire university.

Of course each university has its own code of conduct, and each class its own rules for specific assignments. In the next chapter I'll discuss these detailed rules and explain how to follow them in papers, labs, study groups, and exams.

I'll also discuss how to use the internet properly for assignments and what you can—and cannot—do with your laptop and cell phone on those assignments and exams. I'll show you how to cite websites, social media, and podcasts as well as books, articles, poems, films, and many other types of sources. With this brief book you can avoid plagiarism and handle nearly every citation you'll ever do, from computer science to visual arts.

Speaking of sciences, what about honesty in study groups and labs? That can be confusing because you sometimes work with fellow students and sometimes by yourself. What exactly are you supposed to do on your own, without any help? I'll pass along useful advice from lab supervisors, who explain how to use study groups effectively and how to avoid any problems.

On all these issues, I'll report on conversations with deans of students. They deal with academic honesty every day and know the issues well. Believe me, it's a lot better to read their advice here than to have them explain it to you privately! That is a meeting you do *not* want to have.

The most important advice is to *listen* to your professors' rules for each assignment, *ask* for clarification if you're unsure, and then *follow the three basic principles*: If you say you did this work, then you really did it. If you quoted others or used their research, you acknowledge it openly. If you say the data or lab experiment came out a particular way, then it really did. Never make up data, hide bad results, or present others' work as your own.

The most basic point is this: your work should be presented fairly and honestly. Don't misrepresent your findings or anyone else's. Don't misrepresent their ideas. Don't misrepresent the paper or exam as solely your own if you relied on someone else. Give credit where it is due. In a paper, cite your sources. In an exam, do the work yourself.

If you follow this straightforward advice, you'll stay on the right side of your university's rules and meet the highest standards of academic integrity. You will actually learn the material, and your grades will be honestly earned.

Now let's get down to nuts and bolts.

2

ACADEMIC HONESTY FROM YOUR FIRST CLASS TO YOUR FINAL EXAM

· · · · · · · · · · · · · · ·

What does it mean to do honest work in college? This chapter explores everyday issues and offers practical solutions, beginning with reading assignments and exams. From the first day of classes, you'll be required to read books and articles, and perhaps watch videos, perform lab experiments, and do group assignments. It's important to know what's expected. It's also important to know what's expected in seminars and discussion sections, as well as specialized classes such as foreign languages. I'll cover all of those and offer concrete advice, all of it to help you do your best work.

Within a few weeks you'll be taking midterm exams. Whether they are in-class or take-home, all exams share one basic rule: you have to do your own work without "borrowing" from others. But beyond that, the rules vary. I'll discuss these different rules and explain what to do if you're unsure about them.

Next I'll turn to one of the most important tasks in college: writing papers. Research for these papers requires you to draw on others' work and combine it with your own ideas. That means taking clear notes and using quotes and citations properly. I'll explain how to do that in this chapter and the next, showing you how to take notes that clearly separate your words and ideas from another author's. I'll explain how to quote and paraphrase in your papers and how to cite the works you rely on, whether they're in print or online.

Readings, exams, and papers are all individual assignments. Other assignments, however, require you to work closely with fellow students. In chemistry and biology, for example, you'll work alongside a lab partner. In statistics and computer science you may join a study group. What are you supposed to do together? And what are you supposed to do separately? I'll explain.

I'll also explain what to do about a low grade. One thing you can always do is get advice about how to do better next time. Teachers *want* to help students. Most are happy to aid students who want to improve and are willing to work at it. You can also appeal if you think your paper was graded too harshly. To do that, though, you need to follow some basic guidelines. You can't change anything on the paper or exam, and you should offer a clear, sensible reason for the appeal. I'll explain that later in the chapter.

Finally, I'll discuss honor codes, which some colleges use to encourage honest work and personal responsibility.

The aim of this chapter, then, is to give you an overview of what it means to do honest work in college and take you step by step through the issues you'll confront. I'll discuss reading assignments, exams, papers, study groups, and labs, and I'll offer some suggestions about problems that occasionally crop up. I'll also pass along some tips about studying more effectively. All these ideas point toward a single goal: honest learning.

READING ASSIGNMENTS

From the first day of class, you'll get reading assignments. It's a mistake to skip the reading—but it's not cheating. Some students read summaries (such as SparkNotes or CliffsNotes) to supplement their readings or even to substitute for them. As supplements they're fine, if you think they help. As substitutes, however, they shortchange your education. You're missing a chance to read and learn from books of lasting value. But you aren't violating any academic rules.

> *Tip on reading more efficiently*: Don't sit down, start reading the first page of an article or nonfiction book, and try to read it straight through. It helps to get an overview first. Look at the introduction, conclusion, and table of contents. If it's an article, read the abstract and section headings. Then read the introduction and conclusion. You don't have to keep the ending secret. It's not a mystery novel. After this overview, you'll have a good sense of the overall work and can begin more detailed reading. That's exactly how your professors do it.

EXAMS

Exams come in two delicious flavors: in-class and take-home. Because the formats are different, so are the rules governing them. Let's consider each briefly.

In-Class Exams

Most in-class exams are "closed book." They don't allow you to consult any materials such as handwritten notes or data stored on your computer or mobile device. You might be asked to bring your own blue books to an exam—blank ones, of course. Those are the default rules for in-class exams, and they are rarely changed. Stick to them unless you are explicitly told otherwise. If you are unsure about a particular exam, simply ask your professor.

Along the same lines, you should not have access to an exam before it is given. You may be able to guess what's on the exam, and it's fine to look at last year's or last semester's. But current exams are off limits until you take them. It's cheating to pass the questions from this morning's exam to a friend who takes it this afternoon.

Occasionally teachers give open-book exams in class. Students can use their notes, thumb through their books, consult their mobile devices, and type answers on their laptops during the test (though not prior to it). At least those are the normal rules for open-book tests. They certainly cut down on dull work and rote memorization, but they don't make the tests any easier. Students still need to know the material well so they can write compelling answers and, if necessary, find essential information quickly. Just remember: even if the test is open book, you can't drag and drop material from an online source into your answer. Instead you can consult other sources to write your own answer. Follow the usual rule: you can't present someone else's work as your own, whether it's an exam, paper, or lab assignment.

In one legendary test, a teacher explained that his next exam would be open book and students could use "anything you can carry into class." One arrived carrying a graduate student. That student deserves an A for effort and has a bright future as a lawyer!

Actually, you have to write your exams without any help. That's true whether they are open or closed book. No glances at other students' papers. No downloading precooked answers from the internet or your laptop. No text messages. No using others' words and ideas without proper quotes and citations. And, unfortunately, no carrying in graduate students, even very light ones.

> *Tip on in-class exams*: The default rule for exams is that they are "closed book." You can't use notes, books, articles, or online materials when you write your answers, unless you are specifically told otherwise.

It's fine to study together before exams. Practicing answers is a great way to study—or, rather, it's great *if* you participate actively in the group. It doesn't help much if you just sit and listen. (That's one reason why small study groups are better than large ones.) Once you are inside the exam room, however, you are on your own. That's a central pillar of academic honesty.

Learn from Woody Allen's experience: "I was thrown out of NYU my freshman year for cheating on the metaphysics final. . . . I looked within the soul of the boy sitting next to me."[1]

Take-Home Exams

Take-home exams are usually open book. You are permitted to use books, articles, notes, and the web. That's the standard policy, although it pays to check the rules for each exam.

Even if you are allowed to use published works and your own notes, you cannot ask others for help. That's cheating, just as it would be in class.

Similarly, if you incorporate ideas from books, articles, or the internet, you need to indicate that they are others' ideas. Even though it's an exam rather than a research paper, play it safe and cite any work you rely on. (Later I'll show you exactly how to do that.) If it's a direct quote, enclose it in quotation marks and include a specific citation. If you've paraphrased something, use your own words, not a close imitation of the author's. And, of course, you still need to cite the original source.

Even with proper citations and quotes, the work has to be your own. You can't copy chunks of text off the internet, drop them into your exam or research paper, pop in a citation or two, and call it your own. It's not. Cutting and pasting doesn't make it truly *your* exam or *your* paper; it's simply a patchwork quilt of others' work.

---

1. The quote is from *Annie Hall*, directed by Woody Allen, written by Woody Allen and Marshall Brickman (MGM/UA Studios, 1977; DVD, Santa Monica: MGM Home Video, 2003).

Actually the rules are even stricter, for both exams and papers. You cannot copy as much as a single sentence—from the web, a book, or anything else—*unless* you clearly mark it as a quote and cite it properly. Remember the basic principle: when you rely on someone else's work, you cite it; when you use their words, you quote them openly and accurately.

> *Tip on take-home exams:* You are usually permitted to use books, articles, notes, and the web for take-home exams, although it always pays to check. What you can *never* do is copy answers or ask anyone for help. The exam is still yours alone to complete. Whatever sources you use, phrase the answers in your own words and cite the source. If you copy anything directly from these sources, place it in quotation marks and cite it.

PAPERS

Paper assignments are almost always meant to be done individually. (Later I'll discuss group assignments. For now, let's concentrate on individual work.) You need to do the reading, research, and writing by yourself and take responsibility for the results. It's great to talk about the project, and it's fine to consult teachers, writing tutors, and friends. Feel free to show them a draft version and get their feedback. But you need to do your own research, organize the paper, and write it yourself.

You will almost always utilize the work of others. That's essential to good research. You should read the best works and draw on them with a critical eye—sometimes agreeing, sometimes disagreeing. Learning to do that well is a major goal of higher education. It's one way you'll become a more thoughtful and informed person.

This is not the place to discuss how to write papers. My goal here is more limited. I simply want to say what it means to write papers honestly. That's really very simple. First, whenever you rely on the work of anyone else, cite it so your readers know. That's true whether you agree or disagree with the cited works. If you use anyone else's ideas, include a citation. If you use their exact words, use quotation marks *and* a citation.

Second, whenever you quote someone directly, use quotation marks. Longer quotes, running more than a few sentences, are indented rather than enclosed with quotation marks, but the principle is the same. Readers will understand this block indent is a quotation:

Fourscore and seven years ago our fathers brought forth on this continent, a new nation, conceived in Liberty, and dedicated to the proposition that all men are created equal.

Now we are engaged in a great civil war, testing whether that nation, or any nation so conceived and so dedicated, can long endure.[2]

No one will ever think you meant to plagiarize the Gettysburg Address. Still, you need to cite it. Citations are especially important when your sources are obscure or controversial. You must show readers exactly which sources you used, whether they're for data, analysis, or direct quotes.

To put it a little differently, your references (or their absence) shouldn't mislead readers. Use them to strengthen your analysis and amplify your ideas, never as a substitute for doing your own work.

One more important point about papers: you cannot hand in the same paper to more than one class. That's also true for homework assignments. If you write a paper on the Great Depression for an economics class, you can't turn it in to an American history class too. You have to write another paper. You're not allowed to plagiarize your own work. You are still welcome to write about the Great Depression and even to rely on some of the same books and articles, but the paper itself should be substantially different. (If you *really* want to expand on an earlier paper, explain that to your current teacher and get approval. If you want to turn in the same paper to two current classes, talk to both teachers and get their approval.)

Tips on writing honest papers

- Cite others' work whenever you rely on it.
- When you use someone's words, quote them accurately, mark them as a quotation, and include a citation.
- When you paraphrase, use your own distinctive voice, not a facsimile of the author's. Be sure to include a citation.
- Never represent anyone else's work as your own.
- Never hand in the same paper to two classes unless you have permission from both instructors.
- Never buy, sell, or "borrow" papers. Do your own work.

---

2. Abraham Lincoln, Gettysburg Address, November 19, 1863, reprinted in Gary Wills, *Lincoln at Gettysburg: The Words That Remade America* (New York: Simon and Schuster, 1992), app. I, pp. 202–3, and app. III D 2, p. 263.

In the next chapter I'll expand on how to write papers honestly. But these are the key ideas: do the work yourself, quote accurately, cite the work you use and the ideas you draw upon, and present all materials fairly.

Buying Papers on the Internet
Don't.

It's dishonest to buy (or sell!) papers. For that matter, it's dishonest to turn in papers you have lifted from friends, downloaded from the internet, or cut-and-pasted from two or three sources. It doesn't matter whether your friends gave you permission or whether the information is freely available on the web. It is dishonest to represent anyone else's work as your own. It's just as dishonest to provide your work to others.

This kind of cheating is often caught. Professors have seen lots of papers, and they have developed good antennae to pick up dishonest ones. There are usually telltale signs. Some papers just don't sound like a particular student. Others don't quite address the assignment. Occasionally the introduction doesn't sound like the conclusion. For example, a paper might begin: "It's for sure America will sign to this international treaty." Then it might conclude, without quotation marks: "Having ratified this pact with such lofty ideals and soaring hopes, America will soon confront its harsh realities." The writer who fumbled through the first sentence could not have written the last one. Someone else did, and the student copied it. Still other papers include obvious signs of cheating such as antiquated citations or out-of-date references. "President Lincoln will probably defeat the Confederacy and win reelection." I'm betting he will. I just hope he doesn't go to the theater.

Faculty are sophisticated about detecting fraud via the internet, and they have a variety of tools to help them. Although it's easy to cheat using the web, it's easy to catch cheating the same way. Faculty simply select some text from a questionable student paper and do a Google search for it. They can also use computer services that work with universities to detect plagiarism and cheating. These services compare newly submitted student papers to everything in their databases, which include thousands of previously submitted student papers, all publicly available websites, and nearly all published articles. They automatically flag sentences in new papers matching those in the database. Then each newly submitted paper, honest or not, becomes part of this ever-expanding database.

This may sound like a cat-and-mouse game, but it's not. It's about honest work, personal integrity, and real learning. Buying papers is cheating.

Universities take it seriously with good reason. It's a direct assault on honest learning. Equally important, it's a self-inflicted wound on your own education.

ONLINE RESEARCH

The web has become integral to academic work. It's the fastest way to scan lots of sources, compare authors, gain access to specialized materials, and much more. It's a great research tool and an easy way to grab some quick facts. When did women get the vote in America? Does India have more people than China? How many miles, roughly, is the Indianapolis 500?

When you use the internet, just remember a few basic points. One is that the quality of information varies widely. Anybody with a website or blog or Twitter account can say whatever they want. There's no quality control. If the *Encyclopaedia Britannica* website says D-Day was June 6, 1944, you can count on it. If the *Encyclopedia BetaTest* says it was April 1, 1984, check somewhere else. You need to use solid sources, and even then you may want to cross-check them. If you're unsure which sources to use, ask your professor or a reference librarian for guidance. They know the literature and can help.

One encyclopedia deserves special mention. Wikipedia. Everyone, including faculty, uses it. But you need to be careful and double-check the material you include in your papers. The text is entirely written by volunteer contributors. Their knowledge and biases vary greatly, and you have no way of knowing them. The contributions are not verified by editors either. My advice: feel free to use Wikipedia, but use it with caution. Try to find an additional source for important information. And be sure to credit Wikipedia, as you would any other sources, in your footnotes.

The great advantage of online research is efficiency. You can zero in on a topic, and you can do it from anywhere. The drawback is that targeted online research often strips away the context from the material you find; the context may be essential, however, for you to understand the topic and explore its significance. If you search for "ISIS + 2018," for instance, you'll get thousands of hits on the terrorist group and the fighting, but you may not learn much about its relationship to political instability across the Middle East or homeland security in Europe, Canada, or the United States. If those issues are important to you, you'll need to do additional reading and additional online searches, such as "ISIS and Saudi Arabia" and "ISIS and homeland security."

Third, it's soooo easy to drag and drop information from the web into your computer. That's great for taking notes, but it can easily become great trouble. Since you already know the value of online research, let me mention a couple of potential problems so you can avoid them. One is that it's often easier to copy information than to read or understand it. (That's true of scanning and photocopying too.) Another is that it invites cheating. Unless you quote and cite what you've dropped into your paper, you're plagiarizing. Finally, even if you are not trying to cheat, it's easy to lose track of what you copied and what you actually wrote yourself.

How should you handle these problems? First, you need to screen your sources of information. Some, like online journals, publish only high-quality articles evaluated by professionals in their field. They reject papers that fall short of their standards. At the other extreme are websites run by the same people who write emails explaining that their father was a corrupt Nigerian millionaire and that they will generously share his fortune with you if you simply send them your bank account and credit card numbers.

There are no gatekeepers online, no global editors to guarantee the quality of information. You have to judge it yourself. You have to determine which sources are reliable and which ones aren't.

Second, you need to decide whether the wider context is important for understanding your topic. If it is, then you'll need to expand the scope of your research. You'll probably want to search online for additional text strings (for example, "ISIS + Saudi Arabia" or "ISIS + homeland security") and follow hyperlinks to background readings. To provide the political, social, and historical setting, you'll want to read significant articles and books. That's not always necessary, but for some issues it's crucial. To hit the bull's-eye, it helps to see the surrounding circles.

Third, don't drag and drop too much from the web into your notes. It's hard to keep straight just who wrote what, and it invites trouble. When you do drag and drop some material, use a consistent system to mark these words and ideas as someone else's and identify where they came from. You need to identify the source page, first in your notes and later in your paper. Also, once you begin writing and drawing on your notes, you need a way to keep your words separate from those you've copied. In the next chapter I'll describe a simple method for doing that—a way that works with quotations from books, articles, and electronic sources. Just put the letter Q at the beginning and end of any quoted materials. It works well because it's simple and stands out clearly in your notes. It's equally effective in your handwritten notes.

When you copy something from a website, be sure to copy the URL or DOI so you can cite it later or return to the document if you need to.[3] It's a good idea to write down the date you accessed it too. Some citation styles require it, mainly because online content changes so often. If you use a professional database like Medline or MathSciNet, jot down the document ID number so you can add it to citations or return easily for more research.

Tips on online research

- Screen the quality of information you get off the internet.
- Move beyond your targeted search and look for background materials to provide essential context. That means browsing books and articles, not just briefer items.
- Don't drag and drop too much into your notes. Summarize the information in your own words. You'll learn more by doing it.
- Have a clear system, such as Q-quotes, to mark any material you drag and drop.
- Be sure to write down the URL of web pages you use and the date you accessed them so you can cite them later. It's also a time-saver if you need to return to the site. That's true for database identification numbers too. Be sure to write them down.

LANGUAGE CLASSES

Learning a foreign language is one of the most common college experiences. Fortunately, it presents very few difficulties for doing honest work. The rules are straightforward and familiar. You can't copy homework or exams from anyone—from classmates, answer books, or published translations. You can't use your mobile phone for a quick computer-assisted

---

3. A DOI, or digital object identifier, is a string of numbers and letters that permanently tag an article or document, and only that one. A document keeps the same, unique DOI even if it moves from one URL to another.

translation either. You know the basic principle: when you say you did the work yourself, you actually did it. That's as true for classes in Mandarin as it is for classes in Chinese art or history.

What about using a Chinese-English dictionary? Rules vary from teacher to teacher, and sometimes from assignment to assignment. You can generally use dictionaries for take-home work. They may help you learn new words and remind you of old ones. On the other hand, some teachers don't permit them for in-class quizzes and translations, since they want you to master the vocabulary. One student passed along an important practical point, based on her classes in Arabic. Although she was allowed to use dictionaries for all her assignments, the translations in class "were generally timed, so thumbing through dictionaries was a disadvantage."[4] That's true for online dictionaries too, although they are usually faster. The main point is to use dictionaries for occasional assistance and to learn vocabulary, not as a constant crutch.

Beyond these basic issues, it's important to know how honest work actually helps you learn a foreign language.

"My goal," says one Italian professor, "is to help students become good listeners, good readers, and spontaneous speakers and writers." For classical languages, the goal is to read easily and translate accurately. Whatever the language, you'll master it only with practice. That means repeating oral exercises, listening to conversations, working on grammar and vocabulary, and writing translations. Homework exercises are designed to guide you along this path by immersing you in the language and gradually building on what you've already covered. Besides giving you practice, the exercises allow you to learn from your mistakes. "Mistakes are actually quite important," one professor told me. "Correcting them is how you learn the language."

That's why it undercuts learning to simply copy the answers instead of working on the assignments. (It's obvious to teachers too, according to everyone I spoke with.) To learn, you need to practice. It will give you an easy familiarity with what you already know and a chance to identify and

---

4. Some students need more time for other important reasons. Some have learning disabilities, and others are still mastering English. If you need more time for an exam or an assignment, speak with your teacher *in advance* and explain your situation. You may be asked to provide a letter documenting your needs.

correct mistakes. Remember that the goal is not simply to translate a few paragraphs correctly. The goal is to understand the language, to grasp the general rules of Spanish, Russian, or Japanese, and to learn how they apply to specific words and sentences.

Can you ever use published translations or answer keys? Yes, occasionally, if your teacher doesn't mind. But use them *only* to double-check your work or solve a sticky problem. "Don't use them until you've already wrestled with the problem yourself," one Latin professor cautions. "Then you can turn to a published translation to check your work or get past a rough spot." In other words, use prepared translations for self-guided learning, not as substitutes for doing your own work.

Faculty in physics, chemistry, math, and economics told me exactly the same thing about answer books in their fields. As a way to check your work, they can serve as silent teachers. As a way to avoid work, they are dishonest and self-defeating.

> *Tip for all classes*: Don't use answer keys, published translations, or work by others as substitutes for doing your own work. You can use them occasionally, if your teacher approves, as guides to help you learn—to check your work, for example, or to overcome specific obstacles.

GROUP ASSIGNMENTS

While most class assignments are meant to be done individually, some are designed for small groups. Your professor may assemble these groups, or you may form your own. "I tell my students that this is an extremely efficient way to study," one scientist explained to me. "By looking for questions that will show up on the exam, students end up looking at the material differently. Three or four folks working together will put slightly different emphases on the information, and [they] may even have taken different notes."

When you work in small groups, it's important to know the professor's rules. They vary across classes and assignments, and that variation matters for doing honest work. Sometimes you are asked to study together but then to produce your own individual written work. Sometimes you are asked to produce a joint paper or group presentation. Sometimes you are simply encouraged to study together with no written assignment. It's important to know which one applies to your group and to your assignment. When in doubt, ask.

Tips on group assignments: Know what the professor expects. What is to be done by the group, and what is to be done individually? If you are unsure, ask before doing the work. If one member of the group doesn't do his share, speak privately with the student first and then with the professor.

If the assignment is to study as a group and then turn in individual papers, it violates the rules to incorporate other students' work directly into yours. Talk with them, learn from them, but don't share their writing and don't copy their ideas word for word. "Shared writing like this will be obvious," one professor told me.

On the other hand, you may be asked to prepare a true group assignment, such as a class presentation. Encourage everyone in the group to pitch in and work honestly. When the group presents its work, give everyone credit. Working well in groups like this is rewarding in its own right. "It's good practice for the rest of [students'] lives," one scientist pointed out, "since so much of what we do is in collaboration with others." The downside is that you may also get some practice dealing with someone who doesn't pull a fair share of the load. If someone doesn't participate, or might be cheating, first speak privately with that student and then, if necessary, with the professor.

All this advice applies to group assignments. Of course if the assignment is given to you individually, rather than as part of a group, you have to do it individually. That's true even if you study with a group. You can discuss the assignment with group members or other friends—in person, by email and text messages, or in internet chat rooms. It's fine to toss around ideas, but it's cheating to swap actual answers and submit them as your own. You have to write the assignment by yourself, in your own words.

What crosses the line and counts as "too much cooperation" for assignments given to you individually? That differs from subject to subject and sometimes from professor to professor. Nearly all professors encourage general discussion. What they prohibit is more detailed help, unless it's a group assignment. Take an individual assignment to write a computer program. You need to write, edit, and debug the software yourself. You need to warrant how well it works and what the problems are. That's the heart of the assignment, and it needs to be done alone, without help. There may be some gray areas about giving or receiving minor assistance, such as checking the program's syntax. Some professors encourage it; some don't allow it. All you need to do is ask. In fact, that's the best advice I can give, whether you're taking a class in computer programming, macroeconomics, or cell biology. Ask your professor what work you can do jointly and what you must do alone.

Problem Sets as Group Activities

The most common group task is to work together on problem sets. Teachers in math, economics, statistics, and the sciences encourage it, and for good reason. It's a great way to learn.

To avoid any suspicion of cheating, however, it's important to know your professor's rules about doing problem sets. What's perfectly fine for one teacher or one assignment may not be fine for another. You may be encouraged to write answers together, as a group. Or you may be explicitly told not to. There's nothing right or wrong about these varied assignments. They're just different, the same way open- and closed-book exams are different. Listen carefully to the rules governing each problem set, ask for clarification if you are unsure, and then respect the rules you are given.

There are really two issues here. One is avoiding dishonesty. If your name stands alone on a paper, it means you solved the problems yourself. You can consult others in the group—that's why it was formed—but you must do all the written work yourself. On the other hand, if you are listed as coauthor of a group paper, then you participated in the joint work.

Tip on authorship: If your name is alone on a paper, it means you did the work entirely yourself. If you are listed as a coauthor, you contributed to the group's work.

The other issue is how best to learn from group activity. This is not usually a question of cheating (although the lines are sometimes fuzzy), but it is important to your education. If there are four students in the group and four problem sets to do, the temptation is to divide the assignment. Even if your teacher permits the group to parcel out work this way, it still may not be the best way to learn. After all, you can't take exams that way, by passing the hard questions over to friends in the study group. You need to learn how to think about the questions and solve the problems—all of them, not just 25 percent.

It's not enough just to "get the answers." That's why simply copying them cheats your own education. The goal of learning is not only finding answers but finding the best *paths* to answers. It's about the journey, as well as the destination. Problem sets are tools for finding these paths, or finding out if you've lost your way. It's a lot better to discover that on practice problems than on high-stakes exams.

That's why it's usually best if each group member does *all* the problem sets individually. Then you can go over some or all of them with the group, check each other's work, suggest corrections, and learn together. You'll know the material much better when it comes time to write papers and exams.

> *Tip on problem sets as group activities*: When you do problem sets as a joint activity, each person should do the entire assignment individually and then go over it with the group. That's not a rule about honesty; it's a tip about how to learn.

What if you don't understand how some problems are solved? What if you're unsure about the right methods to use? Then it's fine to ask others to explain them, whether they're in your group or not. Before you ask for help, though, try to work out the solutions yourself. If you are still puzzled, go over the questions as often as you wish with friends, roommates, professors, tutors, TAs, and members of your study group. Focus on *how to solve problems*, rather than on the solutions themselves. Try to diagnose exactly where you are having difficulty. When you understand the right methods, you'll be able to solve the problems yourself. You'll be able to explain *why* you chose one technique or solution rather than another. In fact, that's a good test of whether you really understand the solution.

This advice applies to foreign languages as well as math, science, and economics. "Based on my own experience teaching introductory Latin," one professor told me, "it can sometimes be useful for students to consult each other on a particularly tough assignment or tough patch." But don't consult others, he said, "until you've already tackled the problem yourself." If the help you receive is extensive or crucial, he suggests acknowledging it in the written assignment. That's not required, but it's a good idea for a couple of reasons. It eliminates any confusion about who did what work, and, just as important, it lets your teacher know exactly which issues are troublesome and need more instruction. If they are hard for you, they are probably hard for your classmates too.

Tips on how to set up an effective study group of your own: You can learn a lot if you study with the right people in the right setting. With the wrong people in a noisy place, though, you'll simply waste time. Here are some tips based on conversations with experienced undergraduates:

- Study with one to three other students. Larger groups spend too much time chatting. That's fun, but it's not studying.
- Work together in a quiet place where you can talk without bothering others. The library may have some rooms for study groups. Or there may be a coffee shop near campus that's not too crowded. Do not study together in a dorm room; there are too many distractions. (Speaking of distractions, shut off your mobile devices.)
- Set a specific time to begin and end the session. Make sure everybody knows you will begin on time. Most sessions last about sixty to ninety minutes, perhaps a little longer when you are studying for finals. Setting a time to end the session will push you to work efficiently.
- Pick specific topics in advance to discuss, and make sure everybody studies the same thing beforehand. Do not parcel out the work you'll discuss, with some people studying one thing and some another. Hypothetically that seems efficient. In practice it doesn't work. If there is a study guide, decide in advance which part you'll discuss. If there are ten assigned problems and you want to discuss only half, make sure everybody does the same odd (or even) ones.
- Select people you'll enjoy working with.
  - They should be at about your academic level, so you can keep up with them and they can keep up with you. That way you can teach each other, and it won't be a one-way street.
  - Choose people who want to work and will contribute to the group. Avoid those who don't study for class and just want a free ride. Again, you want a two-way street for mutual teaching and learning.

How do you select the right study partners? One student told me his approach. "I try to pick other students who always come to class and show up on time instead of fifteen minutes late. I like those who say something valuable in class instead of just trying to impress the teacher. They'll have something to say in the study group, too." Excellent advice.

As you learn together, don't cross the line and copy down answers directly from someone else and hand them in as your own work (unless you are specifically allowed to coauthor assignments and include others' names on the paper). The same standards apply to copying from answer books or old problem sets. If your name stands alone on the paper, then you must write all the answers yourself, in your own words. Discuss. Contribute. Learn from friends or your study group. Feel free to ask for help again and again. Then do your own work. That's the best way to learn.

At the Blackboard—or Whiteboard—with Your Study Group

The most inviting time to copy answers is when everyone works together at the blackboard. After one student solves a physics or engineering problem, it's easy for everyone else to scribble down the answer. "Most teachers consider this cheating," the head of one math program told me, "and we can easily spot identical work like this."

There's a better approach and a more honest one, she explained. Work through the problems—individually and collectively—and make sure everyone understands them. Then *erase the solutions on the blackboard* and let everyone do the work individually. Reworking the solutions for yourself is not useless "make work." It's useful practice and genuine learning.

That's true even if the person writing answers on the blackboard is the teaching assistant for your section. It's not cheating to copy the TA's answers. After all, they are written out for the whole class. But you won't learn much by rote copying. The goal is to understand the process and master the technique, not repeat the answers mechanically. If the TA skips over these key elements or if you still don't understand, be sure to ask.

Final Thoughts on Group Learning

One scientist summarized his advice on group work like this: "I generally want the students to figure out *how* to solve the problem together. The actual solution should be done individually. The point [of solving problems individually] is to give each student practice with skills that can only be acquired by doing them." To see if you've actually acquired these skills, try to defend your answer to the group or even to yourself. *Why* is this answer the right one? *How* exactly did you reach it? Be sure you can answer these questions.

Time and again, teachers mention the importance of participating actively in group sessions. "You can't really learn in groups if you're passive," one physicist told me. "After all, it's not about getting the answers to specific questions. It's really about understanding the process, learning how to answer hard questions." You can learn that in groups, but only if you join in. First, work together to master the process; then solve the problems yourself. If you're still stumped, ask for help. Then try again—on your own.

Once you understand the material, you should write your own answers in your own words. That's probably the best approach even if your teacher permits joint written work. *Students who simply copy the answers might not understand them. Unfortunately, their learning gaps will show up later, when it really counts, on exams, papers, and more advanced topics in class.*

Tips on how to use study groups

- Be active, not passive, in study groups.
- Learn how to answer questions and how to think about problems, rather than what the specific answers are. Once you truly understand the process, you'll be able to answer the questions yourself—on homework, papers, and exams—and you'll be able to defend the answers you've got.

That's also why published answer manuals can impede learning. They're easy to buy or find online, and they provide ready solutions to problem sets in major textbooks. Some teachers think it's okay to use them; others don't. In any case, it's not a good idea to lean too heavily on them. As a quick way to check your answers, they can be a useful source of feedback. As a substitute for doing the work, they short-circuit your education. Just remember how we all learned to ride a bicycle. Eventually the training wheels had to come off.

These manuals also raise the crucial issue of honest work. If you copy the answers from a book, you're cheating. It's the same as copying answers from another student or downloading them. It's simply not your own work.

Tips on honesty in group assignments: In some classes you work with study groups but are expected to complete assignments individually (rather than hand in joint projects). It's vital to know what you can and cannot do together. A few pointers:

- Know your professor's expectations for group work *before you hand in your work*. What should the group do together and what should be done individually?
- It's fine for the group to discuss problem sets, class topics, and so forth. It's fine to ask others to explain methods and solutions you don't understand. Together you can go over the problems several times until you understand.
- But it's cheating for others to provide answers to you—on paper, on the blackboard, or in an answer manual—and for you to copy them and turn them in as your own individual work. It's also a terrible way to learn and will come back to bite you on exams and in more advanced work.

LABS

The most common group assignments, aside from problem sets, are science labs. Together with your lab partner, you calibrate instruments, perform experiments, collect data, clean up explosions, and call the fire department. Better yet, you can follow safety procedures. After doing all this activity together, however, you should write your lab reports separately and reach your own conclusions.

The rules here are straightforward. Do the lab experiments jointly (if that's the assignment), but keep your own personal lab notes and write your own reports. *Never* borrow data or written work without your professor's explicit permission.

Accurate Lab Notes

Whenever you do lab work, keep accurate records of both your procedures and your results. Different laboratories do this in different ways. Some use traditional lab notebooks; others use computer programs or apps; and still others use questionnaires designed for specific experiments. Whichever method you use, write down the results as soon as possible. Don't trust your memory. Don't fudge the results. And don't use anyone else's data without your teacher's permission.

Be sure to check the protocol for recording results at your lab and your university. Some are flexible; others, very strict. If you are unsure, ask your professor or lab assistant. A leading science university, Rice, offers guidelines explaining why accurate recordkeeping is so important:

> A well-kept notebook provides a reliable reference for writing up materials and methods and results for a study. It is a legally valid record that preserves your rights or those of an employer or academic investigator to your discoveries. A comprehensive notebook permits you or another researcher to reproduce any part of a methodology completely and accurately.[5]

Professors follow the same record-keeping procedures themselves, so they know exactly what to expect and why it is so important.

Tip on working with lab partners: It's fine to do lab work together with your partners, but you should keep your own lab notes and write up the results individually.

Teachers *do* sometimes give permission to use others' data. If an experiment misfires, for example, your instructor may give you other results to evaluate. Or she may provide some data to the entire class. The reason is simple: labs are designed to teach you how to analyze data as well as how to conduct experiments. But unless your instructor allows you to use other data, stick with your own. If you are unsure, just ask.

Tips on lab records

- Check with your instructor (or head of your lab) about recordkeeping. You may be asked to use lab notebooks, computers, or packets designed for specific experiments.
- Enter data as soon as possible after an experiment. Don't rely on your memory.
- Record even your experimental mistakes. Later, after performing the experiment correctly, neatly cross out the errors in your lab notebook or follow the procedure in your program or app. If you are using a physical notebook, don't rip out pages or use correction fluid. The original data should still be readable. If you record data on computers, label the old data "incorrect" (or use a strikethrough font) but don't wipe it out. With some help from your instructors, you may be able to learn from these mistakes.

---

5. Rice University, "Guidelines for Keeping a Laboratory Record," Experimental Biosciences, accessed November 18, 2017, http://www.ruf.rice.edu/~bioslabs/tools/notebook/notebook.html.

Traditionally scientists record their results in special notebooks—bound volumes with numbered pages—which are tailor-made for the purpose. It's hard to cover up mistakes using notebooks like this. That's the point. "Never use Wite-Out or rip pages from a lab notebook," one chemistry professor told me. "That's one reason the notebooks have numbered pages. If you make an error, cross it out neatly and continue documenting your observations and results."

Why should you save your mistakes? "Because your observations and procedures are just as important as your results," one scientist emphasized to me. "If you record your procedures and results accurately, your teachers can help you figure out the problems, if there are any." The notes are a record of *work in progress*, and they should show each step as you made it. That's exactly what math and physics professors say about showing your work. It shows them how you think about a problem. If any difficulties crop up, it helps you pin them down—and correct them.

Today most labs have replaced notebooks with computers, equipped with software for data analysis. The technologies may change, but the rules for entering data remain the same.

- Do it as soon as possible after the experiment.
- Record your results accurately, even if the experiment failed.
- When you repeat an experiment, don't erase the old data. Label it as "incorrect," but keep it so you can check what went wrong, or perhaps discover it was okay after all.
- Use only your own data, unless you are explicitly told otherwise.

Then write up the conclusions on your own.

Honest Data

The crux of honest lab work is the truthful presentation of experimental data. Your lab notebook and electronic records should be honest, complete, and reliable, showing exactly how you conducted the experiments and what results you obtained, even if they weren't up to expectations.

Never make up lab results, borrow them from others, or bend the results to fit your needs. Don't modify the results arbitrarily. Don't draw perfect graphs and fill in the observations later.

The National Science Foundation calls such violations "scientific misconduct." Misconduct, it says, means "fabrication, falsification, plagiarism, or other serious deviations from accepted practices in preparing, carrying out, or reporting results" from scientific activities.[6] You may not be working on an NSF grant, but the same sensible rules apply: don't cheat on your data.

There are temptations, of course. Sometimes you are running late and could finish quickly if you invented some numbers or "borrowed" them from a friend. Sometimes your experimental results don't match the expected numbers. Again, it's tempting to insert the "right" numbers rather than figure out exactly what went wrong. Were the measurements off? Was the equipment calibrated incorrectly? Did you make a simple mistake in the experiment? Everybody makes mistakes. One way to learn how science is practiced is to review the proper procedures and compare them with what you actually did.

The most common lab mistakes, one biologist told me, come *before* the experiments begin. Students sometimes fail to read the instructions carefully or forget to line up all the equipment and materials. If you're missing a chemical or beaker in the midst of an experiment, it may be too late to recover. You'll learn much more by using orderly procedures, and you'll generate much better data to work with.

> *Tip*: Before beginning any experiment, read the instructions carefully and assemble all the equipment and materials you need. Also, be prepared to record your data.

When you're finished, your instructor or lab supervisor might ask to see your records. That's perfectly appropriate. In introductory courses, it's to teach you the best methods. In more advanced work, it's to evaluate your research progress, improve collaboration, and ensure integrity throughout the lab.

Honest data is the foundation of lab integrity, and it is expected from everyone, from undergraduates to professors. Violations are treated seriously at all levels, involving all types of data. One of Japan's most eminent cell biologists was forced to withdraw multiple articles after his university concluded he had faked images in five research publications.[7] This investi-

---

6. *Federal Register* 56 (May 14, 1991): 22286–90. Additional rules on research misconduct are in *Federal Register* 65 (December 6, 2000): 76260–76264.

7. Aggie Mika, "Investigation Finds Cell Biologist Guilty of Misconduct," *Scientist*, August 2, 2017, https://www.the-scientist.com/?articles.view/articleNo/50015/title/Investigation-Finds-Cell-Biologist-Guilty-of-Misconduct/.

gation, like so many discoveries of fraud, began when other scientists could not repeat his experimental results. Duke University was sued over more than $200 million in federal grants, based on fraudulent biological data used in sixty grant applications.[8] A physicist was dismissed from Berkeley's Lawrence Livermore National Laboratory after his celebrated discovery of elements 116 and 118 proved fraudulent.[9] All these cases involve senior scientists, but the same standards of integrity apply to students doing lab assignments. Everybody has to play by the rules. Good science depends on it.

It's not just scientists who must present honest, complete data. So should researchers in every field, just as they should present reliable quotes and citations. A prize-winning book on early American gun ownership raised questions when no one else could locate many key documents on which it was allegedly based.[10] Outside experts, brought in to investigate, sustained the most serious charges of misconduct, and the professor was dismissed.

Not only must your data be honest, but you must present it fairly. You can't deliberately leave out the bad news. Let's say you are testing a hypothesis and some of your experimental results don't support it. It's perfectly fine to double-check the experiment, see if you made a mistake, and try again. All that should be recorded faithfully in your lab notes. But once you have completed the reevaluation and fixed any problems, you should present the results fully and candidly, whether they agree with your hypothesis or not.

---

8. In this landmark case of research misconduct, the accused scientist pled guilty, lost her job, and had to withdraw multiple published papers. Duke is liable for up to $600 million if the whistleblower's lawsuit is successful. Jef Akst, "Duke Sued for Millions over Fraudulent Data," *Scientist*, September 6, 2016, https://www.the-scientist .com/?articles.view/articleNo/46974/title/Duke-Sued-for-Millions-over-Fraudulent -Data/. "Duke Admits Faked Data 'Potentially Affected' Grant Applications," *Retraction Watch* (blog), June 29, 2017, http://retractionwatch.com/2017/06/29/duke-admits-faked -data-potentially-affected-grant-applications/.

9. Robert L. Park, "The Lost Innocence of Physics," *Times Education Supplement* (London), July 24, 2002.

10. Michael A. Bellesiles, *Arming America: The Origins of a National Gun Culture* (New York: Alfred A. Knopf, 2000). Bellesiles was both professor of history and director of Emory University's Center for the Study of Violence.

> *Tips on honest lab work*
>
> - Lab partners may work together on experiments and discuss their work, but they are always required to keep their own notebooks and write up the results individually, without assistance.
> - Never copy or make up data on experiments.
> - Don't omit or hide unfavorable results. Record them in your lab notes.
> - Present your experimental results honestly, even if you know they are "wrong" and even if they contradict your hypothesis.

The same is true in history, sociology, political science, economics . . . in every field. One of the most damning findings about the book on gun ownership was its "egregious misrepresentation" of historical data. Outside experts found the author simply excluded some findings that disagreed with his.[11]

Whatever your subject, it violates basic research ethics to leave out unfavorable results. It's tempting to omit them from your papers or presentations, but you shouldn't. Remember, this is not a court case or debating contest where you present only selected facts, chosen to help your side. Your aim should be to present the results honestly and completely, warts and all. That's how good scholarship moves forward. Using this data, you may come up with a better hypothesis or more powerful interpretation. Or maybe someone else will. In any case, you should present your results fully and accurately.

---

11. When Bellesiles's critics could not find some crucial documents he had cited, they cried foul. Emory appointed an outside committee of eminent historians to investigate. They reached a number of damning conclusions and used the term "egregious misrepresentation," quoted above. "No one," they said, "has been able to replicate Professor Bellesiles' results [of low percentage of guns] for the places or dates he lists." They also found he had excluded data that contradicted his findings, notably Alice Hanson Jones's higher figures on gun ownership. They concluded that Bellesiles's "scholarly integrity is seriously in question." Stanley N. Katz, Hanna H. Gray, and Laurel Thatcher Ulrich, "Report of the Investigative Committee in the Matter of Professor Michael Bellesiles," Emory University, Atlanta, July 10, 2002, http://www.emory.edu/news/Releases/Final_Report.pdf; Michael Bellesiles, "Statement of Michael Bellesiles on Emory University's Inquiry into Arming America," Emory University, Atlanta, July 10, 2002, http://www.emory.edu/news/Releases/B_statement.pdf.

CLASS PARTICIPATION

In many classes, especially seminars, part of your grade depends on class participation. Teachers *love* active discussions where students raise useful questions, listen to each other, and make thoughtful points based on the readings. There's no more rewarding way to teach—or learn.

Honesty is not an issue in class discussions, but students do have legitimate questions about what counts as "participation" and what grade they should receive for it. Some questions are inevitable since judgments about participation are subjective. Others arise because teachers rarely specify what counts as participation.

Although there's no way to avoid subjective judgments, it's easy to say what counts as effective participation:

- Do you attend class regularly?
- Have you done the assigned work so your comments and questions are solidly based?
- Do your contributions advance the class discussion?

You can contribute in lots of ways—by raising questions, offering answers, or playing off other student comments. To do that effectively, though, you need to keep pace with the assignments and listen respectfully to your classmates as well as your teacher. That way you can respond to each other and to the material, a fruitful give-and-take from which everyone can learn.

Keep in mind that a seminar is *not* a lecture where you sit quietly, take notes, and perhaps ask a question or two. A seminar (or weekly discussion section for a lecture course) is a guided dialogue, based on assigned work. You won't get the most out of it if you sit mute, talk over others, or arrive without preparing. "Passive learning is not the way we do things," one seminar leader told me. "It is expected that a student plays an active part in learning."

To play that active part, you need to do the readings beforehand. Your goal should be to engage the material fully—to grapple with it—first when you read it and later when you discuss it in class.

Don't worry about "showing the teacher what you know." Papers and exams give you plenty of opportunity to do that. Don't worry about agreeing with everyone else. It's perfectly fine to take a different perspective, as long as you keep an open mind, respect others' opinions, and offer reasons

for your views. As one professor put it, "Dialogue and debate are fundamental norms of our system of higher education."

It's also fine to try out new ideas, new angles on the subject, even if
you're not completely sure what you think about them. Consider it a "test
drive" for your ideas. You have my permission (and your teachers'!) to
probe your own thinking in these group discussions. Just make sure you
have done the readings and homework first.

The focus should be on joining the conversation, exploring the material,
and discussing it openly with your classmates. That fosters a more lively
seminar and a richer learning experience. In the process, it reveals how you
approach the subject and what you think about it.

> *Tips on how to participate profitably in class discussions*
>
> - Attend regularly and arrive on time.
> - Keep up with the assigned work.
> - Listen to your fellow students as well as your teacher.
> - Advance the discussion with your own questions, answers, and
>   responses to others' comments.

One final point: try to say something during the first or second class session, even if it's just a small comment. Make an effort to break the ice early.
Don't wait silently, hoping you'll find the perfect moment to say the perfect
thing. Class discussions don't work that way. They are not about making
perfect comments. They're about learning through give-and-take, through
questions and answers, including mistakes and missteps. Believe me, we all
make them. If you don't speak during the first few sessions, you can easily
slip into the routine of never participating. There's a simple solution: pitch
in early, even if it's just a small comment or question. Once you've joined
the conversation, you'll feel more comfortable participating again.

Your teacher wants exactly the same thing: to get the discussion rolling, with lots of students contributing. One experienced professor told
me he "might begin by calling on students and asking them to share their
thoughts on a reading or on another student's previous comment. Students
should not feel as though they are being picked on. [My goal] is not to 'test'
or 'intimidate' students" but to foster discussion and encourage students
to "feel confident sharing their ideas with their classmates and teacher."

If you are shy or simply uncomfortable about speaking in class, you may need to push yourself a little. If you're nervous about speaking off the cuff, jot down an idea or two from the readings and use them to ask a question or make a comment in class. If you are uncomfortable speaking in groups, drop by the professor's office hours and begin a conversation there. After a one-on-one discussion, you may feel better about participating in class. You can also get some help from your college learning skills center. Its staff deal with these issues all the time and will have lots of useful suggestions.

Tip on class participation: Try to say something during the first session or two, even if it's only a small comment. It will open the door to more participation later.

Another tip: Sit at the table in seminars and discussion sections. Slouching in the back row, behind everyone else, invites passive listening instead of active participation.

APPEALING A LOW GRADE

Sometimes when your professor hands back lab reports, papers, or exams, you think your grade is too low. As you hear the answers explained, you realize yours was correct and think you weren't given full credit. My advice: give yourself some time to calm down, mull it over, and review your answer. Maybe, on second look, it's not quite the Nobel Prize winner you remembered.

If you still think you deserve additional credit, it's perfectly fine to discuss it with your professor and appeal the grade. But don't do that until you have reread the exam and settled on specific reasons for your appeal. "I really need a better grade" is *not* a reason. You need to explain *substantively* why your answer is better than the grade it was given.

A little courtesy helps too. Keep the discussion positive and concrete. Snarling about incompetent grading will only make your teacher grumpy. Generally speaking, you should avoid all phrases that include the word *moron*. Instead you might say, "I think my answer is very close to what you outlined in your last lecture, and I'd really appreciate your taking another look." Or "You said the answer should cover three main points, and I think mine did." And it's always fine to ask, "How could I do better?"

Your professor undoubtedly has some standard procedures for regrading, and you should ask about them. For example, some professors ask you to explain your reasons in writing; others don't. In larger classes some professors ask you to work with your TA before appealing to them.

If your reasons are solid, your grade might be raised. Even if it isn't, you might learn what you did wrong so you can do better next time. That's valuable too, because there will be many "next times," in many other classes.

One common problem, especially in math, statistics, and some sciences, is failing to show all your work. It's not enough simply to write down the answer, even if it's correct. You won't get full credit if you don't show full work. That's partly to prevent cheating, but there are other reasons too. It also allows the professor to give you partial credit for what you got right. If you got the answer wrong, it allows the professor to identify the problem and show you how to correct it.

By showing your work, you're showing how you think through a problem. That's exactly what teachers want to know. "Just writing down an answer merits no (or almost no) credit at all," one physicist told me. "We're trying to teach students how to approach problems: how to set them up, how to carry through the calculations, and how to interpret the final results. In other words, how to think physically. . . . *If a student does not show his work, he is leaving out the very thing I'm trying to assess.*"

So follow the advice you've heard from every math teacher since third grade: show your work.

Finally, if you appeal your grades, you must follow one hard-and-fast rule. You cannot modify your work in any way before regrading. That's cheating.

Tips on appealing low grades

- Reread your answer before deciding whether to appeal.
- Courteously explain the specific reasons for your appeal.
- Never change anything on the exam before regrading.

HONOR CODES

Some schools use honor codes to ensure academic integrity. Students typically sign a pledge to do honest work, monitor each other, and report violations. Not only are they responsible for doing honest work themselves; they must report cheating by others. They also promise to behave responsibly outside class and play a major role in judging infractions.

Problems are usually dealt with by honors councils rather than college deans. Some councils are run entirely by students; others include faculty and administrators. In either case, students play a critical role in making honor codes work, mostly by taking responsibility for academic honesty and by emphasizing its central place in education.

The actual content of honest work and responsible behavior is no different from that of other schools. Students pledge to do their own work; not to plagiarize, cheat, or purchase papers; and to follow their professors' rules for papers, lab reports, and exams. Outside class, they pledge not to harass, intimidate, or threaten others—the same rules that apply in most universities, whether or not they use honor codes.

What is different is the responsibility students take upon themselves, individually and collectively, for maintaining and promoting these high ethical standards. "Students should constantly evaluate their own actions, inside or outside of the classroom," one student told me. "This covers everything from day-to-day interactions between students to academic honesty to the manner in which the [university] senate allocates student body funds."

Professors rely on students living up to these standards, and students count on each other. Faculty don't monitor in-class exams, for instance, and often allow students to take closed-book exams in the library or their dorm rooms. They are confident that students will adhere to the rules. Everyone knows that widespread violations would sabotage the whole system.

The purpose of honor codes goes well beyond catching dishonesty or even discouraging it by monitoring and punishment. As one student put it, "The feeling of being watched runs completely counter to the point of the [honor code], as it leaves people feeling infantilized and mistrusted. The benefit of the [honor code] is that students can feel secure in making their own ethical choices because they know that they will be treated like adults, that is, rationally, with compassion and understanding."

I heard that again and again from students. *The most profound goal of the honor system, they said, was a positive one: to create an ethos of honesty and responsibility in academic and social life. The aim is to create a shared norm of integrity, one strong enough to be self-enforcing.*

These codes are more common in teaching colleges than in large universities. That's no surprise. They work best where students know each other well and have a strong sense of community. Indeed, the codes usually become central pillars of that community, vital elements in the school's self-definition. They encourage a student culture of fairness and integrity, promote individual and collective responsibility, and foster strong bonds of trust between students and faculty.

These are goals well worth aspiring to, whether or not your school uses an honor code.

TAKING GOOD NOTES

. . . .

3

Good notes can help you learn more from readings, seminars, and lectures. Whether you are preparing for a final exam or writing a research paper, you'll need notes that highlight the main ideas, organize the materials, and remind you what you have read and heard. In this chapter I'll show you how to take effective notes and avoid problems.

The most important advice I can give you is actually the simplest: *listen carefully in class and take thoughtful notes on all your lectures and readings.* Don't let note-taking substitute for good listening or reading. And don't try to transcribe everything. The goal is not to be comprehensive. The goal is to write down what really matters.

"The simple act of writing notes in class really helps," a biologist told me. "It forces students to pay attention, write down what they think is important, and look for whatever is coming next." That advice applies with equal force to books, articles, and other sources. Taking notes will help you organize the materials and understand them. It helps a second time when you review the notes.

> *Tip:* Take notes on all your readings and lectures, and be sure to review them. The top line should say what they cover, such as "Coleridge and English Romantic Poetry." If it's a lecture, include the course, topic, and date. If it's a written source, include all the bibliographic information.

WHAT ARE GOOD NOTES?

As long as you are taking notes, you might as well take good ones. But what exactly *are* good notes? They are notes and reminders you actually find useful when you write papers, study for exams, or prepare for the next class session. To do that, your notes need to

- highlight the key points and conclusions in the readings or lectures;
- say how these points fit together; and
- remind you what evidence and reasoning were used.

You should include *all* definitions, plus the most important equations, formulas, and algorithms. In English class you can skip the equations.

Of course it's fine to include some helpful details: a few choice quotes, key dates, or other data you might need for papers and exams. Add them when you think they are important in their own right or illustrate some larger point. But don't let the details swamp your notes. The goal is to understand the important issues: the argument, the supporting logic and evidence, and the connective tissue that ties it all together. That's what you should focus on. You are not a dictation app, capturing every word to play back later on your phone.

Tip: The goal of notes is not to include everything but to highlight and organize the most important material.

This point about selectivity is supported by research showing students learn more when they take notes by hand, rather than by keyboard. The reason, apparently, is that typing encourages students to copy the material verbatim, without thinking much about it. Handwriting is more difficult, so students are more selective. They think more about what really matters before writing it down. That seems to encourage deeper processing and better performance on exams.[1]

The key point, I think, is not to switch from your laptop to a spiral notebook but to be discerning in taking notes and then to review them carefully—multiple times if possible. Transcribing isn't learning.

To take good notes,

- listen carefully to your lectures and class discussions;
- select what really matters and include that in your notes;
- review your notes after class and before exams;
- add your own thoughts to your notes as you review them.

1. Pam A. Mueller and Daniel M. Oppenheimer, "The Pen Is Mightier than the Keyboard: Advantages of Longhand over Laptop Note Taking," *Psychological Science* 25, no. 6 (April 23, 2014): 1159–68, https://doi.org/10.1177/0956797614524581.

Clear, simple notes like this are an effective way to review what you have covered. But that's only half the story. To understand the material, you need to do more than repeat it. You need to think about it, grapple with it, figure out what it means. Good notes will help you do that. They should be active learning, not passive transcription.

LECTURE NOTES AND SOURCE NOTES

Notes on lectures and written sources differ in a few obvious ways and a few less obvious ones. With books, articles, and other sources, you can read and take notes at your own pace. With lectures, you have to dash along with the professor. That means your lecture notes are probably incomplete, so you'll need to fill them in after class. It's smart to do that the same day, while you still remember the lecture. Again, concentrate on major points and helpful examples, not minor details. Figuring out what really matters is a critical part of your education. Your notes should reflect that judgment.

Most of the time it's easier to organize your notes on articles, books, and web pages than on lectures and seminars. That's because written work comes with its own built-in structure. The text is divided into major sections, usually with titles. You should use these sections and titles to organize your notes. Take Robert Lieber's book *Retreat and Its Consequences: American Foreign Policy and the Problem of World Order.*[2] His chapter on US policy toward Europe has sections such as "The Cold War Era and Global Order," "What's Wrong with Europe?" and "Europe and a Reluctant USA." Each one should translate into a heading in your notes.

A lecture has a structure too, but it's not always so clear. That's why you should pay special attention to the introduction and conclusion, where the professor emphasizes the central elements. Listen for phrases that indicate what's coming, such as "the three main theories are" or "turning to a slightly different topic." When you hear phrases like this, you'll want to list the three theories or signal a new topic in your notes with a section heading.

Tip: Your notes should be organized into sections, reflecting the structure of the reading or lecture.

---

2. Robert J. Lieber, *Retreat and Its Consequences: American Foreign Policy and the Problem of World Order* (Cambridge: Cambridge University Press, 2016).

Third, while notes on lectures are often skimpy and hurried, notes on sources are often too detailed. That's because you can copy materials so easily from online texts into your notes. That's fine, up to a point. But remember, you still need to read the material—copying is *not* reading—and you still need to select what to copy. In fact, you need to select it carefully. It's enticing to copy paragraph after paragraph instead of choosing what's important. But you cannot produce sharp, useful notes unless you pare down what you include. Remember, too, that you still need to organize it into meaningful sections and highlight what's vital.

> *Tip*: Good notes highlight what's really important. If you are typing, you can do that with boldface. If you are scribbling, you can do it with arrows or underlining. If you don't understand something, signal it to yourself with three question marks (???). Later you can look it up or ask your professor, teaching assistant, or classmate.

As you accumulate these notes, be sure to differentiate anything you copy from anything you write yourself. Otherwise, when you use the notes to write a paper, you might inadvertently treat words you copied as if you wrote them yourself. Big mistake. Even if it's an accident, it's no fun trying to prove that to a skeptical professor or dean.

Fortunately it's a mistake that's easy to avoid. In a section below I'll show you a few simple techniques, beginning with Q-quotes, to keep your notes straight. By using them you can tell exactly what you wrote and what someone else did. Problem solved.

> *Tip*: When taking notes on written sources, clearly mark any direct quotations and note the page they are on. Doing that will prevent inadvertent plagiarism if you use the quote later. Put the letter Q before and after each quote so it stands out in your notes.

These differences between notes on sources and lectures are significant, but so are the similarities. All your notes should help you recall the central points, organize them into coherent sections, and integrate them into a meaningful whole. That's why they should always emphasize the introduction and conclusion and why you should reread those sections. The introduction lays out the main topics to be covered. The conclusion recaps these topics, draws them together, and offers some insights into what they mean. That's exactly what you want to grasp.

> *Tip*: Before reading a book or article closely, read the introduction and conclusion and glance at the section headings. That will give you a quick overview, let you to focus on the main issues as you read, and help you take better notes.

REVIEWING AND IMPROVING YOUR NOTES

The main reason you are taking these notes is so you can review them and think about them. To file them away and forget them is to lose most of your effort—and most of the benefits. My suggestion is to review your notes a few hours after you draft them and then to review them again before writing an exam or paper.

This initial review has two goals. One is to recall the material. The other is to annotate and expand your notes, especially those on lectures and seminars. Sometimes you'll discover that they're too brief, too cryptic, especially if you are jotting them down rapidly. It helps to expand them now, while your memories are fresh.

As you review your notes, you can improve them. You can add that example the professor mentioned. You can clarify your writing if it's hard to decipher. You can insert your own conclusions or observations. (I do that in brackets to keep my comments separate.) Finally, you can organize your notes by inserting a few major headings along the way. If you are reviewing lecture notes on the French Revolution, for instance, you might label one section "The Fall of the Bastille" and the next one "Deposing the King." Adding headers like this clarifies the basic structure of the lecture. Later it helps you prepare for exams.

> *Tip*: Your notes are *not* complete when you have finished reading the article or listening to the lecture. You've still got two brief but vital jobs to do. The first is to review your notes. The second is to clarify and expand them. Although it is easier to add material to computerized notes, you can add them to handwritten notes in the margins or at the end.

None of this takes very long—a few minutes at most—and it has some obvious benefits. It will imprint the material more deeply. It will give you a better overview of the course. Most important of all, it will turn you from a passive recipient into an active learner.

Each time you review your notes, ask yourself: What's the overall point here? What are the three or four most important subsidiary points? How does the author or teacher develop them? What's the evidence? What's the logic? What are the best examples? You should be able to reconstruct these central elements of a lecture or article *by yourself, in your own words.* If you cannot explain them to yourself in plain, sensible language, then you don't really understand the material. That's important to know right now, while you still have time to go over the material or ask the professor or teaching assistant.

TAKING NOTES WITH Q-QUOTES

Some honest writers find themselves in hot water, accused of plagiarism, because their notes are so bad they cannot tell what they copied and what they wrote themselves. You can avoid that by clearly distinguishing your words from others'.

All you need is a simple way to identify quotes and keep them separate from your own words and ideas.

The common solution—using ordinary quotation marks in your notes—doesn't actually work so well in practice. For one thing, quotation marks are small, so it's easy to overlook them later when you return to your notes to write a paper. Second, they don't tell you which page the quote comes from, something you need to know for proper citations. Third, if there's a quote within a quote, it's hard to keep your markings straight.

There's a better way. To avoid all this confusion, simply use the letter Q and the page number to begin all quotations in your notes. To end the quote, write Q again. It's painless, and it's easy to spot the Qs when you read your notes and write your papers.

Begin your notes for each new item by writing down the author, title, and other essential data. (The exact information you need is specified in part 2, in the citation chapters.) You'll need this information for each book, article, and online source you use. With this publication data plus Q-quotes, you'll be able to cite effectively from your own notes without having to return to the original publication.

Tip on using Q-quotes to identify exact words: Q157 Churchill's eloquence rallied the nation during the worst days of the war.Q

This system is simple, clear, and effective. It works equally well for typed and handwritten notes. It easily handles quotes within quotes. Looking at your notes, you'll know exactly which words are the author's and which page they are on. You'll know if the author is quoting anyone else. And you'll know that anything *outside* the Q-quotes is your own paraphrase.

Tip on paraphrasing: Make sure your paraphrase does not closely resemble the author's words. When in doubt, double-check your wording against the original.

Because quotes can be complicated, let's see how these Q-quotes work in more detail. First, some quotes begin on one page and end on another. To show where the page break falls, insert a double slash (//) inside the quote. (A double slash stands out, just as Q does.) That way if you use only part of the quote, you can cite the correct page without having to chase down the original again. To illustrate:

Q324–25 Mark Twain's most important works deal with his boyhood on the river. He remembered // that distant time with great affection. He returned to it again and again for inspiration.Q

The first sentence is on page 324; the next one is on both pages; the third is only on page 325. Using Q-quotes with a double slash gives you all this information quickly and easily.

Quotes can be complicated in other ways too. You may wish to cut out some needless words or add a few to make the quote understandable. Fortunately, there are straightforward rules to handle both changes.

SHORTENING QUOTATIONS WITH ELLIPSES . . .

Although quotes need to be exact, you are allowed to shorten them if you follow two rules. First, your cuts cannot change the quote's meaning. Second, you must show the reader exactly where you omitted any words. That's done with an ellipsis, which is simply three dots . . . with spaces before and after each one.

If the omitted words come in the middle of a sentence, an ellipsis is all you need.

Original   I walked downtown, which took at least thirty minutes, and saw her.
Shortened   I walked downtown . . . and saw her.

If the two parts of your quote come from two separate sentences but work together as one sentence, use an ellipsis to separate the two parts.

Original   I walked downtown. After walking more than thirty minutes,
         I rounded the corner and saw her.
Shortened   I walked downtown . . . and saw her.

Because ellipses are sometimes confusing, it may help to go over them again. Remember that they have a simple purpose: to signal deliberate omissions from any text you quote. The difference is only whether to include a period before an ellipsis.

	LOCATION OF OMISSION	HOW YOU SIGNAL THE OMISSION
A	In the middle of a single sentence, or between quotations that work as a single sentence	Simple ellipsis
B	Between clauses that read as complete sentences	Period in its normal place, followed by an ellipsis (then capitalize the beginning of the second sentence, even if it didn't originally begin a sentence)

Omissions like these are perfectly acceptable as long as you signal them (with ellipses) and you don't change the quoted author's meaning.

ADDING WORDS [IN BRACKETS] TO CLARIFY A QUOTE

Occasionally you need to add a word or two to clarify a quote. Perhaps the original sentence uses a pronoun instead of a person's name. For clarity, you might wish to include the name. Again, you cannot change the quote's meaning, and you need to signal the reader that you are modifying it slightly. You do that by using [brackets] to show exactly what you have inserted. Consider this original text:

Original text   Q237 Secretary of Defense James Mattis was speaking in New York that day. The President called and asked him to return to Washington immediately.Q

Now, let's say you want to quote only the second sentence. An exact quote wouldn't make much sense since the reader won't know whom the president was summoning. To correct that, you need to add a few words and bracket them to make it clear that you've added them to the original:

Your quote with brackets
"The President called and asked [his secretary of defense, James Mattis,] to return to Washington immediately."

That's an accurate quote even though you added several bracketed words. If you added the same words without brackets, however, it would be a misquotation.

One important rule: these additions [with brackets] and omissions (with ellipses . . .) should not change the quote's meaning in any way. The statement belongs to another writer, not to you. You are welcome to interpret it, praise it, or damn it, but not to twist it.

QUOTES WITHIN QUOTES

The phrase you are quoting may itself contain a quotation. One advantage of using Q-quotes for your notes is that you can simply put quotation marks wherever they appear in the text. For example: Q47 He yelled, "Come here, quick," and I ran over.Q Since you are using Qs to mark off the entire quote, there will be no confusion later when you write a paper with these notes.

USING Q-QUOTES TO HANDLE COMPLICATED QUOTATIONS

Now that we've covered the basics of Q-quotes plus ellipses, brackets, and quotes within quotes, you are equipped to handle even the most complex quotes, first in your notes and then in your papers. To illustrate that, let's combine all these elements in one example:

Q157–58 Some of Churchill's most famous speeches // were actually recorded by professional actors imitating his distinctive voice and cadence. . . . The recordings were so good that [one friend] said, "I knew Winston well and still can't tell who is speaking."Q

This notation makes it clear that

- the first few words appear on page 157 and the rest are on page 158;
- some words from the original are omitted after the word "cadence";
- there is a period after "cadence" and then three dots, indicating that the first sentence ended at the word "cadence" and that the omission came after that;
- the bracketed words "one friend" are not in the original text; and
- the final words are actually a quotation from someone else. They are included as a quote by the author you are citing.

With clear notation like this, you will be able to cite portions of this complicated quote later without returning to the original article and with no chance of accidental plagiarism. It's not difficult. Actually it takes more time to explain it than to use it!

PLAGIARISM AND
ACADEMIC HONESTY

4

. . . .

The last chapter included some basic ideas about taking notes to write honest, effective papers. In this chapter I'll expand on them and show you how to avoid problems.

The biggest problem is misrepresenting someone else's work as your own. That's plagiarism, and it's a serious breach of academic rules, whether it involves borrowed words, proofs, data, drawings, computer code, or ideas. When it's caught—and it often is—it leads to severe consequences, anything from failing a paper to failing a course. In extreme cases it leads to suspension or expulsion. It's not a parking ticket. It's a highway crash. If it looks deliberate, it's a highway crash without seat belts.

Plagiarism is rare, but it does happen occasionally. The reason is sometimes a simple, innocent mistake. If book notes are garbled, a student may be unable to separate another author's words from her own. Later, when she uses those notes for writing a paper, she might inadvertently treat the other author's words as her own original language. Even if it's an accident, it's no fun trying to prove that to a skeptical professor or dean.

Fortunately, this problem is easily prevented. I'll show you a few simple techniques, beginning with Q-quotes, to keep your notes straight. Using them, you can tell exactly what you wrote and what someone else did. Problem solved.

Of course bad notes are not the only reason for plagiarism. Students rushing to finish a paper may forget to include the necessary citations. Some students are just sloppy, and others don't understand citation rules. Sadly, a few cheat deliberately.[1]

---

1. It is always wrong to use others' work without proper attribution. The most troubling cases involve intentional use of another author's work without full attri-

Whatever the cause, plagiarism is a serious violation of academic rules—for undergraduates, graduate students, and faculty. Misrepresenting someone else's words or ideas as your own constitutes fraud. Remember the basic principles of academic integrity: When you say you did the work yourself, you actually did it. When you rely on someone else's work, you cite it. When you use someone else's words, you quote them openly and accurately. When you present research materials, you present them fairly and truthfully. Quotations, data, lab experiments, and the ideas of others should never be falsified or distorted. They should never be fabricated.

CITE OTHERS' WORK TO AVOID PLAGIARISM

Citation rules follow from these basic principles of openness and honesty. If the words are someone else's, they must be clearly marked as quotations, either by quotation marks or with block indentation, followed by a citation. It's not enough merely to mention an author's name. If it's a direct quote, use quotation marks and a full citation. If it's a paraphrase of someone else's words, use your own language, not a close imitation of the work being cited, and include a proper reference.

The same rules apply to visual images, architectural drawings, databases, graphs, statistical tables, computer algorithms, spoken words, and information taken from the internet. If you use someone else's work, cite it. Cite it even if you think the work is wrong and you intend to criticize it. Cite it even if the work is freely available in the public domain. Cite it even if the author gave you permission to use the work. All these rules follow from the same idea: acknowledge what you take from others. The only exception is when you rely on commonly known information. (What counts as "commonly known" depends on your audience.) When you discuss gravity, you don't need to footnote Isaac Newton.

The penalties for violating these rules are serious. For students, they

---

bution. That is the classic definition of plagiarism. Some use a wider definition that includes *unintentional* copying and borrowing. I call that "accidental plagiarism." Even if it's accidental borrowing—the spoiled fruits of sloppy notes rather than deliberate theft—it is still a serious problem. Whether or not you call it plagiarism, it's a major breach of academic rules.

can lead to failed courses and even expulsion. For faculty, they can lead to demotion or even loss of tenure. The penalties are severe because academic honesty is central to the university.

> *Tips on avoiding plagiarism*: When in doubt, give credit by citing the original source.
>
> - If you use an author's exact words, enclose them in quotation marks and include a citation.
> - If you paraphrase another author, use your own language. Don't imitate the original. Be sure to include a citation.
> - If you rely on or report someone else's ideas, credit their source, whether you agree with them or not.

USING ONLINE SOURCES WITHOUT PLAGIARIZING

You need to be especially alert to these citation issues when you use online sources. Internet research is very efficient, especially when you don't need to read long stretches of text. You can do extensive targeted searches, quickly check out multiple sources, access sophisticated databases, click on article summaries or key sentences, and then drag and drop material into your notes. That's all perfectly fine. In fact, it's often the best way to conduct research and certainly the most common. But it's also crucial to be a good bookkeeper. You need to use a simple, consistent method to keep straight what some author said and what you paraphrased.

The easiest way is to stick with the method for taking notes on printed books and articles, described in chapter 3: *put Q-quotes around everything you drag and drop from electronic sources.* You can supplement that, if you wish, by coloring the author's text red or blue, or by using a different font. Just be consistent. That way you won't be confused in three or four weeks, when you are reviewing your notes and writing your paper.

One more thing: be sure to copy the URL or DOI for the site into your notes so you can cite it or return to it for more research. It's probably a good idea to include the date you accessed it too. Some citation styles ask for it. If the item appears in a database and has a document identification number, copy that too.

QUOTING AND PARAPHRASING WITHOUT
PLAGIARIZING: A TABLE OF EXAMPLES

A simple example can illustrate how to quote and paraphrase properly and
how to avoid some common mistakes. The following table shows the main
rules for citation and academic honesty, using a sentence written by "Jay
Scrivener" about Joe Blow. I'll use footnote 99 to show when that sentence
is cited.

QUOTING WITHOUT PLAGIARIZING

Joe Blow was a happy man, who often walked down the road whistling and singing.	**Sentence in the book *Joe Blow: His Life and Times*, by Jay Scrivener**

WHAT'S RIGHT

"Joe Blow was a happy man, who often walked down the road whistling and singing."[99]	**Correct:** Full quote is inside quotation marks, followed by citation to *Joe Blow: His Life and Times*.
According to Scrivener, Blow "often walked down the road whistling and singing."[99]	**Correct:** The partial quote is inside quote marks, followed by a citation. The partial quote is not misleading.
"Joe Blow was a happy man," writes Scrivener.[99]	**Correct:** The partial quote is inside quote marks, followed by a citation.
According to Scrivener, Blow was "a happy man," who often showed it by singing tunes to himself.[99]	**Correct:** Partial quote is inside quotation marks; nonquoted materials are outside. The paraphrase (about singing tunes to himself) accurately conveys the original author's meaning without mimicking his actual words. Citation properly follows the sentence.
Joe Blow seemed like "a happy man," the kind who enjoyed "whistling and singing."[99]	**Correct:** Two partial quotes are each inside quotation marks; nonquoted materials are outside. Citation properly follows sentence.
Joe appeared happy and enjoyed whistling and singing to himself.[99]	**Correct:** This paraphrase is fine. It's not too close to Scrivener's original wording. The citation acknowledges the source.

Joe Blow was a happy man, who often walked down the road whistling and singing. (no citation)	**Wrong:** It is plagiarism to quote an author's exact words or to paraphrase them closely without *both* quotation marks and proper citation. Acknowledge your sources!
Joe Blow was a happy man, who often walked down the road whistling and singing.[99]	**Wrong:** These are Scrivener's exact words. It is plagiarism to use them without indicating explicitly that it is a quote. It is essential to use quotation marks (or block indentation for longer quotes), *even if* you give accurate citation to the author. So this example is wrong because it doesn't use quotation marks, even though it cites the source.
Joe Blow was a happy man and often walked down the road singing and whistling. (no citation)	**Wrong:** Although the words are not exactly the author's, they are *very similar*. (The words "singing" and "whistling" are simply reversed.) Either use an exact quote or paraphrase in ways that are clearly different from the author's wording. Either way, include a citation.
Joe Blow was a happy man. (no citation)	**Wrong:** There are two problems here. First, it's an exact quote so it should be quoted *and* cited. Second, even if the quote were modified slightly, Scrivener should still be cited because it is *his personal judgment* (and not a simple fact) that Joe Blow is happy.
Joe Blow often walked down the road whistling and singing. (no citation)	**Wrong:** Same two problems as the previous example: (1) exact words should be both quoted and cited; and (2) Scrivener's personal judgment needs to be credited to him.

Joe Blow appeared to be "a happy man" and often walked down the road whistling and singing.[99]	**Wrong:** Despite the citation, some of Scrivener's exact words are outside the quotation marks. That creates the misleading impression that the words are original, rather than Scrivener's. This is a small violation, like going a few miles over the speed limit. But if such miscitations occur often or include significant portions of text, then they can become serious cases of plagiarism.
"Joe Blow was an anxious man, who often ran down the road."[99]	**Wrong:** The quote is not accurate. According to Scrivener, Joe Blow was not anxious; he was "happy." And he didn't run, he "walked." Although this misquotation is not plagiarism, it is an error. You should quote properly, and your work should be reliable. If such mistakes are repeated, if they are seriously misleading, or, worst of all, if they appear to be intentional, they may be considered academic fraud. (Plagiarism is fraud, too, but a different kind.)
Joe Blow "walked down the road" quietly.[99]	**Wrong:** The words inside the partial quotation are accurate, but the word following it distorts Scrivener's plain meaning. Again, this is not plagiarism, but it does violate the basic principle of presenting materials fairly and accurately. If such mistakes are repeated or if they show consistent bias (for example, to prove Joe Blow is a quiet person or hates music), they may be considered a type of academic fraud. At the very least, they are misleading.

The table refers to single sentences, but some citation issues involve paragraphs or whole sections of your paper. Let's say you are writing about urban poverty and William Julius Wilson's analysis of the subject is central to one section. Whether or not you quote Wilson directly, you should include several citations of his work in that section, reflecting its importance for your paper. You could accomplish the same thing by including an explanatory citation early in the section. The footnote might say, "My analysis in this section draws heavily on Kathryn Sikkink's work, particularly *Evidence for Hope: Making Human Rights Work in the 21st Century* (Princeton, NJ: Princeton University Press, 2017), 55–93." You could include a similar comment in the text rather than a footnote. However you handle it, you want to acknowledge your debt openly. Of course you still need to include citations for any direct quotes.

PARAPHRASING

When you paraphrase an author's sentence, don't veer too close to her words. That's plagiarism, *even if it's unintentional and even if you cite the author.*

So what's the best technique for rephrasing a quote? Set aside the other author's text and think about the point *you* want to get across. Write it down in your own words (with a citation) and then compare your sentence to the author's original. If they contain several identical words or yours merely substitutes a couple of synonyms, rewrite yours. Try to put aside the other author's distinctive language and rhythm as you write. That's sometimes hard because the original sticks in your mind or seems just right. Still, you have to try. Your sentences and paragraphs should look and sound different from those of anyone you cite.

If you have trouble rephrasing an idea in your own words, jot down a brief note to yourself stating the point you want to make. Then back away, wait a little while, and try again. When you begin rewriting, look at your brief note but *don't look at the author's original sentence.* Once you have finished, check your new sentence against the author's original. You may have to try several times to get it right. Don't keep using the same words again and again. Approach the sentence from a fresh angle. If you still can't solve the problem, give up and use a direct quote (perhaps a whole sentence, perhaps only a few key words). It should either be a direct quote or your distinctive rephrasing. It cannot be lip-synching.

Why not use direct quotes in the first place? Sometimes that's the best solution—when the author's language is compelling, or when it says something important about the writer. When Franklin Roosevelt spoke about the attack on Pearl Harbor, he told America: "Yesterday, December 7, 1941—a date which will live in infamy—the United States was suddenly and deliberately attacked . . ."[2] No one would want to paraphrase that. It's perfect as it is, and it's historically significant. When you analyze novels and poems, you'll want to quote extensively to reveal the author's creative expression. Other phrases speak volumes about the people who utter them. That's why you might quote Islamic fundamentalists calling the United States "the Great Satan" and Donald Trump's response calling them "losers." Quotes like these convey the flavor of the conflict.

Because there are so many times when direct quotations are essential, you should avoid them where they're not. Overuse cheapens their value. Don't trot them out to express ordinary thoughts in ordinary words. Paraphrase. Just remember the basic rules: you need to cite the source, and you shouldn't mimic the original language.

These rules apply to the whole academic community, from first-years to faculty. A senior professor at the US Naval Academy was stripped of tenure for violating them, to take only one example. Although Professor Brian VanDeMark had written several well-regarded books, his *Pandora's Keepers: Nine Men and the Atomic Bomb* (2003) contains numerous passages that closely resemble sections of other books.[3] Most were footnoted, but as you now know, that doesn't eliminate the problem.[4]

Here are a few of the questionable passages, compiled by Robert Norris. (Norris compiled an even longer list of similarities between VanDeMark's work and his own 2002 book *Racing for the Bomb*.)

---

2. President Franklin D. Roosevelt, Joint Address to Congress Requesting a Declaration of War against Japan, December 8, 1941, http://docs.fdrlibrary.marist.edu/tmirhdee.html.

3. Brian VanDeMark, *Pandora's Keepers: Nine Men and the Atomic Bomb* (Boston: Little, Brown, 2003).

4. Jacques Steinberg, "U.S. Naval Academy Demotes Professor over Copied Work," *New York Times* (national ed.), October 29, 2003, A23.

BRIAN VANDEMARK, *PANDORA'S KEEPERS* (2003)	RICHARD RHODES, *THE MAKING OF THE ATOMIC BOMB* (1986) AND *DARK SUN* (1995)
". . . Vannevar Bush. A fit man of fifty-two who looked uncannily like a beardless Uncle Sam, Bush was a shrewd Yankee . . ." (60)	"Vannevar Bush made a similar choice that spring. The sharp-eyed Yankee engineer, who looked like a beardless Uncle Sam, had left his MIT vice presidency . . ." (*Making of the Atomic Bomb*, 336)
"Oppenheimer wondered aloud if the dead at Hiroshima and Nagasaki were not luckier than the survivors, whose exposure to radiation would have painful and lasting effects." (194–95)	"Lawrence found Oppenheimer weary, guilty and depressed, wondering if the dead at Hiroshima and Nagasaki were not luckier than the survivors, whose exposure to the bombs would have lifetime effects." (*Dark Sun*, 203)
"To toughen him up and round him out, Oppenheimer's parents had one of his teachers, Herbert Smith, take him out West during the summer before he entered Harvard College." (82)	"To round off Robert's convalescence and toughen him up, his father arranged for a favorite English teacher at Ethical Culture, a warm, supportive Harvard graduate named Herbert Smith, to take him out West for the summer." (*The Making of the Atomic Bomb*, 120–21)
"For the next three months, both sides marshaled their forces. At Strauss's request, the FBI tapping of Oppenheimer's home and office phones continued. The FBI also followed the physicist whenever he left Princeton." (259)	"For the next three months, both sides marshaled their forces. The FBI tapped Oppenheimer's home and office phones at Strauss's specific request and followed the physicist whenever he left Princeton." (*Dark Sun*, 539)

Source: Robert Norris, "Parallels with Richard Rhodes's Books [referring to Brian VaDeMark's *Pandora's Keepers*]," History News Network, http://hnn.us/articles/1485.html (accessed June 22, 2004). For convenience I have rearranged the last two rows in the table, without changing the words.

Unfortunately, VanDeMark does not cite Rhodes or quote him directly in any of these passages. Some, like the last one, are virtual quotations and would raise red flags even if they occurred only once. A few others are a little too close for comfort but raise problems mostly because there are so many of them in VanDeMark's book.[5] This is only one of several tables covering VanDeMark's poor paraphrasing or unquoted sources. Each was prepared by a different author who felt violated. According to the Naval Academy's academic dean, "The whole approach to document-ing the sources of the book was flawed."[6] The dean and VanDeMark himself attributed the problem to sloppiness rather than purposeful theft (which is why VanDeMark was demoted rather than fired outright). Still, the pun-ishment was severe and shows how seriously plagiarism is taken at every level of the university.

PLAGIARIZING IDEAS

Plagiarizing doesn't just mean borrowing someone else's words. It also means borrowing someone else's ideas. Let's say you are impressed by an article comparing *Catcher in the Rye* and *Hamlet*.[7] The article concludes that these works are variations on a single theme: a young man's profound anguish and mental instability, as shown through his troubled internal monologues. If your paper incorporates this striking idea, credit the author who proposed it, *even if every word you say about it is your own.* Otherwise

---

5. Besides copying words and phrases from Richard Rhodes and Robert Norris, VanDeMark took passages from Greg Herken, William Lanouette, and Mary Palevsky without proper quotations or full attribution. Some passages are *not* obvious cases of plagiarism—deliberate or accidental—but some are nearly identical to other works, and still others are too close for comfort. The overall pattern is troubling.

These parallels between VanDeMark's work and other books are documented online with similar tables. See History News Network, "Brian VanDeMark: Accused of Plagia-rism," May 31, 2003, http://hnn.us/articles/1477.html. That page links to several tables comparing VanDeMark's wording to various authors'.

6. Nelson Hernández, "Scholar's Tenure Pulled for Plagiarism: Acts Not Deliberate, Naval Academy Says," *Washington Post*, October 29, 2003, B06, http://www.washington post.com/wp-dyn/articles/A32551-2003Oct28.html.

7. Although I thought of this comparison between Hamlet and Holden Caulfield myself, I suspected others had too. Just to be on the safe side, I decided to do a Google search. The top item offered to sell me a term paper on the subject! After this depress-ing discovery, I decided to search for "Catcher in the Rye + phony." I was deluged with offers. What a delicious irony: to buy a term paper on Holden Caulfield's hatred of all things phony.

your paper will wrongly imply you came up with the idea yourself. Holden Caulfield would call you a phony. The moral of the tale: it's perfectly fine to draw on others' ideas, as long as you give them credit. The only exception is when the ideas are commonplace.

DISTORTING IDEAS

A recurrent theme of this chapter is that you should acknowledge others' words and ideas and represent them faithfully, without distortion. When you paraphrase them, you should keep the author's meaning, even if you disagree with it. When you shorten a quote, you should indicate that you've shortened it and keep the essential idea.

There are really two goals here. One is to maintain honesty in your own work. The other is to engage others' ideas fully on a level playing field. That's the best way to confront diverse ideas, whether you agree with them or not. That's fair play, of course, but it's more than that. It's how you make your own work better. You are proving the strength of your approach by passing a tough, fair test—one that compares your ideas to others without stacking the deck in your favor.

The danger to avoid is setting up flimsy straw men so you can knock them down without much effort. That's not only dishonest; it's intellectually lazy. Believe me, your own position will be much stronger and more effective if you confront the best opposing arguments, presented fairly, and show why yours is better.

CONCLUSION: THE RIGHT WAY
TO PARAPHRASE AND CITE

The rules for paraphrasing and citation are based on a few core ideas:

- You are responsible for your written work, including the ideas, facts, and interpretations you include.
- Unless you say otherwise, every word you write is assumed to be your own.
- When you rely on others' work or ideas, acknowledge it openly.
  - When you use their ideas or data, give them credit.
  - When you use their exact words, use quotation marks plus a citation.

- ○ When you paraphrase, use your own distinctive voice and cite the original source. Make sure your language doesn't mimic the original. If it still does after rewriting, then use direct quotes.
- When you draw on others' work, present it fairly. No distortions. No straw men.
- When you present empirical material, show where you acquired it so others can check the data for themselves. (The exception is commonly known material, which does not need to be cited.)

These principles of fairness and disclosure are more than simple rules for citation. They are more than just "good housekeeping" in your paper. They are fundamental rules for academic integrity. They promote real learning. They apply to teachers and students alike and encourage free, fair, and open discussion of ideas—the heart and soul of a university.

Citations in Every Format
A Quick Guide

• • • • • • • • • • • •

In this part of the book I'll cover citation styles in nearly every field you might encounter as a student. If the world were simple, they'd all be the same. In fact, each one has its little idiosyncrasies, its own twists and turns. Fortunately, none of them is complicated.

Chapter 5 covers some basics of citation for all fields. After that I'll describe each style in its own chapter. Each chapter shows you exactly how to cite the works you'll use, from a journal article, to the second volume of a three-volume work, to a podcast. Because each style is presented separately, you only need to turn to one chapter when you write a paper.

Which style should you use? That depends on which field your paper is in, what your professor suggests, and which one you prefer. If your paper is in the humanities, you'll use either Chicago or MLA citations. If it's in the social sciences, engineering, education, or business, you'll use either Chicago or APA. The biological sciences, chemistry, computer sciences, mathematics, and physics all have their own individual styles and sometimes more than one per field. I'll cover each one and include plenty of examples.

In the final chapter I'll answer some frequently asked questions dealing with all types of citations, in all styles. For example, should you cite your background readings? How many sources should your paper have? Can you include analysis in your footnotes?

Now on to the basics of citation and, after that, the specifics of each style.

THE BASICS OF CITATION

5

· · · · · · · · · · · · · ·

Acknowledging your sources is crucial to doing honest academic work. That means citing them properly, using one of several styles. The one you choose depends on your field, your professor's advice if you are a student, and your own preferences.

There are three major citation styles:

- Chicago (or Turabian), used in many fields
- MLA, used in the humanities
- APA, used in social sciences, education, and business

Several sciences have also developed their own distinctive styles:

- CSE for the biological sciences
- AMA for the biomedical sciences, medicine, nursing, and dentistry
- ACS for chemistry
- AIP for physics, plus other styles for astrophysics and astronomy
- various styles for mathematics, computer sciences, and engineering

I will cover each one, providing clear directions and plenty of examples so you won't have any trouble writing correct citations. That way you can concentrate on your paper, not on the type of citation you're using. I'll cover each style separately so you can turn directly to the one you need. Using this information, you'll be able to cite books, articles, websites, films, musical performances, government documents, text messages, podcasts, tweets—whatever you use in your papers.

Why would you ever want to use different citation styles? Why can't you just pick one and stick with it? Because different fields won't let you. They have designed citation styles to meet their special needs, whether it's genetics or German, and you'll just have to use the appropriate one. In some sciences, for instance, proper citations list only the author, journal, and pages. They omit the article's title. If you did that in the humanities or social sciences, you'd be incorrect because proper citations for those fields *require* the title. Go figure.

Compare these bibliographic citations for an article of mine:

Chicago   Lipson. Charles. "Why Are Some International Agreements Informal?" *International Organization* 45, no. 4 (Autumn 1991): 495–538.

APA   Lipson, C. (1991). Why are some international agreements informal? *International Organization, 45,* 495–538.

ACS   Lipson, C. *Int. Org.* 1991, 45, 495.

None of these is complicated, but they *are* different. When you leave the chemistry lab to take a course on Shakespeare, you'll leave behind your citation style as well as your beakers. Not to worry. For chemistry papers, just turn to chapter 8. For Shakespeare, turn to chapter 4, which covers MLA citations for the humanities. Both chapters include lots of examples, presented in simple tables, so it won't be "double, double toil and trouble."

Despite their differences, *all these citation styles have the same basic goals*:

- to identify and credit the sources you use; and
- to give readers specific information so they can access these sources themselves if they wish.

Fortunately, the different styles include a lot of the same information. That means you can write down the same things as you take notes, without worrying about what kind of citations you will ultimately use. You should write down that information as soon as you start taking notes on a new source. If you print out or photocopy an article, write all the reference information on the first page. If you do it immediately, you won't forget. You'll need it later for citations.

Or maybe you will be working with an online citation generator. These programs can do a lot of the work of gathering and formatting the information for you. But some of them are better and more reliable than others. Some can handle only the most common citation styles or source types (good luck if you need to cite a podcast in CSE style!). It's your responsibility to make sure your citations are accurate and complete, and this book can help you get the details right for a wide range of styles and sources.

How these citations will ultimately look depends on which style you use. Most styles include some kind of marker in the text, immediately following the material you need to cite, and a fuller listing of the details of the source elsewhere in the paper, usually at the end. The in-text marker might be a number, given as a superscript [99] or in brackets [99] or parentheses (99). Or it might be a note in parentheses including a couple of key pieces of the citation, such as the author's last name plus the publication date or page number. The fuller listing usually includes the author's name, the title of the source, the publication date, and other details.

For example, Chicago (or Turabian)[1] style uses notes keyed to superscript numbers in the text. You place the notes either at the bottom of each page (footnotes) or at the end of the document (endnotes). Footnotes and endnotes are identical, except for their placement. Word processors give you an easy choice between the two. The notes contain either complete citations or shortened versions, plus a bibliography at the end of the paper.

The other two major citation styles—MLA and APA[2]—look a little different. They use in-text citations such as (Stewart 154) or (Stewart, 2018) with full information provided only in a reference list at the end.[3]

Your department, school, or publisher may prefer one style or even require it, or they might leave it up to you. Check on that as soon as you begin writing papers with citations. Why not do it consistently from the beginning?

> *Tip on selecting a citation style*: Check with your teachers in each class to find out what style citations they prefer. Then use that style consistently.

---

1. As explained in chapter 3, these two names refer to the same style, as covered in two different books published by the University of Chicago Press. *The Chicago Manual of Style*, 17th ed. (Chicago: University of Chicago Press, 2017) is the most comprehensive treatment of the style. Students can find everything they need in a separate book, Kate L. Turabian, *A Manual for Writers of Research Papers, Theses, and Dissertations,* 9th ed., rev. Wayne C. Booth, Gregory C. Colomb, Joseph M. Williams, Joseph Bizup, William T. FitzGerald, and the University of Chicago Press Editorial Staff (Chicago: University of Chicago Press, 2018).

2. In case you are wondering about the initials: MLA stands for the Modern Language Association and APA stands for the American Psychological Association. See chapters 4 and 5 for more details.

3. Reference lists are similar to bibliographies, but there are some technical differences. In later chapters I'll explain the details (and nomenclature) of each style.

Speaking of consistency, it's important for proper citations. Stick with the same abbreviations and capitalizations, and don't mix styles within a paper. It's easy to write "Volume" in one citation, "Vol." in another, and "vol." in a third. We all do it, and then we have to correct it. We all abbreviate "chapter" as both "chap." and "ch." Just try your best the first time around, and then go back and fix the mistakes when you revise. That's why they invented the search-and-replace function.

My goal here is to provide a one-stop reference so that you can handle nearly all citation issues you'll face, regardless of which style you use and what kinds of items you cite. For each style, I'll show you how to cite books, articles, unpublished papers, websites, and lots more. For specialized documents such as musical scores or scientific preprints, I show citations only in the fields that actually use them. Physicists often cite preprints, but they don't cite Beethoven. The physics chapter reflects those needs. Students in the humanities not only cite Beethoven; they cite dance performances, plays, and poems. I have included MLA citations for all of them. In case you need to cite something well off the beaten path, I'll explain where to find additional information for each style.

HANGING INDENTS

One final point about shared bibliographic style. Most bibliographies and reference lists—Chicago, MLA, APA, and some of the sciences—use a special style known as "hanging indents." This applies only to the bibliography and not to footnotes or endnotes. It is the opposite of regular paragraph indention, where the first line is indented and the rest are regular length. In a hanging indent, the first line of each citation is regular length and the rest are indented. For example:

Rothenberg, Gunther E. "Maurice of Nassau, Gustavus Adolphus, Raimondo Montecuccoli, and the 'Military Revolution' of the Seventeenth Century." In *Makers of Modern Strategy from Machiavelli to the Nuclear Age*, edited by Peter Paret, 32–63. Princeton, NJ: Princeton University Press, 1986.

Spooner, Frank C. *Risks at Sea: Amsterdam Insurance and Maritime Europe, 1766–1780*. Cambridge: Cambridge University Press, 1983.

There's a good reason for this unusual format. Hanging indents are designed to make it easy to skim down the list of references and see the authors' names. To remind you to use this format, I'll use it myself when

I illustrate references in the citation styles that use it. (The only ones that don't use hanging indents are science styles with numbered citations. It's actually not complicated, and I'll explain it later.)

To make the authors' names stand out further, most bibliographies or reference lists put their last names first. If an author's name is repeated, however, the styles differ. APA repeats the full name for each citation. Chicago used to call for three em dashes (that is, long dashes), followed by a period, but now encourages repeating the author's name, like APA.[4] MLA uses three hyphens followed by a period.

> Talbot, Ian. *A History of Modern South Asia: Politics, States, Diasporas.* Yale UP, 2016.
> ---. *Pakistan: A Modern History.* Palgrave Macmillan, 2010.

You can arrange hanging indents easily on your word processor. Go to the format feature and, within it, the section on paragraphs. Choose hanging indentation instead of regular or none.

WHERE TO FIND MORE

So far I have covered some basic issues that apply to most citation styles. There are, of course, lots more questions, some that apply to all styles and some that apply only to one or two. Rather than cover these questions now, I'll handle them in the chapters on individual citation styles and in a final chapter on frequently asked questions (FAQs).

If you have questions that aren't covered in the chapter on your citation style, be sure to check the FAQs chapter. If you still have questions, you can always go to the reference book for a given style. Most styles have them (but not all). I'll list them in the chapters for individual styles.

ON TO THE NUTS AND BOLTS

I have organized the references so they are most convenient for you, putting all the documentation for each style in its own chapter.

---

4. Because em dashes are longer than hyphens, they show up differently on screen and in print. The em dashes show up as a solid line, the hyphens as separate dashes. Three em dashes: ———. Three hyphens: ---. Frankly, you don't need to worry about this for your papers. Use the preferred one if you can, but either is fine.

Chapter 3: Chicago (or Turabian) citations

Chapter 4: MLA citations for the humanities

Chapter 5: APA citations for the social sciences, education, and business

Chapter 6: CSE citations for the biological sciences

Chapter 7: AMA citations for the biomedical sciences, medicine, nursing, and dentistry

Chapter 8: ACS citations for chemistry

Chapter 9: Physics, astrophysics, and astronomy citations

Chapter 10: Mathematics, computer science, and engineering citations

Within each chapter I've started with some general information about the style covered, and then moved on to examples of how to cite specific kinds of sources. I've put the most common types of sources at the beginning—usually books or journal articles—and grouped similar sources together. For the first three chapters, which are the longest and most detailed, I've also provided an index of the source types early in the chapter. You can use the index to go right to the examples for journal articles or blog posts or whatever you need to cite.

I've included a wide range of online and other electronic sources. In some cases the official style guides don't cover things like podcasts or text messages, either because the field that follows that style doesn't use them as sources or because the style guide hasn't been updated lately. Where I thought you might need to cite a source like this, I have provided examples based on the style's general rules. Since there are new types of sources to cite all the time, you might need to do the same thing if there isn't an example here.

Don't bother trying to memorize any of these styles. There are simply too many minor details. Just follow the tables, and you'll be able to handle different sources—from journal articles to podcasts—in whichever style you need to use. Later, as you write more papers, you'll become familiar with the style you use most.

After explaining each style and answering questions about it, I will also answer some common questions that apply to every style. That's in chapter 11. Now let's see how to do citations and bibliographies in the specific style you want to use.

6

CHICAGO (OR TURABIAN) CITATIONS

. . . .

Chicago citations are based on the authoritative *Chicago Manual of Style*, published by the University of Chicago Press. The manual, now in its seventeenth edition (2017), is the bible for references and academic style, and is also available online at www.chicagomanualofstyle.org. A briefer version, covering most aspects of student papers, is Kate L. Turabian's *A Manual for Writers of Research Papers, Theses, and Dissertations*, now in its ninth edition (2018). This section, however, should cover all you need to document your sources, even if they're unusual.

FULL NOTES, SHORT NOTES, AND BIBLIOGRAPHY

Chicago-style notes come in two flavors, and I include both in this section.[1]

1. A complete first note + short follow-up notes

The first note for any item is a full one, giving complete information about the book, article, or other document. Subsequent entries for that item are brief. There is no need for a bibliography since all the information is covered in the first note (but your department or publisher may require one, so check with them first).

2. Short notes only + bibliography

All notes are brief. Full information about the sources appears only in the bibliography.

---

1. *The Chicago Manual of Style* and Turabian also describe another style, the author-date system. These citations appear in parentheses in the text, listing the author and the date of publication. For example: (Walls 2017). Full citations appear in a reference list at the end. For simplicity, I have omitted this style since it is similar to APA, discussed in chapter 5.

This means there are three ways to cite individual items. All of them are illustrated in this chapter.

A. Full first notes
B. Short notes
C. Bibliographic entries

The first flavor combines A + B, the second combines B + C.

This chapter covers everything from edited books to online journals, from sheet music to music videos, and lots of things in between. To make it easy to find what you need, I've listed them here alphabetically, together with the pages they are on. At the end of this chapter I answer some questions about using this style.

INDEX OF CHICAGO CITATIONS IN THIS CHAPTER

CHICAGO MANUAL OF STYLE: NOTES AND BIBLIOGRAPHY

Book, one author	Full first note	[99] Charles Lipson, *Reliable Partners: How Democracies Have Made a Separate Peace* (Princeton, NJ: Princeton University Press, 2003), 22–23.

    ▸ This is note number 99 and refers to pages 22–23.

    ▸ Footnotes and endnotes do not have hanging indents. Only the bibliography does.

[99] Terry McDermott, *Off Speed: Baseball, Pitching, and the Art of Deception* (New York: Pantheon, 2017), 1028.

    ▸ Chicago abbreviates consecutive page numbers as follows: if the first number is two digits or less, repeat all digits (1–12, 44–68); if the first number is three digits or more and not a multiple of one hundred, include only the changed part (203–6, 345–52, 349–402 *but* 200–223). If this sounds confusing, it is. Fortunately, it's always acceptable to repeat all digits.

Short note

[99] Lipson, *Reliable Partners*, 22–23.
[99] McDermott, *Off Speed*, 102–8.

    ▸ Shorten titles to four words or fewer, if possible.

Bibliography

Lipson, Charles. *Reliable Partners: How Democracies Have Made a Separate Peace*. Princeton, NJ: Princeton University Press, 2003.

McDermott, Terry. *Off Speed: Baseball, Pitching, and the Art of Deception*. New York: Pantheon, 2017.

Books, several by same author	First note	[99] Ian Talbot, *A History of Modern South Asia: Politics, States, Diasporas* (New Haven, CT: Yale University Press, 2016). [100] Ian Talbot, *Pakistan: A Modern History* (London: Palgrave Macmillan, 2010).
	Short note	[99] Talbot, *History of Modern South Asia*. [100] Talbot, *Pakistan*.

Books, several by same author (*continued*)	Bibliography	Talbot, Ian. *A History of Modern South Asia: Politics, States, Diasporas*. New Haven, CT: Yale University Press, 2016. Talbot, Ian. *Pakistan: A Modern History*. London: Palgrave Macmillan, 2010.

▸ For multiple books by the same author, simply repeat the author's name in the bibliography. You may instead use three em dashes (which are simply long dashes), followed by a period, but this method is not recommended because it may obscure important information in the entry. If you're not sure how to create the em dash, just use three hyphens.

▸ List works for each author alphabetically by title. In alphabetizing, disregard any initial article: *A*, *An*, *The*.

Book, multiple authors	First note	[99] John Martin Fischer and Benjamin Mitchell-Yellin, *Near-Death Experiences: Understanding Visions of the Afterlife* (Oxford: Oxford University Press, 2016), 15–18.

▸ For four or more authors, use only the first author's name plus "et al." (Latin *et alii*, "and others"). For example, if this one had four-plus authors: John Martin Fischer et al., *Near-Death* . . .

	Short note	[99] Fischer and Mitchell-Yellin, *Near-Death Experiences*, 15–18.

▸ Titles with four words or fewer are not shortened.

	Bibliography	Fischer, John Martin, and Benjamin Mitchell-Yellin. *Near-Death Experiences: Understanding Visions of the Afterlife*. Oxford: Oxford University Press, 2016.

▸ Only the first author's name is inverted.

▸ List up to ten coauthors in the bibliography. If there are more, list the first seven, followed by "et al."

Book, multiple editions	First note	⁹⁹ Annelise Orleck, *Common Sense and a Little Fire: Women and Working-Class Politics in the United States, 1900–1965*, 2nd ed. (Chapel Hill: University of North Carolina Press, 2017). ⁹⁹ William Strunk Jr. and E. B. White, *The Elements of Style*, 50th anniversary ed. (New York: Longman, 2009), 12.
	Short note	⁹⁹ Orleck, *Common Sense*. ⁹⁹ Strunk and White, *Elements of Style*, 12. ▸ To keep the note short, the title doesn't include the initial article (*The Elements of Style*) or the edition number.
	Bibliography	Orleck, Annelise. *Common Sense and a Little Fire: Women and Working-Class Politics in the United States, 1900–1965*, 2nd ed. Chapel Hill: University of North Carolina Press, 2017. Strunk, William, Jr., and E. B. White. *The Elements of Style*. 50th anniversary ed. New York: Longman, 2009.
Book, edited	First note	⁹⁹ Annie Bunting and Joel Quirk, eds., *Contemporary Slavery: Popular Rhetoric and Political Practice* (Vancouver: University of British Columbia Press, 2017). ⁹⁹ Jeffrey Ian Ross, ed., *Routledge Handbook of Graffiti and Street Art* (New York: Routledge, 2016). ⁹⁹ Mirjam Künkler, John Madeley, and Shylashri Shankar, eds., *A Secular Age beyond the West* (Cambridge: Cambridge University Press, 2017).
	Short note	⁹⁹ Bunting and Quirk, *Contemporary Slavery*. ▸ Do not include the abbreviation for editor in short notes. ⁹⁹ Ross, *Graffiti and Street Art*. ▸ Choose the most relevant words when shortening the title.

Book, edited (*continued*)		[99] Künkler, Madeley, and Shankar, *Secular Age.*
	Bibliography	Bunting, Annie, and Joel Quirk, eds. *Contemporary Slavery: Popular Rhetoric and Political Practice.* Vancouver: University of British Columbia Press, 2017. Ross, Jeffrey Ian, ed. *Routledge Handbook of Graffiti and Street Art.* New York: Routledge, 2016. Künkler, Mirjam, John Madeley, and Shylashri Shankar, eds. *A Secular Age beyond the West.* Cambridge: Cambridge University Press, 2017.
Book, anonymous or no author	First note	[99] Anonymous, *The Secret Lives of Teachers* (Chicago: University of Chicago Press, 2015). [99] *Golden Verses of the Pythagoreans* (Whitefish, MT: Kessinger, 2003).
	Short note	[99] Anonymous, *Secret Lives of Teachers.* [99] *Golden Verses of Pythagoreans.*
	Bibliography	Anonymous. *The Secret Lives of Teachers.* Chicago: University of Chicago Press, 2015. *Golden Verses of the Pythagoreans.* Whitefish, MT: Kessinger, 2003. ▸ If a book lists "anonymous" as the author, then that word should be included. If no author is listed, then you may list "anonymous" or simply begin with the title.
E-book	First note	[99] Gary Taubes, *The Case against Sugar* (New York: Alfred A. Knopf, 2016), Kindle. [99] Kate Auspitz, *Wallis's War: A Novel of Diplomacy and Intrigue* (Chicago: University of Chicago Press, 2015), iBooks. ▸ For e-books, include the name of the device or app used to read the book. If a file format such as EPUB or PDF is specified, you can note that in addition to the name of the device or app (e.g., Adobe Digital Editions EPUB).

> ► To specify location within an e-book,
> it's best to cite a chapter number, section
> heading, or other signpost, since page and
> location numbers may vary depending on
> the device or app.

Short note	[99] Taubes, *Case against Sugar*, chap. 2. [99] Auspitz, *Wallis's War*.
Bibliography	Taubes, Gary. *The Case against Sugar*. New York: Alfred A. Knopf, 2016. Kindle. Auspitz, Kate. *Wallis's War: A Novel of Diplomacy and Intrigue*. Chicago: University of Chicago Press, 2015. iBooks. Adobe Digital Editions EPUB.

Book, online

First note	[99] Charles Dickens, *Great Expectations* (1867; Project Gutenberg, 2008), chap. 2, http://www.gutenberg.org/files/1400/1400-h/1400-h.htm. [99] Frederick Jackson Turner, *The Frontier in American History* (New York: Henry Holt, 1921), 6, https://books.google.com/books/about/The_Frontier_in_American_History.html?id=vtF1AAAAMAAJ.

> ► Include the URL as the last part of the
> citation. A URL based on a DOI (appended
> to https://doi.org/) is preferable to a URL.
> ► There are often multiple formats of a
> book available online. When possible, use
> scanned pages of a printed book instead of
> reflowable text (like HTML or EPUB). It
> is more authoritative and will make page
> citation easier. The Turner edition here is a
> scanned version of the original.
> ► If you can't find a version with page numbers, refer to a chapter number, section
> heading, or similar signpost.

Short note	[99] Dickens, *Great Expectations*, chap. 2. [99] Turner, *Frontier in American History*, 6.
Bibliography	Dickens, Charles. *Great Expectations*. 1867. Project Gutenberg, 2008.http://www.gutenberg.org/files/1400/1400-h/1400-h.htm.

Book, online *(continued)*		Turner, Frederick Jackson. *The Frontier in American History*. New York: Henry Holt, 1921. https://books.google.com/books/about/The_Frontier_in_American_History.html?id=vtF1AAAAMAAJ.
Multivolume work	First note	[99] Otto Pflanze, *Bismarck and the Development of Germany*, 3 vols. (Princeton, NJ: Princeton University Press, 1963–90), 1:153. [99] Babette Rothschild, *The Body Remembers*, 2 vols. (New York: W. W. Norton, 2017), 2:16.
	Short note	[99] Pflanze, *Bismarck*, 1:153. [99] Rothschild, *Body Remembers*, 2:16.
	Bibliography	Pflanze, Otto. *Bismarck and the Development of Germany*. 3 vols. Princeton, NJ: Princeton University Press, 1963–90. Rothschild, Babette. *The Body Remembers*, 2 vols. New York: W. W. Norton, 2017.
Single volume in a multivolume work	First note	[99] Robert A. Caro, *The Years of Lyndon Johnson*, vol. 4, *The Passage of Power* (New York: Alfred A. Knopf, 2012), 237. [99] Bruce E. Johansen, *Global Warming in the 21st Century*, vol. 2, *Melting Ice and Warming Seas* (Westport, CT: Praeger, 2006), 71. [99] Akira Iriye, *The Globalizing of America*, vol. 3 of *Cambridge History of American Foreign Relations*, ed. Warren I. Cohen (Cambridge: Cambridge University Press, 1993), 124. ▸ Caro wrote all three volumes. Iriye wrote only the third volume in a series edited by Cohen.
	Short note	[99] Caro, *Years of Lyndon Johnson*, 4:237. ▸ or [99] Caro, *Passage of Power*, 237. [99] Johansen, *Global Warming*, 2:71. ▸ or [99] Johansen, *Melting Ice and Warming Seas*, 71. [99] Iriye, *Globalizing of America*, 124.

Bibliography   Caro, Robert A. *The Years of Lyndon Johnson.*
                  Vol. 4, *The Passage of Power.* New York:
                  Alfred A. Knopf, 2012.
                  Johansen, Bruce E. *Global Warming in the*
                  21st Century. Vol. 2, *Melting Ice and*
                  Warming Seas. Westport, CT: Praeger,
                  2006.
                  Iriye, Akira. *The Globalizing of America.*
                  Vol. 3 of *Cambridge History of American*
                  Foreign Relations, edited by Warren I.
                  Cohen. Cambridge: Cambridge University
                  Press, 1993.

Reprint of   First note   ⁹⁹ Jacques Barzun, *Simple and Direct: A Rhet-*
earlier edition   *oric for Writers*, rev. ed. (1985; repr., Chicago:
                                    University of Chicago Press, 1994), 27.
                                    ⁹⁹ Adam Smith, *An Inquiry into the Nature*
                                    and Causes of the Wealth of Nations (1776),
                                    ed. Edwin Cannan (Chicago: University of
                                    Chicago Press, 1976).

                                    ▸ The year 1776 appears immediately after the
                                       title because that's when Smith's original
                                       work appeared. The editor, Edwin Cannan,
                                       worked only on its modern publication.
                                       The Barzun volume, by contrast, is simply a
                                       reprint so the original year appears as part
                                       of the publication information.

                   Short note   ⁹⁹ Barzun, *Simple and Direct*, 27.
                                    ⁹⁹ Smith, *Wealth of Nations*, vol. I, bk. IV,
                                    chap. II: 477.

                                    ▸ This modern edition of Smith is actually
                                       a single volume, but it retains the volume
                                       numbering of the 1776 original. You could
                                       simply cite the page number, but the full
                                       citation helps readers with other editions.

                   Bibliography   Barzun, Jacques. *Simple and Direct: A Rhet-*
                                    oric for Writers. 1985. Reprint, Chicago:
                                    University of Chicago Press, 1994.
                                    Smith, Adam. *An Inquiry into the Nature and*
                                    Causes of the Wealth of Nations. 1776.
                                    Edited by Edwin Cannan. Chicago: Univer-
                                    sity of Chicago Press, 1976.

Translated volume	First note	[99] Hesiod, *The Poems of Hesiod: Theogony, Works and Days, & The Shield of Herakles*, trans. Barry B. Powell (Oakland: University of California Press, 2017), 30–35. [99] Alexis de Tocqueville, *Democracy in America* (1835), ed. J. P. Mayer, trans. George Lawrence (New York: HarperCollins, 2000). ▸ Translator and editor are listed in the order they appear on the book's title page. [99] Seamus Heaney, trans., *Beowulf: A New Verse Translation* (New York: Farrar, Straus and Giroux, 2000). ▸ For *Beowulf*, the translator's name appears before the book title because Heaney's is the only name on the title page. (The poem is anonymous.) The same treatment would be given to an editor or compiler whose name appeared alone on the title page.
	Short note	[99] Hessiod, *Poems*, 30–35. [99] Tocqueville, *Democracy in America*. [99] *Beowulf*. ▸ or [99] Heaney, *Beowulf*.
	Bibliography	Hesiod. *The Poems of Hesiod: Theogony, Works and Days, & The Shield of Herakles*. Translated by Barry B. Powell. Oakland: University of California Press, 2017. Tocqueville, Alexis de. *Democracy in America*. 1835. Edited by J. P. Mayer. Translated by George Lawrence. New York: HarperCollins, 2000. Heaney, Seamus, trans. *Beowulf: A New Verse Translation*. New York: Farrar, Straus and Giroux, 2000.
Chapter in edited book	First note	[99] Benjamin J. Cohen, "The Macrofoundations of Monetary Power," in *International Monetary Power*, ed. David M. Andrews (Ithaca, NY: Cornell University Press, 2006), 31–50.

	Short note	[99] Cohen, "The Macrofoundations of Monetary Power," 31–50.
	Bibliography	Cohen, Benjamin J. "The Macrofoundations of Monetary Power." In *International Monetary Power*, edited by David M. Andrews, 31–50. Ithaca, NY: Cornell University Press, 2006.

Journal article	First note	[99] Stefan Timmermans, "Matching Genotype and Phenotype: A Pragmatist Semiotic Analysis of Clinical Exome Sequencing," *American Journal of Sociology* 123, no. 1 (July 2017): 137.
		[99] Smita Sahgal, "Situating Kingship within an Embryonic Frame of Masculinity in Early India," *Social Scientist* 43, no. 11/12 (November–December 2015): 5, http://www.jstor.org.pnw.idm.oclc.org/stable/24642382.
		[99] Krista A. Capps, Carla L. Atkinson, and Amanda T. Rugenski, "Implications of Species Addition and Decline for Nutrient Dynamics in Fresh Waters," *Freshwater Science* 34, no. 2 (June 2015): 490, https://doi.org/10.1086/681095.

- ► For journal articles accessed online, include the URL or Digital Object Identifier (DOI) as the last part of the citation. A URL based on a DOI (appended to https://doi.org/) is preferable to another type of URL. If there is no DOI or URL, list the name of the database.
- ► For four or more authors, list only the first author's name plus "et al."
- ► Cite an abstract the same way you would a journal article, but add the word *abstract* after the article title.

	Short note	[99] Timmermans, "Matching Genotype and Phenotype," 137.
		[99] Sahgal, "Situating Kingship," 5.

Journal article (*continued*)		[99] Capps, Atkinson, and Rugenski, "Implications of Species Addition and Decline," 490.

▸ In a note, refer only to the page(s) cited, if any; in a bibliography, give the page range for the whole article.

	Bibliography	Timmermans, Stefan. "Matching Genotype and Phenotype: A Pragmatist Semiotic Analysis of Clinical Exome Sequencing." *American Journal of Sociology* 123, no. 1 (July 2017): 137–77.

Sahgal, Smita. "Situating Kingship within an Embryonic Frame of Masculinity in Early India." *Social Scientist* 43, no. 11/12 (November–December 2015): 3–26. http://www.jstor.org.pnw.idm.oclc.org/stable/24642382.

Capps, Krista A., Carla L. Atkinson, and Amanda T. Rugenski. "Implications of Species Addition and Decline for Nutrient Dynamics in Fresh Waters." *Freshwater Science* 34, no. 2 (June 2015): 485–96, https://doi.org/10.1086/681095.

▸ Only the first author's name is inverted.

▸ List up to ten coauthors in the bibliography. If there are more, list the first seven, followed by "et al."

Journal article, foreign language	First note	[99] Zvi Uri Ma'oz, "Y a-t-il des juifs sans synagogue?," *Revue des Études Juives* 163 (juillet–décembre 2004): 485.

▸ or

[99] Zvi Uri Ma'oz, "Y a-t-il des juifs sans synagogue?" [Are there Jews without a synagogue?], *Revue des Études Juives* 163 (juillet–décembre 2004): 485.

	Short note	[99] Ma'oz, "Y a-t-il des juifs sans synagogue?," 485.

	Bibliography	Ma'oz, Zvi Uri. "Y a-t-il des juifs sans synagogue?" *Revue des Études Juives* 163 (juillet–décembre 2004): 483–93.

▸ or

Ma'oz, Zvi Uri. "Y a-t-il des juifs sans synagogue?" [Are there Jews without a synagogue?]. *Revue des Études Juives* 163 (juillet–décembre 2004): 483–93.

Newspaper or magazine article	First note	⁹⁹ "Retired U.S. General Is Focus of Inquiry over Iran Leak," *New York Times*, June 28, 2013, A18.

> This refers to page A18. You may omit page numbers if you wish, since many newspapers have different editions with different pagination.

⁹⁹ Shivani Vora, "Why Your Airline Says It's Sorry," *New York Times*, July 30, 2017, Sunday edition.

⁹⁹ Evan Halper, "Congress Takes Aim at the Clean Air Act, Putting the Limits of California's Power to the Test," *Los Angeles Times*, August 3, 2017, 3:00 a.m. PDT, http://www.latimes.com/politics/la-na-pol-smog-republicans-20170803-story.html.

> Include the URL or DOI at the end of the citation for articles accessed online.
> If the article is updated often, include a time stamp as posted with the article.

⁹⁹ Ian Parker, "The Greek Warrior: How a Radical Finance Minister Took on Europe — and Failed," *New Yorker*, August 3, 2015, 46.

> Articles in magazines intended for general audiences are treated the same as newspaper articles and cited by date only. Some magazines are more like journals. If you are unsure what you're citing—journal or magazine—look for a volume number. If you spot one without too much trouble, cite as a journal.

Short note

⁹⁹ "Focus of Inquiry," *New York Times*, A18.
⁹⁹ Vora, "Airline Says It's Sorry."
⁹⁹ Harper, "Congress Takes Aim."
⁹⁹ Parker, "The Greek Warrior," 46.

Newspaper or magazine article (*continued*)		▸ Since newspapers and magazines are usually omitted from the bibliography, use a full citation for the first reference.
	Bibliography	▸ Newspaper and magazine articles are left out of bibliographies, but you can include an especially important article:

"Retired U.S. General Is Focus of Inquiry over Iran Leak." *New York Times*. June 28, 2013, A18.

Parker, Ian. "The Greek Warrior: How a Radical Finance Minister Took on Europe — and Failed." *New Yorker*, August 3, 2015, 44–57.

Review	First note	[99] Allison J. Pugh, review of *The Gender Trap: Parents and the Pitfalls of Raising Boys and Girls*, by Emily W. Kane, *American Journal of Sociology* 119, no. 6 (May 2014): 1773–75.

[99] Giovanni Vimercati, "Soviet Pseudo-science: The History of Mind Control," review of *Homo Sovieticus: Brain Waves, Mind Control, and Telepathic Destiny*, by Wladimir Velminski, *Los Angeles Review of Books*, August 20, 2017, https://lareviewofbooks .org/article/soviet-pseudoscience-the -history-of-mind-control.

	Short note	[99] Pugh, review of *Gender Trap*.

[99] Vimercati, "Soviet Pseudoscience."

▸ or

[99] Vimercati, review of *Homo Sovieticus*.

	Bibliography	Pugh, Allison J. Review of *The Gender Trap: Parents and the Pitfalls of Raising Boys and Girls*, by Emily W. Kane. *American Journal of Sociology* 119, no. 6 (May 2014): 1773–75.

Ferguson, Niall. "Ameliorate, Contain, Coerce, Destroy." Review of *The Utility of Force: The Art of War in the Modern World*, by Rupert Smith. *New York Times Book Review*, February 4, 2007, 14–15.

Unpublished paper, thesis, or dissertation	First note	[99] Shaojie Tang, "Profit Driven Team Grouping in Social Networks" (paper presented at the Thirty-First AAAI Conference on Artificial Intelligence, February 4–9, 2017), https://aaai.org/ocs/index.php/AAAI/AAAI17/paper/view/14791/13741. [99] Lance Noble, "One Goal, Multiple Strategies: Engagement in Sino-American WTO Accession Negotiations" (master's thesis, University of British Columbia, 2006), 15. [99] Luis Manuel Sierra, "Indigenous Neighborhood Residents in the Urbanization of La Paz, Bolivia, 1910–1950," (PhD diss., State University of New York at Binghamton, 2013), ProQuest. ▸ If you consult a paper through a commercial database, include the name of the database. Include a URL for papers consulted online.
	Short note	[99] Tang, "Profit Driven Team Grouping." [99] Noble, "One Goal, Multiple Strategies." [99] Sierra, "Indigenous Neighborhood Residents."
	Bibliography	Tang, Shaojie. "Profit Driven Team Grouping in Social Networks." Paper presented at the Thirty-First AAAI Conference on Artificial Intelligence, February 4–9, 2017, https://aaai.org/ocs/index.php/AAAI/AAAI17/paper/view/14791/13741. Noble, Lance. "One Goal, Multiple Strategies: Engagement in Sino-American WTO Accession Negotiations." Master's thesis, University of British Columbia, 2006. Sierra, Luis Manuel. "Indigenous Neighborhood Residents in the Urbanization of La Paz, Bolivia, 1910–1950." PhD diss., State University of New York at Binghamton, 2013. ProQuest (3612828).

Preprint or working paper	First note	[99] John C. Rodda et al., "A Comparative Study of the Magnitude, Frequency and Distribution of Intense Rainfall in the United Kingdom," preprint, October 9, 2009, http://precedings.nature.com/documents/3847/version/1. [99] Daniel P. Gross, "The Ties That Bind: Railroad Gauge Standards and Internal Trade in the 19th Century U.S." (working paper, Berkeley Economic History Lab, University of California, Berkeley, March 2016), http://behl.berkeley.edu/working-papers/.
	Short note	[99] Rodda et al., "Rainfall in the United Kingdom." [99] Gross, "The Ties That Bind."
	Bibliography	Rodda, John C., Max A. Little, Harvey J. E. Rodda, and Patrick E. McSharry. "A Comparative Study of the Magnitude, Frequency and Distribution of Intense Rainfall in the United Kingdom." Preprint, October 9, 2009. http://precedings.nature.com/documents/3847/version/1. Gross, Daniel P. "The Ties That Bind: Railroad Gauge Standards and Internal Trade in the 19th Century U.S." Working paper, Berkeley Economic History Lab, University of California, Berkeley, March 2016. http://behl.berkeley.edu/working-papers/.

Archival materials and manuscript collections, hard copies and online	First note	[99] Isaac Franklin to R. C. Ballard, February 28, 1831, series 1.1, folder 1, Rice Ballard Papers, Southern Historical Collection, Wilson Library, University of North Carolina, Chapel Hill.
		▸ Here is the order of items within the citation:
		  1. Author and brief description of the item
		  2. Date, if possible
		  3. Identification number of item or manuscript

4. Title of the series or collection
5. Library (or depository) and its location; for well-known libraries and archives, the location may be omitted

[99] Mary Swift Lamson, "An Account of the Beginning of the B.Y.W.C.A.," MS, [n.d.], and accompanying letter, 1891, series I, I-A-2, Boston YWCA Papers, Schlesinger Library, Radcliffe Institute for Advanced Study, Harvard University.

▶ "MS" = manuscript = papers (plural: "MSS")

[99] Sigismundo Taraval, journal recounting Indian uprisings in Baja California [handwritten MS], 1734–37, ¶ 23, Edward E. Ayer Manuscript Collection no. 1240, Newberry Library, Chicago.

▶ This journal has numbered paragraphs. Page numbers, paragraphs, or other identifiers aid readers.

[99] Horatio Nelson Taft, diary, February 20, 1862, p. 149 (vol. 1, January 1, 1861–April 11, 1862), Manuscript Division, Library of Congress, http://memory.loc.gov/ammem/tafthtml/tafthome.html.

[99] Henrietta Szold to Rose Jacobs, February 3, 1932, reel 1, book 1, Rose Jacobs–Alice L. Seligsberg Collection, Judaica Microforms, Brandeis Library, Waltham, MA.

▶ Abbreviations: When a collection's name and location are often repeated, they may be abbreviated after the first use:

[99] Henrietta Szold to Rose Jacobs, March 9, 1936, A/125/112, Central Zionist Archives, Jerusalem (hereafter cited as CZA).

[100] Szold to Eva Stern, July 27, 1936, A/125/912, CZA.

Short note

[99] Isaac Franklin to R. C. Ballard, February 28, 1831, series 1.1, folder 1, Rice Ballard Papers.

▶ Short-form citation varies for archival items. The main concerns are readers' convenience and the proximity of full information in nearby notes.

Archival
materials and
manuscript
collections,
hard copies
and online
(*continued*)

[99] Mary Swift Lamson, "Beginning of the B.Y.W.C.A.," MS [1891], Boston YWCA Papers, Schlesinger Library.

[99] Sigismundo Taraval, journal recounting Indian uprisings in Baja California, Edward E. Ayer Manuscript Collection, Newberry Library.

▶ or

[99] Taraval, journal, Ayer MS Collection, Newberry Library.

[99] Horatio Nelson Taft, diary, February 20, 1862, 149.

[99] Henrietta Szold to Rose Jacobs, February 3, 1932, reel 1, book 1, Rose Jacobs–Alice L. Seligsberg Collection.

[100] Szold to Jacobs, March 9, 1936, A/125/112, CZA.

[101] Szold to Eva Stern, July 27, 1936, A/125/912, CZA.

Bibliography

Rice Ballard Papers. Southern Historical Collection. Wilson Library. University of North Carolina, Chapel Hill.

▶ In footnotes and endnotes, the specific archival item is usually listed first because it is the most important element in the note. For example: Isaac Franklin to R. C. Ballard, February 28, 1831. In bibliographies, however, the collection itself is usually listed first because it is more important. Individual items are not mentioned in the bibliography *unless* only one item is cited from a particular collection.

Boston YWCA Papers. Schlesinger Library. Radcliffe Institute for Advanced Study, Harvard University.

▶ or

Lamson, Mary Swift. "An Account of the Beginning of the B.Y.W.C.A." MS [n.d.] and accompanying letter, 1891. Boston YWCA Papers. Schlesinger Library. Radcliffe Institute for Advanced Study, Harvard University.

▶ If Lamson's account is the only item cited
from these papers, then it would be listed in
the bibliography.

Ayer, Edward E. Manuscript collection. Newberry Library, Chicago, IL.

Taft, Horatio Nelson. Diary. Vol. 1, January 1,
1861–April 11, 1862. Manuscript Division,
Library of Congress. http://memory.loc
.gov/ammem/tafthtml/tafthome.html.

Rose Jacobs–Alice L. Seligsberg Collection.
Judaica Microforms. Brandeis Library,
Waltham, MA.

Central Zionist Archives, Jerusalem.

Encyclopedia and dictionary	First note	[99] *Encyclopaedia Britannica*, 15th ed. (1974), s.vv. "Balkans: History," "World War I."

[99] *Merriam-Webster*, s.v. "app (n.)," accessed
April 6, 2016, http://www.merriam-webster
.com/dictionary/app.

▶ The abbreviation s.v. (*sub verbo*) means
"under the word." Plural: s.vv.

▶ For print versions you must include the
edition but you can omit the publisher,
location, and page numbers for well-known
references like the *Encyclopaedia Britannica*.

[99] *Encyclopaedia Britannica Online*, s.v. "Balkans," accessed September 7, 2016, http://
www.britannica.com/EBchecked/topic/
50325/Balkans.

[99] Dictionary.com, s.v. "metropolitan,"
accessed August 4, 2017, http://www
.dictionary.com/browse/metropolitan?s=t.

▶ Some encyclopedias post a recommended
URL alongside each article; use that one
instead of the URL that appears in your
browser's address bar.

[99] George Graham, "Behaviorism," in *Stanford Encyclopedia of Philosophy*, article
published May 26, 2000, revised July 30,
2007, http://plato.stanford.edu/entries/
behaviorism/.

▶ or

Encyclopedia
and dictionary
(*continued*)

[99] *Stanford Encyclopedia of Philosophy,*
"Behaviorism," by George Graham, article
published May 26, 2000, revised July 30,
2007, http://plato.stanford.edu/entries/
behaviorism/.
[99] Wikipedia, s.v. "Sufjan Stevens," last modified July 31, 2017, 15:30, https://en.wikipedia
.org/wiki/Sufjan_Stevens.

▸   If an article lists a publication date, include
     it; a last-modified date can be used instead.
     If neither is available, include an access date.
▸   For reference works with authored entries,
     you may cite the entry by author, as you
     would for a contribution to a multiauthored
     book.

Short note

[99] *Encyclopaedia Britannica,* s.v. "World
War I."
[99] *Merriam-Webster's,* s.v. "chronology."
[99] *Encyclopaedia Britannica Online,* s.v.
"Balkans."
[99] Dictionary.com, s.v. "metropolitan."
[99] Graham, "Behaviorism."

▸   or

[99] *Stanford Encyclopedia,* "Behaviorism."
[99] Wikipedia, "Sufjan Stevens."

Bibliography

▸   Well-known encyclopedias and dictionaries
     are not normally listed in bibliographies,
     but you may wish to include articles from
     more specialized works, especially if they're
     authored.

Graham, George. "Behaviorism." In *Stan-
     ford Encyclopedia of Philosophy.* Article
     published May 26, 2000. Revised July 30,
     2007. http://plato.stanford.edu/entries/
     behaviorism/.

▸   or

Stanford Encyclopedia of Philosophy.
     "Behaviorism," by George Graham. Article
     published May 26, 2000. Revised July 30,
     2007. http://plato.stanford.edu/entries/
     behaviorism/.

Bible, Koran (Qur'an)	First note	⁹⁹ Genesis 1:1, 1:3–5, 2:4.

⁹⁹ Genesis 1:1, 1:3–5, 2:4 (New Revised Standard Version).

- ► Books of the Bible can be abbreviated: Gen. 1:1.
- ► Abbreviations for the next four books are Exod., Lev., Num., and Deut. Abbreviations for other books are easily found with a web search for "abbreviations + Bible."

⁹⁹ Koran 18:65–82.

Short note

⁹⁹ Genesis 1:1, 1:3–5, 2:4.
⁹⁹ Koran 18:65–82.

Bibliography

- ► References to the Bible, Koran, and other sacred texts are not normally included in the bibliography. You may include them, however, if you wish to show that you are using a particular version or translation. Example:

Tanakh: The Holy Scriptures: The New JPS Translation according to the Traditional Hebrew Text. Philadelphia: Jewish Publication Society, 1985.

- ► Thou shalt omit the Divine Author's name.

Classical works **First note**

- ► Ordinarily, classical Greek and Latin works are referred to in the text itself or in notes. They are not included in the bibliography except to reference the specific translation or commentary by a modern author. Here is an in-text reference:

In Pericles' Funeral Oration (2.34–46), Thucydides gives us one of history's most moving speeches.

- ► If you do need to include a note, here is the format:

⁹⁹ Plato, *The Republic*, trans. R. E. Allen (New Haven, CT: Yale University Press, 2006).
⁹⁹ Virgil, *The Aeneid*, trans. David Ferry (Chicago: University of Chicago Press, 2017).

Classical works (*continued*)	Short note	[99] Plato, *Republic* 3.212b–414b.
		[99] Virgil, *Aeneid* 5.6–31.
	Bibliography	▸ Classical Greek and Latin works are not normally included in the bibliography except to reference the specific translation or commentary by a modern author.
		Plato. *The Republic*. Translated by R. E. Allen. New Haven, CT: Yale University Press, 2006.
		Virgil. *The Aeneid*. Translated by David Ferry. Chicago: University of Chicago Press, 2017.

Speech, academic talk, or course lecture	First note	[99] Alison Dagnes, "Circles of Influence: How the Current Partisan Media System Divides Us" (paper presented at the annual meeting of the Northeastern Political Science Association, November 12, 2015).
		[99] Gary Sick, lecture on US policy toward Iran (U.S. Foreign Policy Making in the Persian Gulf, course taught at Columbia University, New York, March 22, 2007).
		▸ The title of Professor Sick's talk is not capitalized or in quotes because it is a regular course lecture and does not have a specific title. I have given a description, but you could simply call it a lecture and omit the description. For example: Gary Sick, untitled lecture (U.S. Foreign . . .).
	Short note	[99] Dagnes, "Circles of Influence"
		▸ or, to differentiate it from Skorton's addresses in subsequent years:
		[99] Skorton, "State of the University Speech," 2006.
		[99] Sick, lecture on US policy toward Iran.
	Bibliography	Dagnes, Alison. "Circles of Influence: How the Current Partisan Media System Divides Us." Paper presented at the annual meeting of the Northeastern Political Science Association, November 12, 2015.

Sick, Gary. Lecture on US policy toward Iran. U.S. Foreign Policy Making in the Persian Gulf, course taught at Columbia University, New York, March 22, 2007.

Personal communication or interview	First note	[99] Robert Alter, personal interview, October 21, 2015. [99] Nicolas Sarkozy, telephone interview, May 5, 2013. [99] George Lucas, video interview (Skype), October 27, 2016. [99] Anonymous US soldier recently returned from Afghanistan, interview by author, February 19, 2017. [99] Discussion with senior official at Department of Homeland Security, Washington, DC, January 7, 2010.

> ▸ Sometimes you may not wish to reveal the source of an interview or conversation, or you may have promised not to reveal your source. If so, then you should (a) reveal as much descriptive data as you can, such as "a police officer who works with an anti-gang unit," instead of just "a police officer," and (b) explain to readers in a footnote why you are omitting names, such as "All interviews with State Department officials were conducted with guarantees of anonymity because the officials were not authorized to disclose this information to the public."

[99] Ta-Nehisi Coates, "On Charlottesville, Trump, the Confederacy, Reparations & More," interview by Amy Goodman and Juan González, *Democracy Now!*, August 15, 2017, https://www.democracynow.org/2017/8/15/full_interview_ta_nehisi_coates_on.

	Short note	[99] Robert Alter, personal interview, October 21, 2015. [99] George Lucas, video interview, October 27, 2016. [99] Nicolas Sarkozy, telephone interview, May 5, 2013.

Personal communication or interview (*continued*)		^{99} Anonymous US soldier, interview by author, February 19, 2017. ^{99} Discussion with senior official at Department of Homeland Security, January 7, 2010. ^{99} Coates, "On Charlotesville."
	Bibliography	▸ Interviews should be included in the bibliography if they are in print, online, or archived because they are available to other researchers. Personal interviews and communications that are not accessible to others should be described fully in the notes and omitted from the bibliography. Hence there is a bibliographic item for Coates but none for Alter, Sarkozy, Lucas, or the anonymous US soldier or senior official.
		Coates, Ta-Nehisi. "On Charlottesville, Trump, the Confederacy, Reparations, & More." Interview by Amy Goodman and Juan González. *Democracy Now!*, August 15, 2017. https://www.democracynow.org/2017/8/15/full_interview_ta_nehisi_coates_on.
Poem	First note	^{99} Elizabeth Bishop, "The Fish," in *The Complete Poems, 1927–1979* (New York: Noonday Press / Farrar, Straus and Giroux, 1983), 42–44. ^{99} Walt Whitman, "Song of Myself," in *Leaves of Grass* (Philadelphia: David McKay, 1891–92), sec. 51, p. 78, http://whitmanarchive.org/published/LG/1891/whole.html.
	Short note	^{99} Bishop, "The Fish," 42–44. ^{99} Whitman, "Song of Myself," sec. 51, p. 78.
	Bibliography	Bishop, Elizabeth. "The Fish." In *The Complete Poems, 1927–1979*, 42–44. New York: Noonday Press / Farrar, Straus and Giroux, 1983. Walt Whitman. "Song of Myself." In *Leaves of Grass*, 29–79. Philadelphia: David McKay, 1891–92. http://whitmanarchive.org/published/LG/1891/whole.html.

Play, text	First note	[99] Shakespeare, *Hamlet, Prince of Denmark*, 2.1.1–9.
		▸ Refers to act 2, scene 1, lines 1–9.
		▸ Examples for citing a specific edition:
		[99] William Shakespeare, *Hamlet, Prince of Denmark*, ed. Constance Jordan (New York: Pearson/Longman, 2005).
		[99] William Shakespeare, *The Three-Text Hamlet: Parallel Texts of the First and Second Quartos and First Folio*, ed. Bernice W. Kliman and Paul Bertram (New York: AMS Press, 2003).
		[99] William Shakespeare, *Hamlet, Prince of Denmark* (1600–1601; University of Virginia Library, Electronic Text Center, 1998), http://etext.virginia.edu/toc/modeng/public/MobHaml.html.
	Short note	[99] Shakespeare, *Hamlet*, 2.1.1–9.
	Bibliography	Shakespeare, William. *Hamlet, Prince of Denmark*. Edited by Constance Jordan. New York: Pearson/Longman, 2005.
		Shakespeare, William. *The Three-Text Hamlet: Parallel Texts of the First and Second Quartos and First Folio*. Edited by Bernice W. Kliman and Paul Bertram. New York: AMS Press, 2003.
		Shakespeare, William. *Hamlet, Prince of Denmark*. 1600–1601. University of Virginia Library, Electronic Text Center, 1998. http://etext.virginia.edu/toc/modeng/public/MobHaml.html.
Performance of play or dance	First note	[99] *Romeo and Juliet*, choreography by Krzysztof Pastor, music by Sergei Prokofiev, Joffrey Ballet, Auditorium Theatre, Chicago, October 13, 2016.
		[99] *Fake*, written and directed by Eric Simonson, performed by Kate Arrington, Francis Guinan, and Alan Wilder, Steppenwolf Theatre, Chicago, October 28, 2009.

Performance of
play or dance
(*continued*)

> If you are concentrating on one person
> or one position such as director, put that
> person's name first. For example, if you are
> concentrating on Kate Arrington's acting:
> [99] Kate Arrington, performance, *Fake*, written
> and directed by Eric Simonson, . . .

Short note

[99] *Romeo and Juliet*.
[99] *Fake*.

Bibliography

Romeo and Juliet. Choreography by Krzysztof
Pastor. Music by Sergei Prokofiev. Joffrey
Ballet. Auditorium Theatre, Chicago,
October 13, 2016.
Fake. Written and directed by Eric Simonson.
Performed by Kate Arrington, Francis
Guinan, and Alan Wilder. Steppenwolf
Theatre, Chicago, October 28, 2009.

> or, if you are concentrating on Arrington's
> acting:

Kate Arrington, performance. *Fake*. Written
and directed by Eric Simonson, . . .

> Live performances are often left out of the
> bibliography, since the performance cannot
> be consulted in person by the reader.

Television
program

First note

[99] *Game of Thrones*, season 4, episode 10,
"The Children," June 15, 2014.

> or a fuller citation:

[99] *Game of Thrones*, season 4, episode 10,
"The Children," directed by Alex Graves,
written by David Benioff and D. B. Weiss, featuring Peter Dinklage, Nikolaj Coster-Waldau,
Lena Heady, Kit Harington, and Maisie Williams, aired June 15, 2014, on HBO.
[99] *30 Rock*, season 4, episode 1, "Season 4,"
directed by Don Scardino, written by Tina
Fey, performed by Tina Fey, Tracy Morgan,
Jane Krakowski, Jack McBrayer, Scott Adsit,
Judah Friedlander, and Alec Baldwin, aired
October 15, 2009 (NBC), http://www.hulu
.com/30-rock.

▸ Yes, this first episode of the fourth season was actually called "Season 4." Episode numbers are helpful. So are original air dates for shows you watched in a medium other than broadcast.

Short note

⁹⁹ *Game of Thrones*, "The Children."
⁹⁹ *30 Rock*, "Season 4."

Bibliography

Game of Thrones. Season 4, episode 10, "The Children," Directed by Alex Graves. Written by David Benioff and D. B. Weiss. Featuring Peter Dinklage, Nikolaj Coster-Waldau, Lena Heady, Kit Harington, and Maisie Williams. Aired June 15, 2014, on HBO.

30 Rock. Season 4, episode 1, "Season 4." Directed by Don Scardino. Written by Tina Fey. Performed by Tina Fey, Tracy Morgan, Jane Krakowski, Jack McBrayer, Scott Adsit, Judah Friedlander, and Alec Baldwin. Aired October 15, 2009, on NBC. http://www.hulu.com/30-rock.

Film

First note

⁹⁹ *Godfather II*, directed by Francis Ford Coppola (1974; Los Angeles: Paramount Home Video, 2003), DVD.
⁹⁹ *Tig*, directed by Kristina Goolsby and Ashley York (Beachside Films, 2015), Netflix.

▸ If you wish to cite individual scenes, treat them like chapters in books. "Murder of Fredo," in *Godfather II* . . .

Short note

⁹⁹ *Godfather II*.
⁹⁹ *Tig*.

Bibliography

Godfather II, DVD. Directed by Francis Ford Coppola. Performed by Al Pacino, Robert De Niro, Robert Duvall, Diane Keaton. Screenplay by Francis Ford Coppola and Mario Puzo based on novel by Mario Puzo. 1974; Paramount Home Video, 2003.

Film
(*continued*)

Tig. Netflix. Directed by Kristina Goolsby and Ashley York. Written by Jennifer Arnold. Performed by Tig Notaro, Stephanie Allynne, Zach Galifianakis, Sarah Silverman. Beachside Films, 2015.

▸ Title, director, studio, and year of release are all required. So is the year the video recording was released, if that's what you are citing.

▸ Optional: the actors, producers, screenwriters, editors, cinematographers, and other information. You can include what you need for your paper, in order of their importance to your analysis. Their names appear between the title and the distributor.

Artwork

First note

[99] Jacopo Robusti Tintoretto, *The Birth of John the Baptist*, ca. 1550, Hermitage, St. Petersburg.

▸ If the exact date of an artwork is not available, give an approximate one. A painting from "circa 1550" would be abbreviated "ca. 1550."

[99] Jacopo Robusti Tintoretto, *The Birth of John the Baptist*, 1550s, in Tom Nichols, *Tintoretto: Tradition and Identity* (London: Reaktion Books, 1999), 47.

▸ For a reproduction, cite where you found the work.

[99] Jacopo Robusti Tintoretto, *The Birth of John the Baptist* (detail), 1550s, Hermitage, St. Petersburg, http://cgfa.acropolisinc.com/t/p-tintore1.htm.

▸ Include a URL for art consulted online.

Short note

[99] Tintoretto, *Birth of John the Baptist*.

▸ Shorten note the same way for an original, reproduction, or artwork found online.

Bibliography

▸ Do not include any artwork, sculptures, or photographs in the bibliography.

Photograph	First note	[99] Ansel Adams, *Monolith, the Face of Half Dome, Yosemite National Park*, 1927, Art Institute, Chicago.
		[99] Ansel Adams, *Monolith, the Face of Half Dome, Yosemite National Park*, 1927, Art Institute, Chicago, http://www.hctc.commnet .edu/artmuseum/anseladams/details/pdf/ monlith.pdf.
	Short note	[99] Adams, *Monolith*.
	Bibliography	▶ Artwork, sculptures, and photographs are not usually included in the bibliography.

Figures: map, chart, graph, or table	Credit for figure or table	▶ Citation for a map, chart, graph, or table normally appears as a credit below the item or within the text, but can be cited in a note if needed.
		Source: Ken Menkhaus, "Governance without Government in Somalia: Spoilers, State Building, and the Politics of Coping," *International Security* 31 (Winter 2006/7): 79, fig. 1.
		Source: "Presidential Election Results: Donald J. Trump Wins" (interactive map), *New York Times*, August 9, 2017, https://www .nytimes.com/elections/results/president.
		[99] Garrett Dash Nelson and Alasdair Rae, *An Economic Geography of the United States: From Commutes to Megaregions, Plos One*, accessed August 29, 2017, https://doi.org/10 .1371/journal.pone.0166083.g001.
		[99] G. M. Wheeler, *Topographical Map of the Yosemite Valley and Vicinity*, preliminary edition, 1883, 43 × 55cm, 1:42,240 scale, David Rumsey Historical Map Collection, http:// www.davidrumsey.com/luna/servlet/detail/ RUMSEY~8~1~405~40014:Topographical -Map-Of-The-Yosemite-V.
		Source: Google Maps, map of 1427 E. 60th St., Chicago, IL 60637, accessed May 5, 2017, http://maps.google.com/.

Figures: map, chart, graph, or table (*continued*)		▸ For maps, include cartographer (if known), the title or description of the map, the scale and size, and publication details or location.
		▸ For undated maps consulted online, include an access or revision date.
	Short citation	▸ Use full citations for all figures.
	Bibliography	Menkhaus, Ken. "Governance without Government in Somalia: Spoilers, State Building, and the Politics of Coping." *International Security* 31 (Winter 2006/7): 74–106.
		▸ Do not list any maps, charts, graphs or tables in the bibliography; *do* include any book, article, or other publication used as the source for such an item. Google Maps does not need to appear in the bibliography; the other sources do.
		"Presidential Election Results: Donald J. Trump Wins." *New York Times*, August 9, 2017. https://www.nytimes.com/elections/results/president.
Musical recording	First note	[99] Robert Johnson, "Cross Road Blues," 1937, *Robert Johnson: King of the Delta Blues Singers*, Columbia Records 1654, 1961.
		[99] Samuel Barber, "Cello Sonata, for cello and piano, op. 6," *Barber: Adagio for Strings, Violin Concerto, Orchestral and Chamber Works*, compact disc 2, St. Louis Symphony, cond. Leonard Slatkin, Alan Stepansky (cello), Israela Margalit (piano), EMI Classics 74287, 2001.
		[99] Jimi Hendrix, "Purple Haze," 1969, *Woodstock: Three Days of Peace and Music*, compact disc 4 of 4, Atlantic/Wea, 1994.
		[99] Vladimir Horowitz, Hungarian Rhapsody no. 2, by Franz Liszt, recorded live at Carnegie Hall, February 25, 1953, MP3 file (241 Kbps).

> ▸ Kbps stands for kilobits per second; MP3 is the name of the popular audio compression format. If the MP3 file is just a copy of a version from compact disc or LP, you can cite the original:

[99] Vladimir Horowitz, Hungarian Rhapsody no. 2, by Franz Liszt, recorded live at Carnegie Hall, February 25, 1953, compact disc, RCA Victor 60523-2-RG, 1991.

[99] Beyoncé, "Formation," TIDAL, track 11 on *Lemonade*, Parkwood Entertainment and Columbia Records, 2016.

> ▸ Include the service or file format for streaming audio.

Short note

[99] Johnson, "Cross Road Blues."
[99] Barber, "Cello Sonata, op. 6."
[99] Hendrix, "Purple Haze."
[99] Horowitz, Hungarian Rhapsody no. 2.
[99] Beyoncé, "Formation."

Bibliography

Johnson, Robert. "Cross Road Blues." 1937. *Robert Johnson: King of the Delta Blues Singers*. Columbia Records 1654, 1961.

Barber, Samuel. "Cello Sonata, for cello and piano, op. 6." *Barber: Adagio for Strings, Violin Concerto, Orchestral and Chamber Works*. Compact disc 2. St. Louis Symphony. Cond. Leonard Slatkin, Alan Stepansky (cello), Israela Margalit (piano). EMI Classics 74287, 2001.

Hendrix, Jimi. "Purple Haze," 1969. *Woodstock: Three Days of Peace and Music*. Compact disc 4. Atlantic/Wea, 1994.

Horowitz, Vladimir. Hungarian Rhapsody no. 2, by Franz Liszt. Recorded live at Carnegie Hall, February 25, 1953. MP3 file (241 Kbps).

Beyoncé. "Formation." TIDAL. Track 11 on *Lemonade*. Parkwood Entertainment and Columbia Records, 2016.

Recording of reading, lecture, or audiobook	First note	[99] Franklin D. Roosevelt, "Fireside Chat: Outlining New Deal Program," May 7, 1933, Recorded Speeches and Utterances of Franklin D. Roosevelt, FDR Presidential Library and Museum, MP3 audio (23:00), http://www .fdrlibrary.marist.edu/archives/collections/ utterancesfdr.html. [99] George Eliot, *Middlemarch*, performed by Juliet Stevenson, Naxos Audiobooks, released on Audible.com, March 18, 2011. ▸ Cite recordings of readings, books, or lectures as you would musical recordings.
	Short note	[99] Roosevelt, "Fireside Chat." [99] Eliot, *Middlemarch*.
	Bibliography	Roosevelt, Franklin D. "Fireside Chat: Outlining New Deal Program." May 7, 1933. Recorded Speeches and Utterances of Franklin D. Roosevelt, FDR Presidential Library and Museum. MP3 audio (23:00). http://www.fdrlibrary.marist.edu/ archives/collections/utterancesfdr.html. Eliot, George. *Middlemarch*. Performed by Juliet Stevenson. Naxos Audiobooks. Released on Audible.com, March 18, 2011.
Music video, comments on music video	First note	[99] Arcade Fire, "Everything Now," music video, directed by the Sacred Egg, released June 1, 2017, https://youtu.be/zC30BYR 3CUk. [99] Rihanna, Kanye West, and Paul McCartney, "FourFiveSeconds," music video, directed by Inez & Vinoodh, produced by Stephanie Bargas and Jeff Lepine, February 3, 2015, http:// vevo.ly/3aZlDK. [99] Bruno Mars, "That's What I Like," music video, directed by Bruno Mars and Jonathan Lia, March 1, 2017, https://youtu.be/PMivT7 MJ41M. [99] Minimanaloto, March 3, 2017, comment on Mars, "That's What I Like."

	Short note	[99] Arcade Fire, "Everything Now."
		[99] Rihanna, Kanye West, and Paul McCartney, "FourFiveSeconds."
		[99] Mars, "That's What I Like."
		[99] Minimanaloto, comment on Mars, "That's What I Like."
	Bibliography	Arcade Fire. "Everything Now." Music video. Directed by the Sacred Egg, released June 1, 2017. https://youtu.be/zC30BYR3CUk.
		Rihanna, Kanye West, and Paul McCartney. "FourFiveSeconds." Music video. Directed by Inez & Vinoodh. Produced by Stephanie Bargas and Jeff Lepine, released February 3, 2015, http://vevo.ly/3aZlDK.
		Mars, Bruno. "That's What I Like." Music video. Directed by Bruno Mars and Jonathan Lia, released March 1, 2017. https://youtu.be/PMivT7MJ41M.
		▸ Viewers' comments on music videos are not included in bibliographies.
Sheet music	First note	[99] Johann Sebastian Bach, "Toccata and Fugue in D Minor," 1708, BWV 565, arranged by Ferruccio Benvenuto Busoni for solo piano (New York: G. Schirmer LB1629, 1942).
	Short note	[99] Bach, "Toccata and Fugue in D Minor."
	Bibliography	Bach, Johann Sebastian. "Toccata and Fugue in D Minor." 1708. BWV 565. Arranged by Ferruccio Benvenuto Busoni for solo piano. New York: G. Schirmer LB1629, 1942.
		▸ This piece was written in 1708 and has the standard Bach classification BWV 565. This particular arrangement was published by G. Schirmer in 1942 and has Schirmer's catalog number LB1629.
Liner notes	First note	[99] Steven Reich, liner notes for *Different Trains*, Elektra/Nonesuch 9 79176-2, 1988.
	Short note	[99] Reich, liner notes.
		▸ or
		[99] Reich, liner notes, *Different Trains*.

Liner notes (*continued*)	Bibliography	Reich, Steven. Liner notes for *Different Trains*. Elektra/Nonesuch 9 79176-2, 1988.

Advertisement	First note	⁹⁹ *Letters from Iwo Jima* advertisement, *New York Times*, February 6, 2007, B4.

⁹⁹ *Letters from Iwo Jima* advertisement, *New York Times*, February 6, 2007, B4.
▸ You may omit pagination from newspapers, if you wish, since these vary from edition to edition.
⁹⁹ Vitamin Water, "Drink outside the Lines" advertisement, *Rolling Stone*, June 15, 2017, 17.
⁹⁹ Tab cola, "Be a Mindsticker," television advertisement, ca. late 1960s, http://www .dailymotion.com/video/x2s3qi_1960s-tab -commercial-be-a-mindstick_ads.

Short note
⁹⁹ *Letters from Iwo Jima* advertisement.
⁹⁹ Vitamin Water, "Drink outside the Lines" advertisement.
⁹⁹ Tab advertisement.

Bibliography
▸ Advertisements are rarely included in bibliographies, but you may include them if they are especially important to your work.
Letters from *Iwo Jima* advertisement. *New York Times*, February 6, 2007.
Vitamin Water. "Drink outside the Lines" advertisement. *Rolling Stone*, June 15, 2017, 17.
Tab cola. "Be a Mindsticker." Television advertisement, ca. late 1960s. http://www .dailymotion.com/video/x2s3qi_1960s -tab-commercial-be-a-mindstick_ads.

Government document — First note
⁹⁹ Senate Committee on Armed Services, *Hearings on S. 758, A Bill to Promote the National Security by Providing for a National Defense Establishment*, 80th Cong., 1st sess., 1947, S. Rep. 239, 13.
▸ "S. Rep. 239, 13" refers to report number 239, page 13.

[99] *Financial Services and General Government Appropriations Act, 2008*, HR 2829, 110th Cong., 1st sess., *Congressional Record* 153 (June 28, 2007): H7347.
[99] *American Health Care Act, 2017*, HR 1628, 115th Cong., 1st sess., June 8, 2017, Congress.Gov, https://www.congress.gov/bill/115th-congress/house-bill/1628/text.
[99] Department of the Treasury, Office of Foreign Assets Control (OFAC), *Sanctions Actions Pursuant to Executive Order 13581*, *Federal Register* 82, no. 166 (August 29, 2017): 41019, https://www.gpo.gov/fdsys/pkg/FR-2017-08–29/pdf/2017-18289.pdf.
[99] US Department of State, Daily Press Briefing, August 9, 2017, https://www.state.gov/r/pa/prs/dpb/2017/08/273288.htm.

Short note

[99] Senate, *Hearings on S. 758*, 13.
[99] *American Health Care Act*, HR 1628.
[99] OFAC, *Sanctions Actions*.
[99] US State Department, Daily Press Briefing, August 9, 2017.

Bibliography

US Congress. Senate. Committee on Armed Services. *Hearings on S. 758, Bill to Promote the National Security by Providing for a National Defense Establishment*. 80th Cong., 1st sess., 1947. S. Rep. 239.

US Congress. House. *Congressional Record*. 110th Cong., 1st sess. June 28, 2007. Vol. 153, no. 106. H7347.

American Health Care Act, 2017. HR 1628, 115th Cong., 1st sess. June 8, 2017. Congress.Gov, https://www.congress.gov/bill/115th-congress/house-bill/1628/text.

Department of the Treasury, Office of Foreign Assets Control. *Sanctions Actions Pursuant to Executive Order 13581*. *Federal Register* 82, no. 166 (August 29, 2017): 41019. https://www.gpo.gov/fdsys/pkg/FR-2017-08-29/pdf/2017-18289.pdf.

Government document (*continued*)		US Department of State. Daily press briefing. August 9, 2017. https://www.state.gov/r/pa/prs/dpb/2017/08/273288.htm.
Website, page or entire	First note	[99] "News and Advocacy," American Historical Association (website), accessed August 1, 2017, https://www.historians.org/news-and-advocacy.

- ▸ Many webpages do not have identifiable authors. List the organization that sponsors the website instead.
- ▸ Include the word *website* or *webpage* if it is not clear from the title.

[99] Digital History (website), ed. Steven Mintz, accessed August 5, 2017, http://www.digitalhistory.uh.edu/.

[99] Yale University, History Department home page, accessed August 5, 2017, http://www.yale.edu/history/.

- ▸ You may omit "home page" if it is obvious.

[99] Charles Lipson, "News and Commentary: US and the World," accessed August 29, 2017, http:// www.charleslipson.com/News-links.htm.

- ▸ Include a publication date or date of revision or modification if possible. If none is available, include access date.

Short note

[99] "News and Advocacy."
[99] Digital History.
[99] Yale History Department.
[99] Lipson, "News and Commentary."

Bibliography

American Historical Association (website). "News and Advocacy." Accessed August 1, 2017. https://www.historians.org/news-and-advocacy

Digital History (website). Edited by Steven Mintz. Accessed August 5, 2017. http://www.digitalhistory.uh.edu/.

Yale University. History Department home page. Accessed August 5, 2017. http://www.yale.edu/history/.

Lipson, Charles. "News and Commentary: US and the World." Accessed August 29, 2017. http://www.charleslipson.com/ News-links.htm.

> ▶ Website citations can be limited to the notes. If you choose to include a website in the bibliography, cite by the owner, author, or sponsor of the website.

Blog post or comment	First note	[99] Greg Weeks, "Venezuela's Core Support," *Two Weeks Notice: A Latin American Politics Blog*, August 2, 2017, http://weeksnotice .blogspot.com/2017/08/venezuelas-core -support.html.

> ▶ If this post had no title, it would be cited thus: Greg Weeks, untitled post, *Two Weeks Notice: A Latin American Politics blog . . .*

[99] Ana Arana, "The Deep Magic of Mexico," *The Big Roundtable* (blog), December 8, 2016, https://thebigroundtable.com/the -deep-magic-of-mexico-2bf1b341d1a1.

[99] Stefanie Fletcher, December 8, 2016 (11:30 a.m.), comment on Arana, "Deep Magic."

> ▶ Stefanie Fletcher made more than one comment on this post, so the time is included to specify which one.
>
> ▶ Comments are cited in reference to the original post.

Short note

[99] Weeks, "Venezuela's Core Support."
[99] Arana, "Deep Magic."
[99] Fletcher, comment on Arana, "Deep Magic."

Bibliography

> ▶ Blog posts are not usually part of the bibliography, but you may include them if the items are important in their own right or are especially significant for your paper. Here is the format:

Weeks, Greg. "Venezuela's Core Support." *Two Weeks Notice: A Latin American Politics Blog*, August 2, 2017. http:// weeksnotice.blogspot.com/2017/08/ venezuelas-core-support.html.

Blog post or comment (*continued*)		Arana, Ana. "The Deep Magic of Mexico." *The Big Roundtable* (blog), December 8, 2016. https://thebigroundtable.com/the-deep-magic-of-mexico-2bf1b341d1a1.

Video	First note	[99] *Duck and Cover*, Federal Civil Defense Administration/Archer Productions, 1951, video file, posted August 19, 2008, http://en.wikipedia.org/wiki/File: DuckandC1951.ogg. [99] Martin Shkreli on Three Counts of Security Fraud," NBC video news clip, August 4, 2017, http://www.nbcnews.com/video/jury-convicts-martin-shkreli-on-three-counts-of-securities-fraud-1017719875664. [99] Franchesca Ramsey, "Turn Your Phone!" Franchesca Ramsey video blog, accessed August 5, 2017, 3:07, http://www.franchesca.net/videos-photos/. [99] Tricia Wang, "The Human Insights Missing from Big Data," filmed September, 2016, TEDxCambridge, TED video, 16:12, https://www.ted.com/talks/tricia_wang_the_human_insights_missing_from_big_data.
	Short note	[99] *Duck and Cover*. [99] "Jury Convicts Martin Shkreli," August 4, 2017." [99] Ramsey, "Turn Your Phone!" [99] Wang, "Human Insights."
	Bibliography	*Duck and Cover*. Federal Civil Defense Administration / Archer Productions, 1951. Video file. Posted August 19, 2008. http://en.wikipedia.org/wiki/File:DuckandC1951.ogg. "Jury Convicts Martin Shkreli on Three Counts of Security Fraud." NBC video news clip, August 4, 2017. http://www.nbcnews.com/video/jury-convicts-martin-shkreli-on-three-counts-of-securities-fraud-1017719875664.

Ramsey, Franchesca. "Turn Your Phone!" Franchesca Ramsey video blog. Accessed August 5, 2017. 3:07. http://www .franchesca.net/videos-photos/.

Wang, Tricia. "The Human Insights Missing from Big Data." Filmed September, 2016, at TEDxCambridge. TED video, 16:12. https://www.ted.com/talks/tricia_wang _the_human_insights_missing_from_big _data.

Multimedia app (video game, other stand-alone application)	First note	99 *Madden NFL 18* (EA Sports, November 2017), PlayStation 4, Xbox One. 99 *Geocaching*, v. 5.6.1 (Seattle: Ground-speak, 2017), Android, iOS 9.0 or later. ▸ Include any relevant information such as version number, release date, and information about the device or operating system necessary to run the app.
	Short note	99 *Madden NFL 18.* 99 *Geocaching.*
	Bibliography	EA Sports. *Madden NFL 18.* November 2017, PlayStation 4, Xbox One. Groundspeak. *Geocaching*, v. 5.6.1. Seattle: Groundspeak, 2017. Android, iOS 9.0 or later.
Podcast	First note	99 Brian Reed, host, "Has Anybody Called You?" *S-Town*, podcast, produced by Brian Reed and Julie Snyder, Serial Productions, March 28, 2017, https://stownpodcast.org/ chapter/2. 99 Ellen DeGeneres, "Ellen's Parenting Advice," *The Ellen Show Podcast*, Telepic-tures Productions, video podcast, June 26, 2015, iTunes. ▸ If no date can be found for the podcast, include the date accessed.
	Short note	99 Reed, "Chapter 2." 99 DeGeneres, "Ellen's Parenting Advice."

Podcast (*continued*)	Bibliography	Reed, Brian, host. "Has Anybody Called You?" *S-Town*, podcast. Brian Reed and Julie Snyder, Serial Productions. March 28, 2017. https://stownpodcast .org/chapter/2.
		DeGeneres, Ellen. "Ellen's Parenting Advice." *The Ellen Show Podcast*. Telepictures Productions. Video podcast. June 26, 2015. iTunes.

Social media (Facebook, Instagram, Twitter)	First note	[99] Neil deGrasse Tyson (@neiltyson), "Always seemed to me that millipedes have more legs than are necessary," Twitter, July 7, 2017, 1:25 p.m., twitter.com/neiltyson/ status/883421859072458752.
		[99] Smithsonian National Museum of African American History and Culture, "For African Americans, the pleasure of swimming at a public pool or beach was not always a right," Facebook, July 28, 2017, 1:50 p.m., https:// www.facebook.com/NMAAHC/.
		[99] Bruce Jackson, "Kennywood closed and paved over the pool rather than integrate," July 30, 2017, 11:49 a.m., comment on Smith-sonian, "For African Americans."
		[99] Cory Richards (@coryrichards), "A quiet if not solemn day on Everest," Instagram photo, May 24, 2017, https://www.instagram .com/p/BUekBZLgDOW/?hl=en.

▸ Publicly available social media content, including comments on others' posts, should be cited in this way. Private content such as direct messages should be cited as a form of personal communication.

▸ Comments are cited in reference to the original post.

▸ If there is no title, use the text of the post, up to 160 characters.

▸ If no real name is known, use the screen name only.

	Short note	[99] Tyson, "Always seemed to me."
		[99] Smithsonian, "For African Americans."
		[99] Jackson, comment on Smithsonian, "For African Americans."
		[99] Richards, "A quiet if not solemn day."
	Bibliography	▸ Do not include individual comments posted to social networking sites in the bibliography. It is fine, however, to include a particular person's page.
		Richards, Corey. Instagram page. https://www.instagram.com/coryrichards/?hl=en.
Email, texts (direct messages)	First note	[99] Jim Abrams, "Fw: a Favor," email from Jim Abrams to Mayor Rahm Emanuel, April 28, 2015, https://assets.documentcloud.org/documents/3516674/Abrams-amp-Bank-Phoenix-Electric.pdf.
		▸ No access date is required when citing email messages.
		▸ Include the URL if the email has been archived.
		[99] Kathy Leis, email message to author, May 5, 2017.
		[99] Kathy Leis, text message to author, May 5, 2017.
		[99] Alison Viup, Facebook direct message to author, July 20, 2016.
		▸ You may include the time of an electronic message if it is important or differentiates it from others. For example:
		[99] Michael Lipson, text message to Jonathan Lipson, May 5, 2017, 11:23 a.m.
		▸ Save copies of electronic messages that you intend to cite.
	Short note	[99] Jim Abrams to Rahm Emanuel, April 28, 2015.
		[99] Kathy Leis, email message to author, May 3, 2017.

Email, texts (direct messages) (*continued*)		▸ You may be able to shorten these notes. If you are citing only one person named Leis, for instance, then you can drop the first name. But if you are citing messages from Alan Leis, Kathy Leis, Elizabeth Leis, and Julia Leis, then it is much clearer to include their first names, even in short notes. [99] Michael Lipson, instant message to Jonathan Lipson, May 5, 2017. [99] Michael Lipson, text message to Jonathan Lipson, May 5, 2017, 11:23 a.m.
	Bibliography	▸ Personal emails, text and other instant messages, and emails to mailing lists are not included in the bibliography unless they can be retrieved by third parties. Abrams, Jim. "Fw: a Favor." Email from Jim Abrams to Mayor Rahm Emanuel, April 28, 2015. https://assets.document cloud.org/documents/3516674/Abrams -amp-Bank-Phoenix-Electric.pdf.

Electronic forum or mailing list	First note	[99] Quinn Ngo, answer to "What Are Some Unknown Truths about College Life?," Quora, July 14, 2017, https://www.quora.com/What -are-some-unknown-truths-about-college -life. [99] Mablegrable, "Cozy spot for a morning coffee," Reddit photo, August 4, 2017, https://i.redd.it/okqb36mkbndz.jpg. [99] VeganSweets, "There's nothing like nature and some coffee/tea," August 4, 2017, 1:28 p.m., comment on Mablegrable, "Cozy Spot." [99] Mark Aaron Polger, "CALL: Call for Proposals," American Library Association mailing list archives, ACRL Campaign for Libraries list, May 10, 2017, http://lists.ala.org/ sympa/arc/academicpr/2017-05/msg00005 .html. ▸ Posts on private email lists or forums are cited as personal communication just as an email or text message would.

Short note   [99] Ngo, Quora, July 14, 2017.
              [99] VeganSweets, comment on Mablegrable, "Cozy Spot."
              [99] Polger, ALA mailing list, May 10, 2017.

Bibliography   ▶ Do not include individual comments posted to forums or mailing lists in the bibliography. You may include an entire thread or forum if it is cited extensively.

Quora. "What Are Some Unknown Truths about College Life?" July 14, 2017. https://www.quora.com/What-are-some-unknown-truths-about-college-life.

CHICAGO: CITATIONS OF TABLES AND NOTES

CITATION	REFERS TO
106	page 106
106n	only note appearing on page 106
107n32	note number 32 on page 107, a page with several notes
89, table 6.2	table 6.2, which appears on page 89; similar for graphs and figures

---

CHICAGO: COMMON ABBREVIATIONS IN CITATIONS

and others	et al.	edited by	ed.	notes	nn.	part	pt.
appendix	app.	edition	ed.	number	no.	pseudonym	pseud.
book	bk.	editor(s)	ed(s).	opus	op.	translator	trans.
chapter	chap.	especially	esp.	opuses	opp.	versus	vs.
compare	cf.	figure	fig.	page	p.	volume	vol.
document	doc.	note	n.	pages	pp.		

Note: All abbreviations are lowercase, followed by a period. Most form their plurals by adding *-s*. The exceptions are note (n. → nn.), opus (op. → opp.), page (p. → pp.), and translator (same abbreviation). (Another exception: when the abbreviation *n.* or *nn.* follows a page number with no intervening space, the period is dropped.)

In citing poetry, do not use abbreviations for "line" or "lines" since a lowercase *l* is easily confused with the number 1.

FAQS ABOUT CHICAGO-STYLE CITATIONS

Are there any differences between the rules for citations in *The Chicago Manual of Style* and those in Kate L. Turabian's *Manual for Writers of Research Papers, Theses, and Dissertations*?

No. Although there used to be some minor differences between them (for example, on whether or not to include access dates for online sources), Turabian and Chicago citation styles are now essentially the same.

For an online source, do I need to list the date when I accessed the source?

Generally not. One exception is when you can't find an official date on the source stating when it was published, posted, or most recently modified. Then the access date is necessary to help establish at least some timeframe for when the material on the site was viewable. Also, instructors sometimes require listing access dates even when those other kinds of dates are available, so it's a good idea to ask.

Why do you put the state after some publishers and not after others?

The Chicago Manual of Style recommends using state names for all but the largest, best-known cities. To avoid confusion, it uses Cambridge, MA, for Harvard and MIT University Presses but just Cambridge for Cambridge University Press in the ancient English university town. Also, you can drop the state name if it is already included in the publisher's title, such as Ann Arbor: University of Michigan Press.

What if a book is forthcoming?

Use "forthcoming" just as you would use the year. Here's a bibliographic entry:

> Godot, Shlomo. *Still Waiting*. London: Verso, forthcoming.

What if the date or place of publication is missing?

Same idea as "forthcoming." Where you would normally put the place or date, use "n.p." (no place) or "n.d." (no date). For example: (Montreal, QC: McGill-Queen's University Press, n.d.).

One book I cite has a title that ends with a question mark. Do I still put a period or a comma after it?

Comma, yes; period, no.

Are notes single-spaced or double-spaced? What about the bibliography?
Space your footnotes and endnotes the same way you do your text.

As for your bibliography, I think it is easiest to read if you single-space within entries and put a double space between the entries. But check what your department or publisher requires. It may require double-spacing for everything.

I'm reading Mark Twain. Do I cite Twain or Samuel Clemens?
When pseudonyms are well known such as Mark Twain or Mother Teresa, you can use them alone, without explanation, if you wish.

If you want to include both the pseudonym and the given name, the rule is simple. Put the better-known name first, followed by the lesser-known one in brackets. It doesn't matter if the "real" name is the lesser-known one.

George Eliot [Mary Ann Evans]
Isak Dinesen [Karen Christence Dinesen, Baroness Blixen-Finecke]
Le Corbusier [Charles-Edouard Jeanneret]
Benjamin Disraeli [Lord Beaconsfield]
Lord Palmerston [Henry John Temple]
Krusty the Clown [Herschel S. Krustofski]

If you wish to include the pseudonym in a bibliographic entry, it reads:

Aleichem, Sholom [Solomon Rabinovitz]. *Fiddler on the Roof . . .*

MLA CITATIONS FOR
THE HUMANITIES

. . . .

The Modern Language Association (MLA) has developed a citation style that is widely used in the humanities. Instead of footnotes or endnotes, it uses in-text citations such as (Strier 125). Full information about each item appears in the bibliography, which MLA calls "Works Cited." Like other bibliographies, it contains three essential nuggets of information about each item: the author, title, and publication data. To illustrate, let's use a book by Amitav Ghosh. The full entry in the Works Cited is

> Ghosh, Amitav. *The Great Derangement: Climate Change and the Unthinkable.* U of Chicago P, 2016.

The eighth edition of the *MLA Handbook*, published in 2016, introduced an overarching approach to citing any source, no matter its format. This represented a major change, since MLA style used to require that you include the medium of publication—print, web, email, television, etc.—along with the full facts of publication. Because content now comes in so many forms, and moves between formats so easily, MLA now works from the idea that writers need an all-encompassing and flexible method for developing citations rather than a list of rigid rules.

In-text citations are brief and simple. Just insert (Ghosh) at the end of the sentence to cite the entire book, or (Ghosh 12) to refer to page 12. If your paper happens to cite several books by Ghosh, be sure your reader knows which one you are referring to. If that's not clear in the sentence, then include a very brief title: (Ghosh, *Great Derangement* 12).

MLA citations can be even briefer—and they should be, whenever possible. They can omit the author and the title as long as it's clear which work is being cited. For example:

As Ghosh notes, climate change is rarely a topic in fiction classified as "literary" (7–9).

You can omit the in-text reference entirely if the author and title are clear and you are not citing specific pages. For instance:

Gibbon's *Decline and Fall of the Roman Empire* established new standards of documentary evidence for historians.

In this case there's nothing to put in an in-text reference that isn't already in the sentence. So, given MLA's consistent emphasis on brevity, you simply skip the reference. You still include Gibbon in your Works Cited.

Because in-text references are so brief, you can string several together in one parenthesis: (Bevington 17; Bloom 75; Vendler 51). The references are separated by semicolons.

If Ghosh's book were a three-volume work, then the citation to volume 3, page 17, would be (Ghosh 3: 17). If you need to differentiate this work from others by the same author, then include the title: (Ghosh, *Great Derangement* 3: 17). If you wanted to cite the volume but not a specific page, then use (Ghosh, vol. 3) or (Ghosh, *Great Derangement*, vol. 3). Why include "vol." here? So readers won't think you are citing page 3 of a one-volume work.

If several authors have the same last name, simply add their first initial to differentiate them: (C. Brontë, *Jane Eyre*), (E. Brontë, *Wuthering Heights*). Of course, full information about the authors and their works appears at the end, in the Works Cited.

Books like *Jane Eyre* appear in countless editions, and your readers may wish to look up passages in theirs. To make that easier, the MLA recommends that you add some information after the normal page citation. You might say, for example, that the passage appears in chapter 1.

Let's say that you quoted a passage from the first chapter of *Jane Eyre*, which appeared on page 7 in the edition you are using. Insert a semicolon after the page and add the chapter number, using a lowercase abbreviation for chapter: (E. Brontë, *Wuthering Heights* 7; ch. 1).

For Shakespeare, you can skip page numbers and cite by act, scene, and lines, separated by periods (*Romeo and Juliet* 1.3.12–15). A similar pattern can be used for other works of poetry or verse that include numbered lines and other divisions. To cite lines alone, spell out "line" or "lines" (lines 12–15).

When you refer to online documents, there are often no pages to cite. As a substitute, include a section or paragraph number, if there is one. Just put a comma after the author's name, then list the section or paragraph: (Padgett, sec. 9.7) or (Snidal, pars. 12–18). If the online document is a PDF file, go ahead and list the page numbers since those will be the same for all users: (Wang 14). If there's no numbering system, though, just list the author.

In-text citations normally appear at the end of sentences and are followed by the punctuation for the sentence itself. To illustrate:

> A full discussion of these issues appears in *Miss Thistlebottom's Hobgoblins* (Bernstein).

In this style you can still use regular footnotes or endnotes for limited purposes. They can be used *only* for commentary, not for citations. If you need to cite some materials within the note itself, use in-text citations there just as you would in the text.

For brevity—a paramount virtue of the MLA system—the names of publishers are also compressed: Princeton University Press becomes Princeton UP, the University of Chicago Press becomes U of Chicago P. For the same reason, most month names are abbreviated.

MLA's penchant for brevity extends to referencing electronic information—to a point. URLs or DOIs are necessary for online sources, but MLA does not include "http://" or "https://" in URLs (though see the exception for DOIs). Access dates are now optional, although encouraged when no date of publication, posting, or modification can be found.

I have provided detailed information and examples in a table below. Because MLA style is often used in the humanities, where citations to plays, poems, paintings, and films are common, I include all of those genres. If you want still more examples or less common items, consult the handbook.

To make it easy to find the citations you need, I've listed them here alphabetically, along with the pages where they are described. At the end of the chapter I have listed some common MLA abbreviations.

INDEX OF MLA CITATIONS IN THIS CHAPTER

MLA: WORKS CITED AND IN-TEXT CITATIONS

| Book,
one author | Works Cited | Lipson, Charles. *How to Write a BA Thesis: A Practical Guide from Your First Ideas to Your Finished Paper.* U of Chicago P, 2005.
Collins, Christopher. *Neopoetics: The Evolution of the Literate Imagination.* Columbia UP, 2016.
Fitzpatrick, Meghan. *Invisible Scars: Mental Trauma and the Korean War.* U of British Columbia P, 2017. |

Book, one author (*continued*)		▸ MLA style omits the publisher's location, unless the book was published before 1900, in which case the city may be listed in place of the publisher's name: Barcelona, 1870
	In-text	(Lipson 80–82) or (80–82) ▸ Refers to pages 80–82. ▸ If it is necessary to differentiate this book from others by the same author, then cite thus: (Lipson, *How* 22–23) ▸ To shorten a title in MLA, include the first noun with any preceding adjectives. If the title does not begin with a noun phrase, just use the first word, as long as it's clear which work you're referencing. (Collins 26) or (26) (Fitzpatrick 136) or (136)
Books, several by same author	Works Cited	Talbot, Ian. *A History of Modern South Asia: Politics, States, Diasporas.* Yale UP, 2016. ---, editor. *The Independence of India and Pakistan: New Approaches and Reflections.* Oxford UP, 2013. ---. *Pakistan: A Modern History.* Palgrave Macmillan, 2010. ▸ The repetition of the author's name uses three hyphens, followed by a period. If the repeated name is that of an editor or translator, place a comma after the three hyphens instead of a period.
	In-text	(Talbot, *History* 34; Talbot, *Independence* 3–5; Talbot, *Pakistan* 456)
Book, multiple authors	Works Cited	Young, Harvey, and Queen Meccasia Zabriskie. *Black Theater Is Black Life: An Oral History of Chicago Theater and Dance, 1970–2010.* Northwestern UP, 2013.

Fischer, John Martin, and Benjamin Mitchell-
    Yellin. *Near-Death Experiences: Under-
    standing Visions of the Afterlife*. Oxford UP,
    2016.

Hall, Jacqueline Dowd, et al. *Like a Family: The
    Making of a Southern Cotton Mill World*.
    U of North Carolina P, 1987.

   ▶ When there are three or more authors, as
     there are for *Like a Family*, use "et al." after
     naming the first one.

In-text

(Young and Zabriskie, *Black Theater* 15–26) or
(Young and Zabriskie 15–26)
(Fischer and Mitchell-Yellin 15–18)
(Hall et al. 67)

Book, multiple editions

Works Cited

Strunk, William, Jr., and E. B. White. *The
    Elements of Style*. 50th anniversary ed.,
    Longman, 2009.

Saller, Carol Fisher. *The Subversive Copy
    Editor: Advice from Chicago*. 2nd ed., U of
    Chicago P, 2016.

Head, Dominic, editor. *The Cambridge Guide
    to Literature in English*. 3rd ed., Cambridge
    UP, 2006.

   ▶ If this were a multivolume work, then the
     volume number would come after the edition:
     3rd ed., vol. 2.

In-text

(Strunk and White 12)
(Saller 97)
(Head 15)

Book, edited

Works Cited

Ross, Jeffrey Ian, editor. *Routledge Handbook
    of Graffiti and Street Art*. Routledge, 2016.

Gilbert, Sandra, and Susan Gubar, editors.
    *Feminist Literary Theory and Criticism:
    A Norton Reader*. Norton, 2007.

Cheng, Jim, et al., editors. *An Annotated Bibli-
    ography for Taiwan Film Studies*. Columbia
    UP, 2016.

   ▶ If there are three or more editors, name the
     first editor followed by "et al."

Book, edited (*continued*)	In-text	(Ross 93) (Gilbert and Gubar 72) (Cheng et al. 12)

Book, anonymous or no author	Works Cited	*Through Our Enemies' Eyes: Osama Bin Laden, Radical Islam, and the Future of America.* Brassey's, 2003. *The Secret Lives of Teachers.* U of Chicago P, 2015. ▸ Do not use "anonymous" as the author. If the author is unknown, alphabetize by title but ignore any initial article (*A*, *An*, or *The*). So *The Holy Koran* is alphabetized under "H."
	In-text	(*Through Our Enemies' Eyes*) (*Secret Lives*)

E-book	Works Cited	Miranda, Lin-Manuel, and Jeremy McCarter. *Hamilton: The Revolution.* Kindle ed., Grand Central Publishing, 2016. Auspitz, Kate. *Wallis's War: A Novel of Diplomacy and Intrigue.* iBooks ed., U of Chicago P, 2015. ▸ MLA treats an e-book as an edition (abbreviated *ed.*).
	In-text	(Miranda and McCarter) (Auspitz, ch. 3) ▸ If the version you are using lacks page numbers or uses reflowable text, cite a chapter or other indicator instead.

Book, online	Works Cited	James, Henry. *The Turn of the Screw.* Martin Secker, 1915. *Internet Archive*, archive.org/details/in.ernet.dli.2015.95031. Skrentny, John David. *After Civil Rights: Racial Realism in the New American Workplace.* Princeton UP, 2014. *eBook Academic Collection, EBSCOhost.* ▸ Following the publication details for the book, list the website that hosts it, followed by the URL.

> ‣ If you consulted the book through a library database, you don't need to list a URL, especially if the URL for the specific item is very long.

	In-text	(James 10) (Skrentny 105)

Multivolume work	Works Cited	Cunningham, Noble E., Jr., editor. *Circular Letters of Congressmen to Their Constituents, 1789–1829*. Omohundro Institute of Early American History and Culture / U of North Carolina P, 2013. 3 vols. ‣ If there is more than one publisher, include both with a slash between them.
	In-text	(Cunningham) or (Cunningham 3: 21) ‣ This refers to volume 3, page 21. (Cunningham, vol. 3) ‣ When a volume is referenced without a specific page, then use "vol." so the volume won't be confused for a page number.

Single volume in a multivolume work	Works Cited	Caro, Robert A. *The Passage of Power*. 2012. *The Years of Lyndon Johnson*, vol. 4, Knopf, 1982–. 5 vols. projected. Iriye, Akira. *The Globalizing of America*. 1993. *Cambridge History of American Foreign Relations*, edited by Warren I. Cohen, vol. 3, Cambridge UP, 1993. 4 vols. ‣ Because these volumes have their own titles, MLA does not require the information for the other volumes. If you want, just cite the single title, with no volume number: Caro, Robert A. *The Passage of Power*. Knopf, 2012. Iriye, Akira. *The Globalizing of America*. Cambridge UP, 1993.
	In-text	(Caro) (Iriye)

Reprint of earlier edition	Works Cited	Barzun, Jacques. *Simple and Direct: A Rhetoric for Writers.* 1985. U of Chicago P, 1994. Smith, Adam. *An Inquiry into the Nature and Causes of the Wealth of Nations.* 1776. Edited by Edwin Cannan, U of Chicago P, 1976.
	In-text	(Barzun, *Simple*) or (Barzun) (Smith, *Inquiry*) or (Smith)
Translated volume	Works Cited	Gan, Aleksei. *Constructivism.* 1922. Translated by Christina Lodder, Editorial Tenov, 2014. Tocqueville, Alexis de. *Democracy in America.* Edited by J. P. Mayer, translated by George Lawrence, Harper, 2000. ▸ Editor and translator are listed in the order in which they appear on the book's title page. *Beowulf: A New Verse Translation.* Translated by Seamus Heaney, Farrar, 2000. ▸ *Beowulf* is an anonymous poem. The translator's name normally comes after the title. But there is an exception. If you wish to comment on the translator's work, then place the translator's name first. For example: Heaney, Seamus, translator. *Beowulf: A New Verse Translation.* Farrar, 2000. Lodder, Christina, translator. *Constructivism.* By Aleksei Gan, 1922. Editorial Tenov, 2014.
	In-text	(Gan, *Constructivism*) or (Gan) (Tocqueville, *Democracy in America*) or (Tocqueville) (Heaney, *Beowulf*) or (*Beowulf*) (Lodder)
Chapter in edited book	Works Cited	Jones, Kima. "Homegoing, AD." *The Fire This Time: A New Generation Speaks about Race*, edited by Jesmyn Ward, Scribner, 2016, pp. 15–18.
	In-text	(Jones, 16)

Journal article	Works Cited	Sampsell, Gary. "Popular Music in the Time of J. S. Bach: The Leipzig Mandora Manuscript." *Bach*, vol. 48, no. 1, 2017, pp. 1–35.

Domínguez Torres, Mónica. "Havana's Fortunes: 'Entangled Histories' in Copley's *Watson and the Shark*." *American Art*, vol. 30, no. 2, Summer 2016, pp. 8–13.

▸ If the article title includes a term in quotation marks, use single quotation marks in your citation.

Ünal, Yusuf. "Sayyid Quṭb in Iran: Translating the Islamic Ideologue in the Islamic Republic." *Journal of Islamic and Muslim Studies*, vol. 1, no. 2, Nov. 2016, pp. 35–60, https://doi.org/10.2979/jims.1.2.04.

Judd, David, and James Rocha. "Autonomous Pigs." *Ethics and the Environment*, vol. 22, no. 1, Spring 2017, pp. 1–18, https://doi.org/10.2979/ethicsenviro.22.1.01.

▸ A DOI is preferable to another kind of URL if one is listed. Add https://doi.org/ to the DOI, despite the normal MLA rule of dropping https:// from URLs.

▸ If there are three or more authors, list as "Judd, David, et al."

Tyler, Tom. "Snakes, Skins and the Sphinx: Nietzsche's Ecdysis." *Journal of Visual Culture*, vol. 5, no. 3, Dec. 2006, pp. 365–85. Abstract.

▸ To cite an abstract, include the word *Abstract* after the article information.

In-text

(Sampsell) or (Sampsell 31)
(Domínguez Torres 12)
(Ünal) or (Ünal 58) or (Ünal, "Sayyid Quṭb" 58)

▸ The title may be needed to differentiate this article from others by the same author.

(Judd and Rocha, 3–5)
(Tyler)

Journal article, foreign language	Works Cited	Joosten, Jan. "Le milieu producteur du Penta-teuque grec." *Revue des Études Juives*, vol. 165, nos. 3–4, juillet–décembre 2006, pp. 349–61. ▸ For inclusive page numbers, MLA requires the full second number up to 99, but only the last two digits for larger numbers, as long as the range is clear.
	In-text	(Joosten) or (Joosten 356)
Newspaper or magazine article	Works Cited	"Retired U.S. General Is Focus of Inquiry over Iran Leak." *The New York Times*, 28 June 2013, p. A18. ▸ If an article has no author, list it by title. Halbfinger, David M. "Politicians Are Doing Hollywood Star Turns." *The New York Times*, 6 Feb. 2007, natl. ed., pp. B1+. ▸ Use European-style dates: day month year. ▸ The plus sign indicates that the article continues, but not on the next page (this one continues on B7). If the article continued on B2 and ran to B3, you'd write B1–B3. Halper, Evan. "Congress Takes Aim at the Clean Air Act, Putting the Limits of California's Power to the Test." *Los Angeles Times*, 3 Aug. 2017, 3:00 a.m. PDT, www.latimes.com/politics/la-na-pol-smog-republicans-20170803-story.html. ▸ Include a time stamp for articles that may be updated frequently. ▸ You do not need to include page numbers for articles consulted online.
	In-text	("Retired U.S. General" A18) (Halbfinger B7) or (Halbfinger, "Politicians" B7) if you cite more than one article by this author. (Halper)

Review	Works Cited	Pugh, Allison J. Review of *The Gender Trap: Parents and the Pitfalls of Raising Boys and Girls*, by Emily W. Kane. *American Journal of Sociology*, vol. 119, no. 6, May 2014, pp. 1773–75. Paxton, Robert O. Review of *The Nazi-Fascist New Order for European Culture*, by Benjamin G. Martin. *New York Review of Books*, 26 Oct. 2017, www.nybooks.com/articles/2017/10/26/nazi-fascist-cultural-axis.
	In-text	(Pugh 1774) or (Pugh, "Gender Trap" 1774) (Paxton) or (Paxton, "Nazi-Fascist New Order")
Unpublished paper, thesis, or dissertation	Works Cited	Levine, Daniel H. "What Pope Francis Brings to Latin America." CLALS Working Paper Series 11, 12 Apr. 2016, papers.ssrn.com/sol3/papers.cfm?abstract_id=2761467. Sierra, Luis Manuel. *Indigenous Neighborhood Residents in the Urbanization of La Paz, Bolivia, 1910–1950*. 2013. State U of New York at Binghamton, PhD dissertation, *ProQuest*, search.proquest.com/docview/1507870239?accountid=14657.
	In-text	(Levine) (Sierra) or (Sierra 49)
Archival materials and manuscript collections	Works Cited	Franklin, Isaac. Letter to R. C. Ballard. 28 Feb. 1831, Rice Ballard Papers. Southern Historical Collection, Wilson Lib. U of North Carolina, Chapel Hill. MS. Series 1.1, folder 1. Lamson, Mary Swift. "An Account of the Beginning of the B.Y.W.C.A." 1891, Manuscript. Boston YWCA Papers. Schlesinger Lib, Radcliffe Institute for Advanced Study, Harvard U. Cambridge, MA. Szold, Henrietta. Letter to Rose Jacobs. 3 Feb. 1932. Rose Jacobs–Alice L. Seligsberg Collection. Judaica Microforms. Brandeis Lib. Waltham, MA. Microform, reel 1, book 1.

Archival materials and manuscript collections (*continued*)		Szold, Henrietta. Letter to Rose Jacobs. 9 Mar. 1936. Central Zionist Archives, Jerusalem. A/125/112. Copland, Aaron. "At the Thought of Mozart." Manuscript / mixed material, Library of Congress, Washington, DC, www.loc.gov/item/copland.writ0036. Accessed 13 Oct. 2017.
	In-text	(Franklin) or (Franklin to Ballard) or (Franklin to Ballard, 28 Feb. 1831) (Lamson) or (Lamson 2) (Szold) or (Szold to Jacobs) or (Szold to Jacobs, 3 Feb. 1932) (Szold) or (Szold to Jacobs) or (Szold to Jacobs, 9 Mar. 1936) (Taraval) or (Taraval, par. 23) ▸ This manuscript uses paragraph numbers, not pages. (Taft) or (Taft 149)

Encyclopedia and dictionary	Works Cited	*Encyclopaedia Britannica*, 15th ed., 1987. *Merriam-Webster*, www.merriamwebster.com. *Oxford English Dictionary*, 2nd ed., 1989. ▸ Cite the work as a whole in the list of works cited; the entries themselves are mentioned or described in the text. ▸ Edition and year are required for print resources. ▸ You can omit the publisher for well-known encyclopedias, dictionaries, and other references. ▸ If you do want to include the specific entry in your works cited, you can do it like this: "App." *Merriam-Webster*. www.merriam-webster.com/dictionary/app. Accessed 24 Oct. 2017 ▸ For undated entries consulted online, include an access date. "pluck, n.1." *OED Online*, www.oed.com/view/Entry/145996. Accessed 24 Oct. 2017. ▸ There are two separate entries for the noun "pluck," and I am citing the first, hence "n.1." The second is for an obscure fish.

Kania, Andrea. "The Philosophy of Music." Revised 11 June 2017. *Stanford Encyclopedia of Philosophy*, plato.stanford.edu/entries/music.

	In-text	("App") or (*Merriam-Webster*) ("Pluck") or (*Oxford English Dictionary*) (Kania)

Bible, Koran (Qur'an)	Works Cited	*Tanakh: The Holy Scriptures: The New JPS Translation according to the Traditional Hebrew Text.* Jewish Publication Society, 1985.

> The Bible, Koran, and other sacred texts do *not* usually appear in Works Cited unless you need to cite a particular version or translation.

	In-text	(*Tanakh*, Genesis 1.1, 1.3–5, 2.4), then Genesis 1.1, 1.3–5, 2.4.

> Books may be abbreviated, such as Gen. 1.1, 1.3–5, 2.4.

> Abbreviations for the next four books are Ex., Lev., Num., and Deut. Abbreviations for other books are easily found with a web search for "abbreviations + Bible."

(Koran 18.65–82)

Speech, academic talk, or course lecture	Works Cited	Zien, Katherine. "Good Neighbor, Good Soldier: Staging Transhemispheric Militarization in the Former Panama Canal Zone." Paper presented at the ASTR/TLA Annual Conference, 4 Nov. 2016, Minneapolis Marriott City Center.

Skeel, David. "Is Justice Possible?" Lecture, 13 Nov. 2014, U of Hong Kong. *YouTube*, uploaded by Faith HKU, 3 Dec. 2014, youtu .be/qeR_Y2KQTts.

Doniger, Wendy. Course on evil in Hindu mythology. 15 Mar. 2007, U of Chicago. Lecture.

> You may indicate a live lecture or address, or another format that is not obvious, at the end of the reference.

Speech, academic talk, or course lecture (*continued*)	In-text	(Zien) (Skeel) (Doniger)

Personal communication or interview	Works Cited	▸ Personal communications can often be mentioned in the text alone. If you'd like to include them in the works cited list, they would look like this:
		Alter, Robert. Personal interview. 21 Oct. 2015.
		Sarkozy, Nicolas. Telephone interview. 5 May 2017.
		Lucas, George. Video interview, Skype. 18 Feb. 2010.
		Anonymous US soldier, recently returned from Afghanistan. Personal interview. 28 Jan. 2014.
		Coates, Ta-Nehisi. "On Charlottesville, Trump, the Confederacy, Reparations & More." Interview by Amy Goodman and Juan González. *Democracy Now!*, 15 Aug. 2017, www.democracynow.org/2017/8/15/full_interview_ta_nehisi_coates_on.
		Rosenquist, James. "Reminiscing on the Gulf of Mexico: A Conversation with James Rosenquist." Interview by Jan van der Marck. *American Art*, vol. 20, no. 3, Fall 2006, pp. 84–107.
	In-text	(Alter) (Sarkozy) (Lucas) (anonymous US soldier) (Coates) (Rosenquist 93)

Poem	Works Cited	Auden, W. H. "The Shield of Achilles." 1952. *Collected Poems*, edited by Edward Mendelson, Random House, 2007, pp. 596–98.
		▸ Auden's poem is dated 1952 by Mendelson. The original date of a poem in a collection or anthology is optional.

Robards, Brooks. "The Front." *On Island:
Poems and Paintings of Martha's Vineyard*,
Summerset Press, 2014, p. 17.

Balakian, Peter. "Near the Border." *Ozone Journal*,
U of Chicago P, 2015, pp. 69–74.

Paredez, Deborah. "St. Joske's." 2012. *Poets.
org*, www.poets.org/poetsorg/poem/st
-joskes.

In-text	(Auden 596) or (Auden, "Shield of Achilles" 596) or ("Shield of Achilles" 596) or (Auden 596; lines 9–11) or (Auden, lines 9–11) or (lines 9–11) or (9–11)

> Do not use abbreviations for "line" or "lines" since a lowercase *1* is easily confused with the number 1.

(Robards)

(Balakian 70) or (Balakian, "Near the Border" 70)

(Paredez) or (Paredez, "St. Joske's")

Play, text	Works Cited	Ruhl, Sarah. *Stage Kiss*. 2011. Theatre Communications Group, 2014.

> The play was first produced in 2011, published in 2014.

Shakespeare, William. *Romeo and Juliet*.

> If you wish to cite a specific edition:

Shakespeare, William. *Romeo and Juliet*.
Edited by Brian Gibbons, Methuen, 1980.

> For an online version:

Shakespeare, William. *Romeo and Juliet*.
Edited by William J. Rolfe, American Book,
1907. Project Gutenberg, www.gutenberg
.org/files/47960/47960-h/47960-h.htm.

In-text	(Ruhl) or (Ruhl, *Stage Kiss*)

(Shakespeare, *Romeo and Juliet* 1.3.12–15) or
(*Romeo and Juliet* 1.3.12–15) or
(1.3.12–15) if the play's name is clear in the text

> This refers to act 1, scene 3, lines 12–15 (separated by periods).

Play, text (*continued*)		► If you refer repeatedly to Shakespeare's plays, you can use MLA's standard abbreviations for them, such as (*Ham.*) for *Hamlet*. The first time you mention a play such as *Romeo and Juliet*, you simply indicate the abbreviation (*Rom.*), and then use it after that for in-text citations, such as (*Rom.* 1.3.12–15).

Performance of play or dance	Works Cited	*Romeo and Juliet*. Choreography by Krzysztof Pastor, music by Sergei Prokofiev, Joffrey Ballet, 13 Oct. 2016, Auditorium Theatre, Chicago. *The Rembrandt*. Written by Jessica Dickey, directed by Hallie Gordon, performance by Francis Guinan and John Mahoney, 6 Oct. 2017, Steppenwolf Theatre, Chicago. ► If you are concentrating on one person's work in theater, music, dance, or other collaborative arts, put that person's name first. For example, if you are focusing on Francis Guinan's acting: Guinan, Francis, performer. *The Rembrandt*. Written by Jessica Dickey, directed by Hallie Gordon, 6 Oct. 2017, Steppenwolf Theatre, Chicago.
	In-text	*(Romeo and Juliet)* (*Rembrandt*) or (Guinan)

Television program	Works Cited	"The Children." *Game of Thrones*, written by David Benioff and D. B. Weiss, directed by Alex Graves, season 4, episode 10, HBO, 15 June 2014. "Pressing the Flesh." *Scandal*, written by Shonda Rhimes, performance by Kerry Washington, Katie Lowes, and Scott Foley, season 7, episode 2, ABC, 12 Oct. 2017. Hulu, www.hulu.com/watch/1156610.
	In-text	("The Children") ("Pressing the Flesh")

Film	Works Cited	*Godfather II*. Directed by Francis Ford Coppola, performance by Al Pacino, Robert De Niro, Robert Duvall, and Diane Keaton, screenplay by Francis Ford Coppola and Mario Puzo, based on the novel by Mario Puzo, Paramount Pictures, 1974. Paramount Home Video, Godfather DVD Collection, 2003.

> Optional information includes actors, producers, screenwriters, editors, cinematographers, etc. Include what you need for analysis in your paper, in order of their importance to your analysis. Their names appear between the title and the distributor.

> If you are concentrating on one person's work, put that person's name and role (such as performer) first, before the title:

Coppola, Francis Ford, director. *Godfather II*. Performance by Al Pacino, Robert De Niro, Robert Duvall, and Diane Keaton, Paramount Pictures, 1974. Paramount Home Video, Godfather DVD Collection, 2003.

Tig. Directed by Kristina Goolsby and Ashley York, Beachside / Netflix, 2015. Netflix, www.netflix.com/title/80028208.

> If there is more than one production company, list both with a slash between them. In the example above, Netflix is both a producer and the name of the website from which the film was retrieved.

	In-text	(*Godfather II*) or (Coppola) (*Tig*)

Artwork	Works Cited	Tintoretto, Jacopo Robusti. *The Birth of John the Baptist*. 1550s, State Hermitage Museum, St. Petersburg. Oil on canvas, 181 × 266 cm.

> The size and medium are optional.

Artwork (*continued*)		Tintoretto, Jacopo Robusti. *The Birth of John the Baptist*. 1550s, State Hermitage Museum, St. Petersburg. *Tintoretto: Tradition and Identity*, by Tom Nichols, Reaktion Books, 1999, p. 47.

➤ For a reproduction, cite where you found the work.

Tintoretto, Jacopo Robusti. *The Birth of John the Baptist*. 1550s, State Hermitage Museum, St. Petersburg, www.hermitage museum.org/wps/portal/hermitage/digital -collection/01.+Paintings/32113/?lng=en.

➤ Include a website and URL for artwork found online, but if the website and museum share the same name, there is no need to list both.

	In-text	(Tintoretto) or (Tintoretto, *Birth of John the Baptist*)

Photograph	Works Cited	Adams, Ansel. *Monolith, the Face of Half Dome, Yosemite National Park*. 1927, Art Institute, Chicago. Adams, Ansel. *Dunes, Oceano, California*. 1963. *MoMA*, www.moma.org/collection/ works/58283.
	In-text	(Adams) or (Adams, *Monolith*) (Adams) or (Adams, *Dunes, Oceano*)

Figures: map, chart, graph, or table	Works Cited	Digout, Delphine. "Climate Change Vulnerability in Africa." Revised by Hugo Ahlenius, UNEP/GRID-Arendal, 2002. *GRID-Arendal*, old.grida.no/graphicslib/detail/climate -change-vulnerability-in-africa_7239.

"Presidential Election Results: Donald J. Trump Wins." 9 Aug. 2017. *The New York Times*, www.nytimes.com/elections/results/ president. Interactive map.

➤ If the format (here an interactive map) is not obvious from the title, you may specify the type of work.

"1427 E. 60th St., Chicago IL 60637." *Google Maps*, www.google.com/maps/place/The +University+of+Chicago+Press,+1427+E +60th+St,+Chicago,+IL+60637/. Accessed 25 Oct. 2017. 2017.

➤ For undated maps consulted online, include an access date.

➤ A map published in a book or journal can usually be mentioned in the text (see "In-text," below); cite the work as a whole in the Works Cited list:

Menkhaus, Ken. "Governance without Government in Somalia: Spoilers, State Building, and the Politics of Coping." *International Security*, vol. 31, no. 7, Winter 2006/7, pp. 74–106.

In-text	("Climate Change Vulnerability in Africa") ("Presidential Election Results") ("Map of Somalia, 2006/7") or (Menkhaus 79, map)

Musical recording	Works Cited	Johnson, Robert. "Come On in My Kitchen (Take 1)." 1936. *Robert Johnson: King of the Delta Blues Singers*, expanded ed., Columbia/Legacy, 1998. Johnson, Robert. "Traveling Riverside Blues." 1937. *Robert Johnson: King of the Delta Blues Singers*, Columbia Records 1654, 1961. LP. Allman Brothers Band. "Come On in My Kitchen." Written by Robert Johnson, *Shades of Two Worlds*. Sony, 1991. Barber, Samuel. Cello sonata, for cello and piano, op. 6. *Barber: Adagio for Strings, Violin Concerto, Orchestral and Chamber Works*, St. Louis Symphony, conducted by Leonard Slatkin, Alan Stepansky, cello, Israela Margalit, piano, EMI Classics 74287, 2001. CD.

➤ Catalog numbers can be listed with publication details to help readers locate a specific recording.

Musical recording (*continued*)		▸ If you consulted a physical medium, add it at the end of the entry. ▸ If you are concentrating on one person's work, such as the pianist, his or her name can come first: Margalit, Israela, piano. Cello sonata, for cello and piano, op. 6. *Barber: Adagio for Strings, Violin Concerto, Orchestral and Chamber Works*, St. Louis Symphony, conducted by Leonard Slatkin, Alan Stepansky, cello, EMI Classics 74287, 2001. Beyoncé. "Formation." *Lemonade*, Parkwood Entertainment, 2016. ▸ You do not need to include the software application or website where you accessed the music. If you choose to do so, it would look like this: Beyoncé. "Formation." *Lemonade*, *iTunes* app, Parkwood Entertainment, 2016.
	In-text	(Johnson) or (Johnson, "Come") (Johnson) or (Johnson, "Traveling") (Allman Brothers) or (Allman Brothers, "Come") (Barber) or (Barber, Cello sonata) (Margalit) or (Margalit, Cello sonata) (Beyoncé) or (Beyoncé, "Formation")
Music video	Works Cited	Arcade Fire. *Everything Now*. *YouTube*, uploaded by ArcadeFireVEVO, 1 June 2017, youtu.be/zC3oBYR3CUk. Rihanna et al. *FourFiveSeconds*. Directed by Inez & Vinoodh, produced by Stephanie Bargas and Jeff Lepine. *Vevo*, 3 Feb. 2015, www.vevo.com/watch/rihanna/fourfiveseconds/QMFUA1590146. Video. ▸ You can specify "Video" if it's not clear from the entry. ▸ Do not include comments on videos (or any web content) in the works cited list.
	In-text	(Arcade Fire) or (Arcade Fire, *Everything Now*) (Rihanna et al.)

Sheet music	Works Cited	Bach, Johann Sebastian. *Toccata and Fugue in D Minor*. 1708. BWV 565, arranged by Ferruccio Benvenuto Busoni for solo piano, G. Schirmer LB1629, 1942.
		▸ This piece was written in 1708 and has the standard Bach classification BWV 565. The arrangement is published by G. Schirmer, with its catalog number LB1629.
	In-text	(*Toccata and Fugue in D Minor*) or (Bach, *Toccata and Fugue in D Minor*)
Liner notes	Works Cited	Reich, Steven. Liner notes. *Different Trains*. Kronos Quartet, Elektra/Nonesuch 9 79176-2, 1988. CD.
	In-text	(Reich, *Different Trains*)
Audiobook	Works Cited	Eliot, George. *Middlemarch*. Narrated by Juliet Stevenson, Audible, 2011. Audiobook.
	In-text	(Eliot) or (Eliot, *Middlemarch*) or (Eliot 01:02:20–27)
		▸ To cite a specific part of the text, refer to the time or range of time in the in-text citation.
Advertisement	Works Cited	Advertisement for *Letters from Iwo Jima*. *The New York Times*, 6 Feb. 2007, p. B4.
		Advertisement for Vitamin Water. *Rolling Stone*, 15 June 2017, p. 17.
		"Be a Mindsticker," advertisement for Tab cola. Coca-Cola Co., circa late 1960s. *Dailymotion*, 8 Aug. 2007, www.dailymotion.com/video/x2s3qd.
	In-text	(*Letters from Iwo Jima* advertisement)
		(Vitamin Water advertisement)
		(Tab advertisement)

Government document	Works Cited	United States, Congress, Senate, Committee on Armed Services. *Hearings on S. 758, a Bill to Promote the National Security by Providing for a National Defense Establishment.* Government Printing Office, 1947. 80th Congress, 1st session, Senate Report 239.

United States, Congress, House. *American Health Care Act. Congress.gov*, 2017, www.congress.gov/bill/115th-congress/house-bill/1628/text.

▶ Number and session of Congress, chamber, and type and number of publication are optional.

United States, Environmental Protection Agency, Office of Air and Radiation. *A Brief Guide to Mold, Moisture, and Your Home.* EPA.gov, 2012, www.epa.gov/mold/brief-guide-mold-moisture-and-your-home.

Freedman, Stephen. *Four-Year Impacts of Ten Programs on Employment Stability and Earnings Growth: The National Evaluation of Welfare-to-Work Strategies.* US Department of Education, 2000, www.mdrc.org/publication/four-year-impacts-ten-programs-employment-stability-and-earnings-growth.

United States, Department of State. Daily Press Briefing. US Department of State, 9 Aug. 2017, www.state.gov/r/pa/prs/dpb/2017/08/273288.htm.

In-text   (US Cong., Senate, Committee on Armed Services)

▶ If you are referencing only one item from that committee, then in-text citations don't need to include the hearing number or report.

(US Cong., Senate, Committee on Armed Services, *Hearings on S. 758*, 1947)

▶ If you refer to several items from the committee, indicate which one you are citing. You can shorten that after the first use:

(*Hearings on S. 758*)

(US, EPA, Office of Air and Radiation 15)
(Freedman 6) or (Freedman, *Four-Year Impacts*)
(US Dept. of State) or (US Dept. of State, *Press Briefing*, 9 Aug. 2017)

Website, page or entire	Works Cited	"News and Advocacy." *American Historical Association*, www.historians.org/news-and -advocacy. Accessed 9 Nov. 2017. de Blasio, Bill. "State of the City 2017." *Office of the Mayor*, City of New York, 13 Feb. 2017, www1.nyc.gov/office-of-the-mayor/ state-of-our-city.page. Lipson, Charles. "News and Commentary: US and the World." *Charles Lipson*, www .charleslipson.com/News-links.htm. Accessed 29 Aug. 2017. ▸ For webpages without identifiable authors, begin the citation with the title of the page or website. ▸ If there is no date of publication, posting, or revision, include an access date. ▸ Webpages and other online documents may not have numbered pages. You may, however, be able to cite to a specific section (Lipson, sec. 7) or paragraph (Lipson, pars. 3–5).
	In-text	("News and Advocacy") (de Blasio) or (de Blasio, "State of the City") (Lipson)
Blog, post or comment	Works Cited	Jayson, Sharon. "Is Selfie Culture Making Our Kids Selfish?" *Well*, *The New York Times*, 23 June 2016, well.blogs.nytimes.com/ 2016/06/23/is-selfie-culture-making-our -kids-selfish. Arana, Ana. "The Deep Magic of Mexico." *The Big Roundtable*, 8 Dec. 2016, thebiground table.com/the-deep-magic-of-mexico -2bf1b341d1a1. ▸ Blog posts (or entries) are cited like articles from newspapers or news sites.

Blog, post or comment (*continued*)		Cheryl. Comment on "Is Selfie Culture Making Our Kids Selfish?" *Well*, *The New York Times*, 23 June 2016, well.blogs.nytimes .com/2016/06/23/is-selfie-culture-making -our-kids-selfish.
	In-text	(Jayson) or (Jayson, "Selfie Culture") (Arana) or (Arana, "Deep Magic")

Video	Works Cited	*Duck and Cover*. Archer Productions / Federal Civil Defense Administration, 1951. *YouTube*, uploaded by Nuclear Vault, 11 July 2009, youtu.be/IKqXu-5jw6o.

▸ This 1951 film was posted online in 2009.

"Jury Convicts Martin Shkreli on Three Counts of Security Fraud." *NBC*, 4 Aug. 2017, www .nbcnews.com/video/jury-convicts-martin -shkreli-on-three-counts-of-securities-fraud -1017719875664.

Wang, Tricia. "The Human Insights Missing from Big Data." *TED*, Sept. 2016, www .ted.com/talks/tricia_wang_the_human _insights_missing_from_big_data. Video.

▸ You can specify "Video" if it's not clear from the entry.

▸ Why is *Duck and Cover* in italics but "Jury Convicts Martin Shkreli" and "Human Insights" placed in quotation marks? Because MLA italicizes films and TV series but "quotes" individual episodes. The emergence of new media blurs this once-bright line. In this case, *Duck and Cover* is italicized because it was produced as a stand-alone film, albeit a brief one. The two other examples, on the other hand, are more like individual episodes in a series.

	In-text	(*Duck and Cover*) ("Jury")

Multimedia app (video game, other stand-alone application)	Works Cited	*Madden NFL 18*. Standard ed., EA Sports, 25 Aug.2017. ▸ Include any other information you think is relevant: *Madden NFL 18*. EA Sports, PlayStation 4, Nov. 2017. *Geocaching*. Groundspeak, v. 5.6.1, 2017.
	In-text	(*Madden NFL 18*) (*Geocaching*)
Podcast	Works Cited	"Has Anybody Called You?" *S-Town*, ch. 2, hosted by Brian Reed, produced by Brian Reed and Julie Snyder, Serial Productions, 28 Mar. 2017, stownpodcast.org/chapter/2. ▸ or Reed, Brian, host. "Has Anybody Called You?" *S-Town*, ch. 2, produced by Brian Reed and Julie Snyder, Serial Productions, 28 Mar. 2017, stownpodcast.org/chapter/2. DeGeneres, Ellen. "Ellen's Parenting Advice." *The Ellen Show Podcast*, Telepictures Productions, 26 June 2015, *iTunes*.
	In-text	("Has Anybody Called You?") or (Reed) (DeGeneres) or (DeGeneres, "Ellen's Parenting Advice")
Social media (Facebook, Instagram, Twitter)	Works Cited	Zuckerberg, Mark. Profile. *Facebook*, www.facebook.com/zuck. Tyson, Neil deGrasse (@neiltyson). "Always seemed to me that millipedes have more legs than are necessary." *Twitter*, 7 July 2017, 1:25 p.m., twitter.com/neiltyson/status/883421859072458752. ▸ For the title, use the text of the post, up to 160 characters. Chicago Manual of Style. "Is the world ready for singular they? We thought so back in 1993." *Facebook*, 17 Apr. 2015, www.facebook.com/ChicagoManual/posts/10152906193679151.

Social media (Facebook, Instagram, Twitter) (*continued*)		Richards, Corey (@coryrichards). "A quiet if not solemn day on Everest." *Instagram*, 24 May 2017, www.instagram.com/p/BUekBZLg DOW/.
		▸ Publicly available social media content should be cited this way. Private content such as direct messages should be cited like text messages.
	In-text	(Zuckerberg) (Tyson) (Chicago Manual of Style) (Richards) or (Richards, "Quiet")
Email, texts (direct messages)	Works Cited	▸ Texts and other personal messages can often be cited in the text alone. If you'd like to include them in the works cited list, they'd look like this: Leis, Kathy. "Re: New Orleans family." Received by Karen Turkish, 3 Mar. 2017. ▸ For title, use the subject of the email. Lipson, Michael. *Facebook* message to Jonathan Lipson. 9 Feb. 2016. ▸ Include the time for instant messages or emails if they are pertinent. For example: 9 Feb. 2010, 3:15 p.m.
	In-text	(Leis) (Lipson) or (Lipson, M.)
Electronic forum or mailing list	Works Cited	Polger, Mark Aaron. "CALL: Call for Proposals." American Library Association mailing list archives, ACRL Campaign for Libraries list, 10 May 2017, lists.ala.org/sympa/arc/ academicpr/2017-05/msg00005.html. Ngo, Quinn. "Re: What Are Some Unknown Truths about College Life?" *Quora*, 14 July 2017, www.quora.com/What-are-some -unknown-truths-about-college-life.
	In-text	(Polger) (Ngo)

A lot of terms that used to be abbreviated in MLA style can now be spelled out, but some things are still usually abbreviated. For example, terms like *editor* are now spelled out, but *edition* is always abbreviated. All months are shortened, except May, June, and July. Here are some other examples:

MLA: COMMON ABBREVIATIONS

and others	et al.	note	n	pseudonym	pseud.
appendix	app.	notes	nn	University [as part	U
book	bk.	number	no.	of a proper noun]	
chapter	ch.	opus	op.	University Press	UP
compare	cf.	opuses	opp.	verse	v.
document	doc.	page	p.	verses	vv.
edition	ed.	pages	pp.	versus	vs.
especially	esp.	paragraph	par.	volume	vol.
figure	fig.	part	pt.		
library	lib.	press	p		

Note: All abbreviations (except for those that shorten publisher names) are lowercase, usually followed by a period. Most form their plurals by adding *s*. The exceptions are note (n → nn), opus (op. → opp.), page (p. → pp.), and translator (same abbreviation).

In citing poetry, do not use abbreviations for "line" or "lines" since a lowercase *l* is easily confused with the number 1. Use either the full word or, if the meaning is clear, simply the number.

In publishers' names, in addition to using the abbreviations U, P, and UP, you can usually omit words and abbreviations like Company, Co., and Inc.

FAQS ABOUT MLA CITATIONS

What's the deal with MLA's "containers"?

Container is just another name for "facts of publication." Most entries in your Works Cited will include an author, a title, and certain facts of publication. (Each of these three categories ends with a period; commas separate items within each category.) These facts consist of information about the work—for example, the publisher and date for a book, or the name of the series and other relevant info for a TV episode.

Sometimes a second container is needed—for example, for a book or a show that you read or watched online. In that case, after the usual facts (the first container, which is followed by a period), you would add the name of the website and a URL.

Not all works found online require a second container. For example, a news article from the *Los Angeles Times* online needs only one, because the name of the newspaper and the website that publishes it are the same.

You'll find lots of examples above.

How do I handle the citation when one author quotes another?

That happens frequently, as in Donald Kagan's book *The Peloponnesian War*, which often quotes Thucydides. Using MLA style, you might write:

> Kagan approvingly quotes Thucydides, who says that Athens acquired this vital site "because of the hatred they already felt toward the Spartans" (quoted in Kagan 14).

In your Works Cited, you include Kagan but *not* Thucydides for this particular quote. You would include the ancient Greek historian in Works Cited only if you quoted him directly elsewhere in your paper.

8

APA CITATIONS FOR THE SOCIAL SCIENCES, EDUCATION, AND BUSINESS

· · · · · · · · · · · · · ·

APA citations are widely used in psychology, education, business, and the social sciences. (Some engineering students are also required to use APA, but most use IEEE or ACSE, which are discussed in chapter 11.) Like MLA citations, APA citations are in text. Notes are used only for analysis and commentary, not to cite references. Unlike MLA, however, APA emphasizes the year of publication, which comes immediately after the author's name. That's probably because as scholarship cumulates in the sciences and empirical social sciences (where APA is used), it is important to know whether the research was conducted recently and whether it came before or after other research. At least that's the rationale.

Detailed information on the APA system is available in the *Publication Manual of the American Psychological Association*, 6th ed. (2010), and *APA Style Guide to Electronic Resources*, 6th ed. (2012).

To get started, let's look at APA references for a journal article, a chapter in an edited book, and a book as they appear at the end of a paper. APA calls this a "Reference List." (MLA calls it "Works Cited," and Chicago calls it "Bibliography.")

Lipson, C. (1991). Why are some international agreements informal? *International Organization, 45,* 495–538.

Lipson, C. (1994). Is the future of collective security like the past? In G. Downs (Ed.), *Collective security beyond the cold war* (pp. 105–131). Ann Arbor: University of Michigan Press.

Lipson, C. (2003). *Reliable partners: How democracies have made a separate peace.* Princeton, NJ: Princeton University Press.

This list for the distinguished author C. Lipson follows another APA rule. All entries for a single author are arranged by year of publication, beginning with the earliest. If there were two entries for a particular year, say 2018, they would be alphabetized by title and the first would be labeled (2018a), the second (2018b). A future publication would be cited as "(in press)." Also note the APAs rules for capitalizing book and article titles. They are treated like sentences, with only the first words capitalized. If there's a colon in the title, the first word after the colon is also capitalized. Proper nouns are capitalized, of course, just as they are in sentences.

In these reference lists, single-author entries precede those with coauthors. So Pinker, S. (as a sole author) would precede Pinker, S., & Jones, B. In the APA system, multiple authors are joined by an ampersand "&" rather than the word *and*. It is not clear why. Just accept it as a rule, like how many minutes are in a soccer game.

The authors' first names are always reduced to initials. That makes APA different from MLA and Chicago, as does its frequent use of commas and parentheses.

When works are cited in the text, the citation includes the author's name unless the author's name has already been mentioned in that sentence. For instance:

These claims are backed up by the most recent data (Nye, 2018).

If the sentence includes the author's name, the citation omits it. For instance:

Nye (2018) presents considerable data to back up his claims.

If you include a direct quote, then you *must* include the page number in the citation. For instance:

"The policy is poorly conceived," according to Nye (2018, p. 12).

The examples in this chapter focus on psychology, education, other social sciences, and business, where APA citations are most widely used, just as the MLA examples focus on the humanities, where that style is common.

To make it easy to find the types of APA citations you need, I've listed them here alphabetically, along with the pages where they are described. At the end of the chapter I have listed some common APA abbreviations.

INDEX OF APA CITATIONS IN THIS CHAPTER

APA: REFERENCE LIST AND IN-TEXT CITATIONS

Book, one author	Reference list	King, B. J. (2017). *Personalities on the plate: The lives and minds of animals we eat.* Chicago, IL: University of Chicago Press.
		▸ APA requires the state even for well-known cities. Exception: if the name of a university publisher includes the state, you can omit it (e.g., Ann Arbor: University of Michigan Press).
		Naughton, B. (2007). *The Chinese economy: Transitions and growth.* Cambridge, MA: MIT Press.

Book, one author (*continued*)		Fitzpatrick, M. (2017). *Invisible scars: Mental trauma and the Korean War.* Vancouver, British Columbia, Canada: University of British Columbia Press.
		► Although US states are abbreviated, Canadian provinces and territories are spelled out and the country name is included.
	In-text	(King, 2017) (Naughton, 2007) (Fitzpatrick, 2017)

Books and articles, several by same author	Reference list	Posner, R. C. (2007a). *Countering terrorism.* Lanham, MD: Rowman & Littlefield with the Hoover Institution. Posner, R. C. (2007b). *Economic analysis of law* (7th ed.). New York, NY: Aspen Law and Business. Posner, R. C. (2007c). *The little book of plagiarism.* New York, NY: Pantheon. Posner, R. C. (2006a). *Not a suicide pact: The Constitution in a time of national emergency.* New York, NY: Oxford University Press. Posner, R. C. (2006b). *Uncertain shield: The U.S. intelligence system in the throes of reform.* Lanham, MD: Rowman & Littlefield with the Hoover Institution. Posner R. C., & Becker, G. S. (2006). *Suicide and risk-taking: An economic approach.* Unpublished paper, University of Chicago.
		► Note that the author's name is repeated. APA does not use dashes for repetition.
		► When the same author or coauthors have several publications in the same year, list them alphabetically (by the first significant word in the title). Label them as "a," "b," and "c." The last 2006 item by Posner is *not* labeled "c" because its authorship is different.

► Coauthored books like Posner & Becker follow a writer's single-author ones, in the alphabetical order of the second author's surname.

In-text	(Posner, 2007a, 2007b, 2007c, 2006a, 2006b; Posner & Becker, 2006)

Book, multiple authors	Reference list	Gazzaley, A., & Rosen, L.D. (2016). *The distracted mind: Ancient brains in a high-tech world.* Cambridge, MA: MIT Press. Useem, M., Singh, H., Neng, L., & Cappelli, P. (2017). *Fortune makers: The leaders creating China's great global companies.* New York, NY: Public Affairs. Butcher, T., Guo., X., Harris, J., Lette, K., Mankell, H., Moggach, D., . . . Welsh, I. (2010). *Because I'm a girl.* New York, NY: Random House. ► Name up to seven authors; for eight or more, list the first six followed by an ellipsis (three spaced periods) and then the name of the last author.
	In-text	(Gazzaley & Rosen, 2016) (Useem, Singh, Neng, & Cappelli, 2017), and then (Useem et al., 2017) ► For two authors, always list both. For three to five authors, name all authors in the first citation. Beginning with the second reference, name only the first author, then add "et al.": (Fubini et al., 2007) ► For six or more authors, name only the first author, then add "et al." for all citations. ► Use "&" within parenthetical references but not in the text itself.

Book, multiple editions	Reference list	DiClemente, C. C. (2018). *Addiction and change: How addictions develop and addicted people recover* (2nd ed.). New York, NY: Guilford Press.

Book, multiple editions (*continued*)		▸ If it says "revised edition" rather than "2nd edition," use "(Rev. ed.)" in the same spot. Strunk, W., Jr., & White, E. B. (2009). *The elements of style* (50th anniversary ed.). New York, NY: Longman.
	In-text	(Strunk & White, 2009) ▸ To refer to a specific page for a quotation: (Strunk & White, 2009, p. 12)
Book, corporate author or no author	Reference list	University of Michigan, Office of Student Publications. (2017). *2017 alumni directory*. Bloomington, IN: University Publishing Corporation. American Psychological Association. (2010). *Publication manual of the American Psychological Association* (6th ed.). Washington, DC: Author. ▸ If the publisher is the same as the author, write "Author" in place of the former. *The bluebook: A uniform system of citation* (20th ed.). (2015). Cambridge, MA: Harvard Law Review Association. ▸ For multiple editions without authors, the form is *Title* (edition). (year). City, STATE: Publisher.
	In-text	(University of Michigan, 2017) ▸ Abbreviate a corporate author on subsequent mentions only, and only if the abbreviation will be immediately recognizable to readers. (American Psychological Association [APA], 2010) ▸ Subsequent references are (APA, 2010) or (*Bluebook*, 2015).
Book, edited	Reference list	Bakker, K. (Ed.). (2007). *Eau Canada: The future of Canada's water*. Vancouver, British Columbia, Canada: University of British Columbia Press.

Bosworth, M., & Flavin, J. (Eds.). (2007). *Race, gender, and punishment: From colonialism to the war on terror*. New Brunswick, NJ: Rutgers University Press.

Matthijs, M., & Blyth, M. (Eds.). (2015). *The future of the Euro*. Oxford, England: Oxford University Press.

In-text	(Bakker, 2007) (Bosworth & Flavin, 2007) (Matthijs & Blyth 2015)

E-book	Reference list	Toy, E. C., & Klamen, D. (2015). *Case files: Psychiatry* (5th ed.) [Kindle Fire HDX version]. Retrieved from http://www.amazon.com

> ► APA says to put important but "nonroutine" information in square brackets following the title (and after any parenthetical information—about edition, volumes, etc.).
>
> ► Electronic retrieval information takes the place of the publisher location and name. That's code for URL. If the URL is very long, cite the home page (as in this example).

In-text	(Toy & Klamen, 2015)

Book, online	Reference list	Reed, J. (1922). *Ten days that shook the world* [Etext 3076]. Retrieved from http://www.gutenberg.org/dirs/etext02/10daz10.txt

> ► APA does *not* put a period after the URL, making it different from most other reference styles.
>
> ► And APA does *not* want access dates—except for sources that may change over time (think *Wikipedia* article).

In-text	(Reed, 1922)

Multivolume work	Reference list	Rothschild, B. (2017). *The body remembers* (Vols. 1–2). New York, NY: Norton. Pflanze, O. (1963–1990). *Bismarck and the development of Germany* (Vols. 1–3). Princeton, NJ: Princeton University Press.
	In-text	(Rothschild, 2017) (Pflanze, 1963–1990)
Single volume in a multivolume work	Reference list	Rothschild, B. (2017). *The body remembers: Vol. 2. Revolutionizing trauma treatment.* New York, NY: Norton. Pflanze, O. (1990). *Bismarck and the development of Germany: Vol. 3. The period of fortification, 1880–1898.* Princeton, NJ: Princeton University Press.
	In-text	(Rothschild, 2017) (Pflanze, 1990)
Reprint of earlier edition	Reference list	Smith, A. (1976). *An inquiry into the nature and causes of the wealth of nations.* E. Cannan (Ed.). Chicago, IL: University of Chicago Press. (Original work published 1776) ‣ There is no period after the parenthesis.
	In-text	(Smith, 1776/1976)
Translated volume	Reference list	Weber, M. (1958). *The Protestant ethic and the spirit of capitalism.* T. Parsons (Trans.). New York, NY: Charles Scribner's Sons. (Original work published 1904–1905)
	In-text	(Weber, 1904–1905/1958)
Foreign-language volume	Reference list	Weber, M. (2005). *Die protestantische Ethik und der Geist des Kapitalismus* [The Protestant ethic and the spirit of capitalism]. Erftstadt, Germany: Area Verlag. (Original work published 1904–1905)
	In-text	(Weber, 1904–1905/2005)

Chapter in edited book	Reference list	Board, J. (2016). The paradox of right and wrong. In R. Bolden, M. Witzel, & N. Linacre (Eds.), *Leadership paradoxes: Rethinking leadership for an uncertain world* (pp. 131–150). New York, NY: Routledge. ▸ Chapter titles are not in quotes or italics.
	In-text	(Board, 2016)

Journal article, one author	Reference list	Ivanov, M. (2016). Dynamic learning and strategic communication. *International Journal of Game Theory, 45*, 627–653. https://doi.org/10.1007/s00182-015-0474-x Massaro, D. W. (2017). Reading aloud to children: Benefits and implications for acquiring literacy before schooling begins. *The American Journal of Psychology, 130*, 63–72. https://doi.org/10.5406/amerjpsyc.130.1.0063 Wettersten, J. (2014). New social tasks for cognitive psychology; or, new cognitive tasks for social psychology [Abstract]. *American Journal of Pyschology, 127*, 403. http://www.jstor.org/stable/10.5406/amerjpsyc.127.4.0403 ▸ Article titles are not in quotes or italics. ▸ The journal's volume number is italicized, but the issue number and pages are not. The word *volume* (or "Vol.") is omitted. ▸ There's no need to name a specific issue if the journal pages are numbered continuously throughout the year. However, if each issue begins with page 1, then the issue's number or month is necessary to find the article: 45(2), 15–30. ▸ To cite an abstract, include "Abstract" in brackets after the article title.

Journal article, one author (*continued*)		▸ Include a Digital Object Identifier (DOI) for every journal article that has one—even if you're citing print. A URL based on a DOI (appended to https://doi.org/) is preferable to another kind of URL. If you're citing an article online and don't see a DOI, list the URL of the journal's home page or the database where you found it.

Mitchell, T. (2002). McJihad: Islam in the U.S. global order. *Social Text, 20*(4), 1–18. https://doi.org/10.1215/01642472 -20-4_73-1

▸ The issue number (4, in parentheses but not in italics) is included because each issue of this journal starts over at page 1.

In-text

(Ivanov, 2016)
(Massaro, 2017)
(Wettersten, 2014)
(Mitchell, 2002)

Journal article, multiple authors

Reference list

Lanis, R., Richardson, G., & Taylor, G. (2017). Board of director gender and corporate tax aggressiveness: An empirical analysis. *Journal of Business Ethics, 144*, 577–596. https://doi.org/10.1007/ s10551-015-2815-x

Guo, S., Chen, D., Zhou, D., Sun, H., Wu, G., Haile, C., . . . Zhang, X. (2007). Association of functional catechol O-methyl transferase (COMT) Val108Met polymorphism with smoking severity and age of smoking initiation in Chinese male smokers. *Psychopharmacology, 190*, 449–456. https://doi.org/10.1007/ s00213-006-0628-4

▸ Name up to seven authors; for eight or more, list the first six followed by an ellipsis and then the last author's name.

In-text

(Lanis, Richardson, & Taylor, 2017)) for first reference.
(Lanis et al., 2017) for second reference and after.

▶ When a work has three to five authors,
name all of them in the first textual reference. After that, use only the first author's
name plus "et al."
(Guo et al., 2007)

▶ When a work has six authors or more,
name only the first one plus "et al." For
example, this would be the first mention of
the Guo article:
In their study of Chinese male smokers,
Guo et al. (2007) find an association . . .

Journal article, foreign language	Reference list	Maignan, I., & Swaen, V. (2004). La responsabilité sociale d'une organisa-tion: Intégration des perspectives mar-keting et managériale. *Revue Française du Marketing, 200*, 51–66. ▶ or Maignan, I., & Swaen, V. (2004). La responsabilité sociale d'une organi-sation: Intégration des perspectives marketing et managériale [The social responsibility of an organization: Integration of marketing and manage-rial perspectives]. *Revue Française du Marketing, 200*, 51–66.
	In-text	(Maignan & Swaen, 2004)
Newspaper or magazine article, with author	Reference list	Wingfield, N. (2017, September 11). The robots of Amazon. *The New York Times* (New York ed.), p. B1. ▶ APA includes an initial *The* in newspaper and magazine titles. ▶ Newspaper page numbers include "p." or "pp." Tsukayama, H. (2017, September 11). The iPhone is 10. Where does Apple go from here? *The Chicago Tribune*. Retrieved from www.chicagotribune.com

Newspaper or magazine article, with author (*continued*)		Pandey, S. (2007, February 11). I read the news today, oh boy. *The Los Angeles Times* (Home ed.), p. M6. Retrieved from http://www.proquest.com ▸ Provide the URL for the homepage of the newspaper, magazine, or database, rather than the URL for the specific article.
	In-text	(Wingfield, 2017) or, if necessary, (Wingfield, September 11, 2017) (Tsukayama, 2017) or (Tsukayama, 2017, September 11) (Pandey, 2007) or (Pandey, 2007, February 11)
Newspaper or magazine article, no author	Reference list	Retired U.S. general is focus of inquiry over Iran leak. (2013, June 28). *The New York Times* (New York ed.), p. A18. America and China talk climate change: Heating up or cooling down? (2009, June 11). *The Economist 391*(8635), 61. ▸ APA treats magazines much like journals. If you can't determine the volume and issue numbers, leave them out and put "p." or "pp." before the page number(s).
	In-text	("Retired U.S. general," 2013) ("Climate change," 2009)
Review	Reference list	Pugh, A. J. (2014, May). [Review of the book *The gender trap: Parents and the pitfalls of raising boys and girls*, by E. W. Kane]. *American Journal of Sociology 119*, 1773–1775. Vimercati, G. (2017, August 20). Soviet pseudoscience: The history of mind control [Review of the book *Homo Sovieticus: Brain waves, mind control, and telepathic destiny*, by W. Velminski]. *Los Angeles Review of Books*. Retrieved from https://lareviewofbooks.org/.
	In-text	(Pugh, 2014) (Vimercati, 2017)

Unpublished paper, poster session, dissertation, or thesis	Reference list	Tang, S. (2017, February). *Profit driven team grouping in social networks*. Paper presented at the Thirty-First AAAI Conference on Artificial Intelligence, San Francisco.
		➤ Only the month and year are needed for papers.
		Tomz, M., & Van Houweling, R. P. (2009, August). *Candidate inconsistency and voter choice*. Unpublished manuscript, Stanford University and University of California, Berkeley. Retrieved from http://www.stanford.edu/~tomz/working/TomzVanHouweling-2009-08.pdf
		➤ Other categories include "Manuscript submitted for publication" and "Manuscript in preparation."
		Noble, L. (2006). *One goal, multiple strategies: Engagement in Sino-American WTO accession negotiations*. Unpublished master's thesis, University of British Columbia, Vancouver, Canada.
		➤ APA considers any thesis or dissertation that's not available from a commercial database to be unpublished.
		Sierra, L. M. (2013). *Indigenous neighborhood residents in the urbanization of La Paz, Bolivia, 1910–1950* (Doctoral dissertation, State University of New York at Binghamton). Retrieved from ProQuest Dissertations and Theses (UMI No. 3612828).
		➤ That parenthetical string of letters and numbers at the end is the accession number—helpful in finding the item in the database.
		➤ APA doesn't require the name of the institution for a thesis or dissertation retrieved from a commercial database, but why not add it anyway?
	In-text	(Tang, 2017)
		(Tomz & Van Houweling, 2009)
		(Noble, 2006)
		(Sierra, 2013)

Preprint	Reference list	Piatti, A. E. (2017). *On the extended stellar structure around NGC 288* [Preprint]. Retrieved from https://arxiv.org/pdf/1709.07284v1.pdf

▸ arXiv is a collection facility for scientific "e-prints." Some of them have been published and some have not. APA recommends updating your references when you're close to finishing your paper; if you've cited a preprint that's since been published, cite the published journal article.

▸ The title is in italics because it hasn't yet been accepted in a journal, and is therefore considered a stand-alone work.

▸ Some journals publish articles online ahead of time. You can cite these in one of two ways (and again, update the reference when the article gets published):

Ravigné, V., Dieckmann, U., & Olivieri, I. (2009). Live where you thrive: Joint evolution of habitat choice and local adaptation facilitates specialization and promotes diversity. *The American Naturalist*. Advance online publication. https://doi.org/10.1086/605369

▸ or

Ravigné, V., Dieckmann, U., & Olivieri, I. (in press). Live where you thrive: Joint evolution of habitat choice and local adaptation facilitates specialization and promotes diversity. *The American Naturalist*, *174*, E141–E169. https://doi.org/10.1086/605369

	In-text	(Piatti, 2017) (Ravigné, Dieckmann, & Olivieri, 2009) or (Ravigné, Dieckmann, & Olivieri, in press)

▸ Subsequent references are (Ravigné et al., 2009) or (Ravigné et al., in press)

Research or technical report, policy paper, other "gray literature"	Reference list	Environmental Protection Agency. (2016, December). *State of the science white paper: A summary of literature on the chemical toxicity of plastics pollution to aquatic life and aquatic-dependent wildlife* [White paper]. Retrieved from https://www.epa.gov/sites/produc-tion/files/2016-12/documents/plastics-aquatic-life-report.pdf Tarullo, D. (2017, October). *Monetary policy without a working theory of infla-tion*. [Working paper]. Retrieved from Hutchins Center on Fiscal & Monetary Policy, Brookings Institute website: https://www.brookings.edu/research/monetary-policy-without-a-working-theory-of-inflation/
	In-text	(Environmental Protection Agency, 2016) (Tarullo, 2017)
Encyclopedia and dictionary	Reference list	Balkans: History. (1987). In *Encyclopaedia Britannica* (15th ed., Vol. 14, pp. 570–588). Chicago, IL: Encyclopaedia Britannica. Balkans. (2017). *Encyclopaedia Britannica online*. Retrieved from https://www.britannica.com/place/Balkans App. (2016, April 6). *Merriam-Webster*. Retrieved from http://www.merriam-webster.com/dictionary/app Protest, *v*. (1971). *Compact edition of the Oxford English dictionary* (Vol. 2, p. 2335). Oxford, England: Oxford University Press. ▸ The word *protest* is both a noun and a verb. Here I am citing the verb. Graham, G. (2015). Behaviorism. In E. N. Zalta (Ed.), *The Stanford encyclopedia of philosophy*. Retrieved from http://plato.stanford.edu/entries/behaviorism/

Encyclopedia and dictionary (*continued*)		Emotion. (n.d.). *Wikipedia*. Retrieved November 8, 2017, from http://en .wikipedia.org/wiki/Emotion
		▸ Though APA does not recommend access dates for most types of sources, they do recommend them for undated sources that are subject to frequent updates—like this *Wikipedia* article.
	In-text	(Balkans: History, 1987)
		▸ You may wish to include the subtitle, "History," in this case to help the reader if the main article is long or if you are citing several articles with similar titles and dates.
		(Balkans, 2017)
		(App, 2016)
		(Protest, 1971)
		(Graham, 2015)
		(Emotion, n.d.)
Bible, Qur'an (Koran)	Reference list	▸ Not needed, except to reference a particular version.
		The five books of Moses: A translation with commentary. (2004). Robert Alter (Trans. & Ed.). New York, NY: Norton.
	In-text	Deut. 1:2 (New Revised Standard Version).
		▸ List the version you are using the first time it is mentioned in the text. After that, omit the version.
		Gen. 1:1, 1:3–5, 2:4.
		▸ Books of the Bible can be abbreviated: Exod., Lev., Num., Cor., and so on.
		Qur'an 18:65–82.
Classical works	Reference list	▸ Not needed, except to reference a particular version.
		Plato. (2006). *The republic*. R. E. Allen (Trans.). New Haven, CT: Yale University Press. (Original work, approximately 360 BC)

Virgil. (2017). *The Aeneid*. D. Ferry (Trans.). Chicago, IL: University of Chicago Press. (Original work, approximately 19–29 BC)

In-text (Plato, trans. 2006)
(Virgil, trans. 2017)

Speech, academic talk, or course lecture

Reference list Wingfield, A. M. H. (2016, August 21. Presidential address at the annual meeting of the American Sociological Association, Seattle, WA.
Rector, N. (2017, March 6). Course lecture at the University of Toronto, Toronto, Ontario, Canada.
Shiller, R.J. (2011). Risk and financial crisis. [recorded lecture]. Retrieved from http://oyc.yale.edu/economics/econ-252-11/lecture-2

In-text (Wingfield, 2016)
(Rector, 2017)
(Shiller, 2011)

Personal communication or interview

Reference list Gates, B. (2014, March 13). Bill Gates: the *Rolling Stone* interview. (J. Goodell, Interviewer). Retrieved from http://www.rollingstone.com/culture/news/bill-gates-the-rolling-stone-interview-20140313
Smith, H. (1941). Interview by J. H. Faulk [Audio file]. Library of Congress, Archive of Folk Culture, American Folklife Center, Washington, DC. Retrieved from http://hdl.loc.gov/loc.afc/afc9999001.5499a

In-text (Gates, 2014)
(Smith, 1941)
(J. M. Coetzee, personal interview, May 5, 2017)
(D. A. Grossberg, personal communication, January 1, 2015)
(anonymous US soldier, recently returned from Afghanistan, interviewed by author, August 22, 2010)

Personal communication or interview (*continued*)		▶ The reference list includes published or archived interviews, like Gates's and Smith's, but not personal communications such as private conversation, faxes, letters, or interviews that cannot be accessed by other investigators. Therefore, in-text citations for personal communications— like the ones for Coetzee, Grossberg, and the anonymous US soldier—should fully describe the item, including the full date. Do not cite interviews conducted with research participants, since those are confidential.
Television program	Reference list	Benioff, D., & Weiss, D. B. (Writers), & Graves, A. (Director). (2014). The children [Television series episode]. In D. Benioff & D. Weiss (Executive Producers) *Game of Thrones*. New York, NY: HBO. Carlock, R. (Writer), & Miller, M. B. (Director). (2009). Into the crevasse [Television series episode]. In T. Fey, L. Michaels, M. Klein, D. Miner, & R. Carlock (Producers), *30 Rock*. NBC. Retrieved from http://www.hulu.com /30-rock
	In-text	(Benioff, Weiss, & Graves, 2014) (Carlock & Miller, 2009)
Film	Reference list	Wallis, H. B. (Producer), & Huston, J. (Director/Writer). (1941). *The Maltese falcon* [Motion picture]. H. Bogart, M. Astor, P. Lorre, S. Greenstreet, E. Cook Jr. (Performers). Based on novel by D. Hammett. Warner Studios. United States: Warner Home Video, DVD. (2000) Goolsby, K., & York, A. (Directors). (2015). *Tig* [Motion picture]. United States: Beachside Films and Netflix. Retrieved from www.netflix.com ▶ Required: You must include the title, director, studio, and year released.

> ► Optional: the actors, producers, screen-
> writers, editors, cinematographers, and
> other information. Include what you need
> for analysis in your paper, in order of
> importance to your analysis. Their names
> appear between the title and the distribu-
> tor.
> ► If a motion picture accessed online is
> behind a paywall or easily available by
> searching a site (such as Netflix or Hulu),
> just provide the home page URL.

	In-text	(Wallis & Huston, 1941/2000) (Goolsby & York, 2015)
Photograph	Reference list	Adams, A. (1927). *Monolith, the face of Half Dome, Yosemite National Park* [Photograph]. Art Institute, Chicago. Adams, A. (1927). *Monolith, the face of Half Dome, Yosemite National Park* [Photograph]. Art Institute, Chicago. Retrieved from http://www.hctc.commnet.edu/artmuseum/anseladams/details/pdf/monlith.pdf
	In-text	(Adams, 1927)
Figures: map, chart, graph, or table	Credit or explanation for figure or table	► Citation for a map, chart, graph, or table normally appears as a credit below the item rather than as an in-text citation. *Note.* 2016 House election results map. *Politico.* Retrieved from http://www.politico.com/mapdata-2016/2016-election/results/map/house/ *Note.* From M. E. J. Newman (n.d.), Maps of the 2016 US presidential election. Retrieved from http://www-personal.umich.edu/~mejn/election/2016// *Note.* K. Smith, Urban Institute, (2013), Distribution of family income [Graph], 1963–2013. Retrieved from http://apps.urban.org/features/wealth-inequality-charts/

Figures: map,
chart, graph,
or table
(*continued*)

Note. From K. Menkhaus (2006/2007), Governance without government in Somalia: Spoilers, state building, and the politics of coping. *International Security*, *31* (Winter), 79, fig. 1.

▸ Give a descriptive title to your maps, charts, graphs, and tables. With this description, the reader should understand the item without having to refer to the text.

Note. All figures are rounded to nearest percentile.

▸ This is a general note explaining information in a table.

*p <.05 ***p* < .01. Both are two-tailed tests.

▸ This is a probability note for a table of statistics.

Reference list

House election results map. (2016). *Politico*. Retrieved from http://www.politico .com/mapdata-2016/2016-election/ results/map/house/

Newman, M. E. J. (n.d.). Maps of the 2016 US presidential election. Retrieved from http://www-personal.umich.edu/ ~mejn/election/2016

K. Smith, Urban Institute. (2013) Distribution of family income [Graph]. 1963– 2013. Retrieved from http://apps.urban .org/features/wealth-inequality-charts

Menkhaus, K. (2006/2007). Governance without government in Somalia: Spoilers, state building, and the politics of coping. *International Security*, *31* (Winter), 74–106. https://doi.org/10 .1162/isec.2007.31.3.74

In-text

(2016 House election results, 2016)
(Newman, n.d.)
(K. Smith, 2013)
(Menkhaus, 2006/2007)

Musical recording	Reference list	Johnson, R. (1998). Last fair deal gone down. On *Robert Johnson: King of the Delta blues singers* (Exp. ed.) [CD]. Columbia/Legacy. (Originally recorded 1936) ▸ "Exp. ed." = expanded edition. Beyoncé. (2016). Formation. On *Lemonade*. Columbia / Parkwood Entertainment. Retrieved from http://tidal.com/us
	In-text	(Johnson, 1936/1998, track 5) (Beyoncé, 2016, track 11)
Advertisement	Reference list	Advertisement for *Letters from Iwo Jima* [Motion picture]. (2007, February 6). *New York Times*, p. B4. Drink outside the Lines. (2017, June 15). [Advertisement for Vitamin Water]. *Rolling Stone*, 17. Tab cola. [ca. late 1960s]. Be a mindsticker [Television advertisement]. Retrieved from http://www.dailymotion.com/ video /×2s3qi_1960s-tab-commercial -be-a-mindstick_ads ▸ Enclose estimated dates in square brackets.
	In-text	(advertisement for *Letters from Iwo Jima*, 2007) (Vitamin Water, 2017) (Tab cola [ca. late 1960s])
Government document	Reference list	*A bill to promote the national security by providing for a national defense establishment: Hearings on S. 758 before the Committee on Armed Service, Senate*, 80th Cong. 1 (1947). ▸ "80th Cong. 1" refers to page 1 (not to the first session). If the reference was to testimony by a specific individual, that would appear after the date: (1947) (testimony of Gen. George Marshall).

Government document (*continued*)		▸ For documents printed by the Government Printing Office, give the full name rather than the initials GPO.

National Institute on Aging. (2015). *Caring for a person with Alzheimer's disease: Your easy-to-use guide from the National Institute on Aging.* Washington, DC: US Government Printing Office.

▸ or

National Institute on Aging. (2015). *Caring for a person with Alzheimer's disease: Your easy-to-use guide from the National Institute on Aging.* Retrieved from https://permanent.access.gpo.gov/ gpo66296/caring-for-a-person-with -alzheimers-disease.pdf

Public Safety Canada (2017, September 24). Minister Goodale pays tribute to fallen police and peace officers. Retrieved from https://www.canada.ca/en/public -safety-canada/news/2017/09/minister _goodalepaystributetofallenpoliceand peaceofficers.html

Federal Bureau of Investigation [FBI]. (1972). *Investigation of John Lennon* (248 pages). Retrieved from http:// foia .fbi.gov/foiaindex/lennon.htm

In-text

(*Bill to promote national security*, 1947)
(National Institute on Aging, 2015)
(Public Safety Canada, 2017)
(FBI, 1972)

Database or data set	Reference list	Maryland Department of Assessments and Taxation. (2017). *Real property data search.* Retrieved from https://sdat.dat .maryland.gov/RealProperty/Pages/ default.aspx

US Copyright Office. (2017). *Search copyright records.* Retrieved from http:// www.copyright.gov/records/

Gleditsch, K. S., & Chiozza, G. (2009). *Archigos: A data base on leaders, 1875–2004* (Version 2.9). Retrieved from http://mail.rochester.edu/%7Ehgoemans/data.htm

Pew Research Center. (2014). *Religious landscape study*. Retrieved from http://www.pewforum.org/religious-landscape-study/

United Nations Treaty Collection. (2010). *Databases*. Retrieved from http://treaties.un.org/

► For a specific item within this database:

Convention on the prevention and punishment of the crime of genocide. (1948). In United Nations Treaty Collection, *Databases*. Retrieved from https://treaties.un.org/doc/Treaties/1951/01/19510112%2008-12%20PM/Ch_IV_1p.pdf

In-text	(Maryland Department of Assessments, 2017) (US Copyright Office, 2017) (Gleditsch & Chiozza, 2009) (United Nations Treaty Collection, 2010) (Convention on the prevention and punishment of the crime of genocide, 1948)

Diagnostic test	Reference list	*MMPI-2: Restructured clinical (RC) scales.* (2003). Minneapolis: University of Minnesota Press. Ben-Porath, Y. S., & Tellegen, A. (2008). *MMPI-2-RF (Minnesota Multiphasic Personality Inventory-2): Manual for administration, scoring, and interpretation.* Minneapolis: University of Minnesota Press. ► Manual for administering the test. Ben-Porath, Y. S. (2012). *Interpreting the MMPI-2-RF.* Minneapolis: University of Minnesota Press. ► Interpretive manual for the test.

Diagnostic test (*continued*)		Q Local (Version 3.3) [Computer software]. (2017). Minneapolis, MN: Pearson Assessments.
		▸ Scoring software for the test.
	In-text	(*MMPI-2 RC scales*, 2003) (Ben-Porath & Tellegen, 2008) (Ben-Porath, 2012) (Q Local, 2017)

Diagnostic manual	Reference list	Lingiardi, V., & McWilliams, M. (Eds.). (2017). *Psychodynamic diagnostic manual* (2nd ed.). New York, NY: Guilford Press. American Psychiatric Association. (2000). *Diagnostic and statistical manual of mental disorders* (4th ed., text rev. [*DSM-IV-TR*]). Washington, DC: Author.
		▸ or
		American Psychiatric Association. (2000). *Diagnostic and statistical manual of mental disorders* (4th ed., text rev. [*DSM-IV-TR*]). https://doi.org/10.1176/appi.books.9780890423349
	In-text	(Lingiardi & McWilliams, 2017) (American Psychiatric Association, *Diagnostic and statistical manual of mental disorders* [*DSM-IV-TR*], 2000) for the first use only. (*DSM-IV-TR*) for second use and later. Title is italicized.

Website, page or entire	Reference list	American Historical Association [Home page]. (2017). Retrieved August 1, 2017, from https://www.historians.org
		▸ Many webpages do not have identifiable authors. List the organization that sponsors the website instead.
		Lipson, C. (2010). "Advice on getting a good recommendation." Retrieved from http://www.charleslipson.com/Getting -a-good-recommendation.htm

The Dick Van Dyke show: Series summary. (n.d.). *Sitcoms online*. Retrieved from http://www.sitcomsonline.com/thedick vandykeshow.html

> If a website or webpage does not show a date when it was copyrighted or updated, then list (n.d.) where the year normally appears.

> It is usually sufficient to provide the address of the website in the text.

In-text	(American Historical Association, 2017)
(Lipson, 2010)
(*The Dick Van Dyke show*: Series summary, n.d.)

Blog, post or comment	Reference list	Pearce, F. (2017, September 18). In a stunning turnaround, Britain moves to end the burning of coal. [Blog post]. *Yale Environment 360*. Retrieved from http:// e360.yale.edu/features/in-a-stunning -turnaround-britain-moves-to-end-the -burning-of-coal

> If this post had no title, it would be cited thus:

Pearce, F. (2017, September 18). Untitled. [Blog post. *Yale Environment 360* . . .

Dinah. (2017, August 1). Inpatient psychiatry: Not all bad. [Blog post]. *Shrink Rap*. Retrieved from http://psychiatrist-blog .blogspot.com/

Catlover. (2017, August 5). Re: Inpatient psychiatry: Not all bad. [Blog comment]. *Shrink Rap*. Retrieved from https:// www.blogger.com/comment.g?blogID =26666124&postID=4980105132352 25858

> If "Catlover" had commented several times the same day and there was no link to a specific comment, then you should include the time: (2017, August 5, 12:53 a.m.).

In-text	(Pearce, 2017)
(Dinah, 2017)
(Catlover, 2017)

Video	Reference list	Archer Productions (Producer). (1951). *Duck and cover* [Video file]. Produced for the Federal Civil Defense Administration. Retrieved from https://en.wikipedia .org/wiki/File:DuckandC1951.ogv Jury convicts Martin Shkreli on three counts of security fraud. (2017, August 4). [Video file]. Retrieved from https:// www.nbcnews.com/video/jury-convicts -martin-shkreli-on-three-counts-of -securities-fraud-1017719875664 Wang, T. (2016, September). The human insights missing from big data. [Video file]. Retrieved from https://www.ted .com/talks/tricia_wang_the_human _insights_missing_from_big_data Stevens, M. (2017, July 17). How much of the earth can you see at once? [Video file]. Retrieved from https://youtu.be/ mxhxL1LzKww Windfall. (July 29, 2017). Re: How much of the earth can you see at once? [Comment on video blog post]. Retrieved from https://youtu.be/mxhx L1LzKww ▸ When the URL is very long and the video can be found on a searchable site, you may choose to include only the site's main page: Retrieved from https://www.ted.com/
	In-text	(Archer Productions, 1951) ("Jury convicts Martin Shkreli," 2017) (Wang, 2016) (Stevens, 2017) (Windfall, 2017)
Multimedia app and software	Reference list	▸ APA cites apps (mobile application software) and computer software the same way.

▸ You do not need to include standard software, like Microsoft or Adobe, in the reference list, but do include specialty software and apps.

EA Sports. (2017). Madden NFL 18 [Video game]. Retrieved from https://www.easports.com/madden-nfl

Groundspeak. (2017). Geocaching. (v. 5.6.1) [Mobile application software]. Retrieved from https://www.geocaching.com/play

Mathworks. (2014). Matlab. (versionR2014b) [Computer software]. Retrieved from https://www.mathworks.com/products/matlab.html

	In-text	(EA Sports, 2017) (Groundspeak, 2017) (Mathworks, 2014) (Microsoft home & business, 2016)

Podcast	Reference list	Burriss, R. (Producer). (2017, August 1). Conflict and reconciliation [Audio podcast]. In *The Psychology of Attractiveness*. Retrieved from http://psychology-ofattractivenesspodcast.blogspot.com/2017/08/conflict-and-reconciliation-01-aug-2017.html

▸ Or to avoid the long URL:

Burriss, R. (Producer). (2017, August 1). Conflict and reconciliation [Audio podcast]. In *The Psychology of Attractiveness*. Retrieved from http://psychology-ofattractivenesspodcast.blogspot.com

Shipping container grow rooms, Uber for dogs, and plutonium on Pluto. (2015, July 27). [Video podcast]. In *Geekbeat*. Retrieved from http://geekbeat.tv/shipping-container-grow-rooms-uber-for-dogs-and-plutonium-on-pluto/

▸ or

Podcast (*continued*)		Draney, G. (Host). (2015, July 27). Shipping container grow rooms, Uber for dogs, and plutonium on Pluto. [Video podcast]. In *Geekbeat*. Retrieved from http://geekbeat.tv
	In-text	(Burris, 2017) "Shipping container," 2015) ▸ or (Draney, 2015)

Social media (Facebook, Instagram, Twitter)	Reference list	Simpson, M. [Maggie]. (n.d.) [Profile]. Retrieved from http://www.facebook.com/maggiesimpson ▸ When initials are not enough (in this case, let's pretend Maggie happened to be listed as an author in the references also), add a first name in square brackets. In text, cite the full name. Grammar Girl. (2017, October 5). Diminutives often express smallness [Facebook status update]. Retrieved from https://www.facebook.com/GrammarGirl/posts/10157671243605228 Tyson, N. D. [neiltyson]. (2017, July 7, 1:25pm). Always seemed to me that millipedes have more legs than are necessary [Tweet]. Retrieved from https://twitter.com/neiltyson/status/883421859072458752 ▸ Provide the address ("permalink") for the archived version of the message or page if possible. On sites like Facebook and Twitter, the archived message URL can be accessed via the date and time stamp. Richards, C. [coryrichards]. (2017, May 4). A quiet if not solemn day on Everest [Instagram photo]. Retrieved from https://www.instagram.com/p/BUekBZLgDOW/
	In-text	(Maggie Simpson, n.d.) (Grammar Girl, 2017) (Tyson, 2017) (Richards, 2017)

Email, texts (direct messages)	Reference list	▸ Personal emails, texts, and other instant messages are not included in the reference list because they cannot be retrieved by third parties. You should include items that can be accessed through a URL.
		Abrams, J. (2015, April 28). Fw: a Favor. [Email]. Retrieved from https://assets .documentcloud.org/documents/ 3516674/Abrams-amp-Bank-Phoenix -Electric.pdf
	In-text	(Abrams, 2015)
		▸ Because personal emails and instant messages are not included in the reference list, they should be fully described in the text.
		(E. Leis, email message to author, 2018, May 3)
		(M. H. Lipson, instant message to J. S. Lipson, 2015, March 9)
		▸ You may include the time of an electronic message if it is important or differentiates it from others. For example:
		(M. H. Lipson, instant message to J. S. Lipson, 2015, March 9, 11:23 a.m.)
Electronic forum or mailing list	Reference list	▸ Nonarchived messages to mailing lists or discussion groups are also not included in the reference list because they cannot be retrieved by third parties. You should include items that can be accessed through a URL.
		Ngo, Q. (2017, July 14). Re: what are some unknown truths about college life? [Online forum comment]. Retrieved from https://www.quora.com/What-are-some -unknown-truths-about-college-life
		▸ Include the user's real name, if known, with screen name in brackets. The screen name is sufficient if the real name is unknown.

| Electronic forum or mailing list (*continued*) | | ▶ If the name of the group or list is not evident from the URL, you must include it in the reference. |
| | In-text | (Ngo, 2017) |

APA does not permit very many abbreviations in its reference lists. When it does, it sometimes wants them capitalized and sometimes not. Who knows why?

APA: COMMON ABBREVIATIONS IN REFERENCE LISTS

chapter	chap.	part	Pt.
edition	ed.	revised edition	Rev. ed.
editor	Ed.	second edition	2nd ed.
no date	n.d.	supplement	Suppl.
number	No.	translated by	Trans.
page	p.	volume	Vol. (e.g., Vols. 2–5)
pages	pp.	volumes	vols. (e.g., 3 vols.)

CSE CITATIONS FOR THE BIOLOGICAL SCIENCES

· · · · · · · · · · · · · ·

CSE citations, devised by the Council of Science Editors, are widely used for scientific papers, journals, and books in the life sciences. The citations are based on international principles adopted by the National Library of Medicine. Detailed information about CSE citations for the sciences can be found in *Scientific Style and Format: The CSE Manual for Authors, Editors, and Publishers*, 8th ed. (Chicago: University of Chicago Press, 2014), which is also available online at www.scientificstyleandformat.org.

Actually the CSE system lets you choose among three ways of citing documents:

- *Citation-sequence*: Citations are numbered (1), (2), (3), in the order they appear in the text. Full references appear at the end of the paper—in the same order. They are *not* alphabetized.
- *Citation-name*: Citations are numbered, with full references at the end of the paper, in alphabetical order. The first item cited in the text might be number 8 on the alphabetical list. It would be cited as (8), even though it appeared first—and (8) if it appears again.
- *Name-year*: Citations in the text are given as name and year, such as (McClintock 2017). Full references appear at the end of the paper in alphabetical order, just as they do in APA citations.

Whichever format you choose, use it consistently throughout the paper. Ask your instructor which one she prefers.

Citation-sequence. Cite the first reference in the text as number 1, the second as number 2, and so on. You can use brackets [1], superscripts[1], or parentheses (1). At the end of the paper, list all the items, beginning with the first one cited. The list is *not* alphabetical. If the first item you cite is by Professor Zangwill, then that's the first item in the reference list. If you cite Zangwill's paper again, it's still [1], even if it's the last citation in your paper. If you want to cite several items at once, simply include the number for each one, separated by commas, such as [1,3,9] or [1,3,9] or (1,3,9). If items have successive numbers, use hyphens: 4–6,12–18.

Citation-name. Begin by assembling an alphabetical list of references at the end of the text and numbering them. Each item in the list will have a number, which is used whenever that book or article is cited in the text. If the Zangwill article is thirty-sixth in the alphabetical list, then it is always cited with that number, even if it's the first item you cite in the paper. The next reference in the text might be [23], the one after that might be [12]. Citations can be set as superscripts, in brackets, or in parentheses. If you want to cite several items at once, include a number for each one, such as [4,15,22] or [4,15,22] or (4,15,22). Use hyphens for continuous numbers (1–3). So a citation of multiple sources could be (4,16–18,22).

Name-year. For in-text citations, use the (name-year) format without commas, such as (Cronin and Siegler 2016) and (Siegler et al. 2017). The reference list is alphabetical by author and includes all cited articles. If an author has several articles, list the earliest ones first. Follow the same method if an author has published several articles in the same year. List the first one as 2017a, the second as 2017b, and so on by the month of publication. To cite several articles by Susan Lindquist, then, the notation might be (Lindquist 2014d, 2013a, 2017h), referring to those three articles in the reference list.

In the same way, you can also cite articles by different authors within the same reference. Separate them with semicolons, such as (Liebman 2017; Ma and Lindquist 2013; Outeiro and Lindquist 2015).

If the author's name appears in the sentence, you do not need to repeat it in the citation. For example, "According to LaBarbera (2010), this experiment . . ."

What if LaBarbera had ten or fifteen coauthors? That's certainly possible in the sciences. Articles sometimes have dozens of authors because they include everyone involved in the experiments leading to publication. My colleague Henry Frisch, a high-energy physicist, told me that one of his articles has nearly eight hundred coauthors![1] I grew up in a town with a phone book shorter than that. Really.

---

1. Professor Frisch's own practice is to list himself as author only if he actually helped write the paper. His practice is unusual, but a number of scientists think that he's right—that current practices are unclear and often lax. To correct the problem,

How many of these authors should you include when you use name-year citations in the text? Don't go overboard. Just list the first seven hundred. If you do that in the first sentence, you'll reach the paper's word limit before you even have to write a second sentence. That's one easy science paper.

Actually, CSE offers clear recommendations, stopping a bit short of seven hundred authors. If there are only two authors, list them both, separated by "and." If there are three or more authors, list only the first one, followed by "et al." For example: (LaBarbera et al. 2010). Later I'll show you how to handle coauthors in the reference list at the end of the paper.

QUICK COMPARISON OF CSE STYLES

Style	In-text citations	Reference list at end of paper
Citation-sequence	(1), (2), (3), (4)	Items listed in order of their text appearance
Citation-name	(31), (2), (13), (7)	Items listed alphabetically, by author surname
Name-year	(Shapiro 2016)	Items listed alphabetically, by author surname

STYLES OF REFERENCE LISTS

All three styles require reference lists following the text. CSE emphasizes brevity and simplicity for these lists. Instead of using the authors' first names, use only their initials. Omit periods after the initials and don't put spaces between them: Stern HK.

Shorten journal names with standard abbreviations, such as those listed in the PubMed journals database available at http://www.ncbi.nlm.nih.gov/journals. CSE doesn't use periods in shortening journal titles. So J Biosci Bioeng (without periods) is the abbreviation for the *Journal of Bioscience and Bioengineering.*

CSE uses sentence-style capitalization for titles. Capitalize only the first word, proper nouns, and the first word after a colon. Format the titles in normal type rather than italics.

If you cite something you've read online rather than in print, cite the electronic version. After all, the two versions may differ. To do that, CSE style requires you to add a couple of items to the citation: (1) the dates the

---

some scientists are circulating proposals that would require coauthors to specify how they contributed to joint papers. For Frisch's comments on the metastasizing growth of coauthors, see his webpage, http://hep.uchicago.edu/~frisch/authorship.pdf.

document was modified or posted and the date you accessed it and (2) the URL and/or DOI. A URL based on a DOI (appended to https://doi.org/) is preferable to another kind of URL.

Print citation　Pantazopoulou M, Boban M, Foisner R, Ljungdahl PO. 2016. Cdc48 and Ubx1 participate in a pathway associated with the inner nuclear membrane that governs Asi1 degradation. J Cell Sci. 129(20):3770–3780.

Online citation　Pantazopoulou M, Boban M, Foisner R, Ljungdahl PO. 2016. Cdc48 and Ubx1 participate in a pathway associated with the inner nuclear membrane that governs Asi1 degradation. J Cell Sci. [accessed 2017 Sep 14];129(20):3770–3780. https://doi.org/10.1242/jcs.189332.

This article, like nearly all printed articles, was not modified after it was published. But preprints are often modified, and so are articles in electronic journals. You need to include that information in the citation so your readers will know which version you are citing. That information appears in the square brackets, immediately before the date you accessed the item.

Modified paper　Pantazopoulou M, Boban M, Foisner R, Ljungdahl PO. 2016. Cdc48 and Ubx1 participate in a pathway associated with the inner nuclear membrane that governs Asi1 degradation. J Cell Sci. [modified 2016 Dec 2; accessed 2017 Sep 14];129(20):3770–3780. https://doi.org/10.1242/jcs.189332.

Don't worry about remembering all these details. There are too many of them. I'll explain them in the tables that follow and include plenty of examples. If you use this style often, you'll gradually grow familiar with the fine points.

These tables show CSE recommendations for in-text citations and reference lists, using all three formats. Not every journal follows them exactly, so you'll see some variation as you read scientific publications. Journals differ, for example, in how many coauthors they include in the reference list. Some list only the first three authors before adding "et al." One lists the first twenty-six. (Imagine being poor coauthor number 27.) The CSE says to name up to ten and then add "et al."

CSE: NAME-YEAR SYSTEM

Journal article	Reference list	Dannemann M, Kelso J. 2017. The contribution of Neanderthals to phenotypic variation in modern humans. Am J Hum Genet. 101(4):578–589.

> CSE does not require the issue number for consecutively paginated journal volumes like this one, but it's always okay to include it.

Wong KK et al. 2007. A comprehensive analysis of common copy-number variations in the human genome. Am J Hum Genet. 80(1):91–104.

> The Wong article has eleven authors. CSE says to list the first ten, followed by "et al." But individual journals vary in their practice. Some would include all of them in the reference list. Most would include only the first two.

Guerrero-Sanchez VM et al. 2017. Holm oak (*Queras ilex*) transcriptome. *De novo* sequencing and assembly analysis. Front Mol Biosci [modified 2017 Oct 6; accessed 2017 Oct 21];4:70. https://doi.org/10.3389/fmolb.2017.00070.

> Note the unusual way that dates are written in this CSE style: 2017 Oct 21.

In-text

(Dannemann and Kelso 2017)
(Wong et al. 2007)

> If your list includes several publications by Wong and other authors in 2007, your in-text reference should include coauthors to clarify exactly which article you are citing. For example: (Wong, deLeeuw, et al. 2007).

(Guerrero-Sanchez et al. 2017)

Book, one author	Reference list	Bickley LS. 2016. Bates' guide to physical examination and history taking. Alphen aan de Rijn (Netherlands): Wolters Kluwer.

Book, one author (*continued*)		Vetter RS. 2015. The brown recluse spider. Ithaca (NY): Cornell University Press.
		▸ If the publisher's city is well known, you may omit the state.
	In-text	(Bickley 2016) (Vetter 2015) ▸ To cite the same author for works written in several years: (Vetter 2015, 2016a, 2016b, 2018) ▸ To cite works by authors with the same surname published in the same year, include the authors' initials: (Vetter RS 2015;Vetter T 2015)
Book, multiple authors	Reference list	Provost JJ, Colabroy KL, Kelly BS, Wallert MA. 2016. The science of cooking: Understanding the biology and chemistry behind food and cooking. Hoboken (NJ): John Wiley & Sons. ▸ In the reference list, name up to ten authors, then add "et al."
	In-text	(Provost et al. 2016) ▸ If there are just two authors, name them both: (Provost and Colabroy 2016)
Book, online or e-book	Reference list	Schmitz OJ. 2016. The new ecology: Rethinking a science for the Anthropocene. Princeton (NJ): Princeton University Press. [accessed 2017 Oct 22]. Google Play Books. ▸ Include a URL or DOI at the end of the reference, instead of device or service, if the book is read online.
	In-text	(Schmitz 2016)
Book, multiple editions	Reference list	Gerard JE. 2014. Principles of environmental chemistry. 3rd ed. Burlington (MA): Jones and Bartlett.

Snell RS. 2007. Clinical anatomy by regions. 8th ed. Philadelphia: Lippincott Williams & Wilkins.

▸ For a revised edition, use the phrase "Rev. ed." instead of "8th ed."

In-text	(Gerard 2014) (Snell 2007)

Book, multiple editions, no author	Reference list	Publication manual of the American Psychological Association. 2010. 6th ed. Washington (DC): American Psychological Association.
	In-text	(Publication manual . . . 2010) ▸ Do not use "Anonymous" in place of the author name. Instead, use the first word or first few words of the title and an ellipsis, followed by the date.
Book, edited	Reference list	Rish, I, Cecchi GA, Lozano A, Niculescu-Mizil A, editors. 2014. Practical applications of sparse modeling. Cambridge (MA): MIT Press.
	In-text	(Rish et al. 2014)
Chapter in edited book	Reference list	McGrath J. 2015. Environmental factors and gene-environment interactions. In: Mitchell KJ, editor. The genetics of neurodevelopmental disorders. Hoboken (NJ): John Wiley and Sons. p. 111–127.
	In-text	(McGrath 2015)
Preprint	Reference list	Muir CD. 2017. Light and growth form interact to shape stomatal ratio among British angiosperms. Preprint. bioRxiv. [posted 2017 Jul 14, accessed 2017 Oct 22]. https://doi.org/10.1101/163873.

Preprint (*continued*)		▸ CSE's 8th edition of *Style and Format* does not specify a style for citing preprints. The format shown here is consistent, however, with other citation rules in that edition.
	In-text	(Muir 2017)
Government document, hard copy or online	Reference list	Marinopoulos SS, Dorman T, Ratanawongsa N, Wilson LM, Ashar BH, Magaziner JL, Miller RG, Thomas PA, Prokopowicz GP, Qayyum R, et al. 2007. Effectiveness of continuing medical education. Rockville (MD): Agency for Healthcare Research and Quality. AHRQ Pub. No. 07-E006. [EPA] Environmental Protection Agency (US), Office of Air and Radiation, Indoor Environments Division. 2012. A brief guide to mold, moisture, and your home. Washington (DC): EPA. [modified 2012 Sep 1; accessed 2015 Nov 28]. https://www.epa.gov/nscep. ▸ If an organization is both author and publisher, the name may be abbreviated as publisher.
	In-text	(Marinopoulos et al. 2007) (EPA 2012)
Video	Reference list	3D human anatomy: Regional edition [DVD-ROM]. 2009. London (England): Primal Pictures. The secret social life of a solitary puma [video]. 2017 Oct 12, 1:43 minutes. Scientific American. [accessed 2017 Nov 19]. https://www.scientificamerican.com/video/the-secret-social-live-of-a-solitary-puma/.
	In-text	(3D human anatomy 2009) (Secret social life 2017)
Database	Reference list	RCSB Protein Data Bank. 1971– . [accessed 2017 Aug 1]. http://www.rcsb.org/pdb/home/home.do.

		Swedish Life Sciences Database. [date unknown]– . Zurich (Switzerland): Venture Valuation. [accessed 2017 Sep 15]. http://www.swedishlifesciences.com/ se/portal/index.php.
		▸ Both databases are continually updated. List the year they began or "[date unknown]," followed by an en dash or hyphen and a space.
	In-text	(RCSB Protein Data Bank 1971–) (Swedish Life Sciences Database [accessed 2017]) ▸ Use the access date if no other date is listed.
Website, webpage, or blog	Reference list	[CSE] Council of Science Editors. c2017. Wheat Ridge (CO): Council of Science Editors; [accessed 2017 Oct 19]. https:// www.councilscienceeditors.org/ resource-library/editorial-policies/cse -policies/. ▸ Include the date of publication or the date copyrighted (c2017) if available. [USDA] US Department of Agriculture, Agricultural Research Service. Washington (DC): USDA; [modified 2017 Feb 2; accessed 2017 Nov 8]. https://www.ars .usda.gov/. Haran M. 2016 Sep 7. Active parenting behaviors of the Caribbean spiny lobster. BMC series blog. [accessed 2017 Jul 29]. https://blogs.biomedcentral .com/bmcseriesblog/2016/09/07/active -parenting-behaviors-caribbean-spiny -lobster. ▸ If it is not obvious that the article is from a blog, insert [blog] after the date.
	In-text	(CSE c2017) (USDA 2017) (Haran 2016)

Podcast	Reference list	Semple I. Tomorrow's technology: From asteroid mining to programmable matter. 2017 Nov 15, 30:42 minutes. The Guardian science weekly podcast. [accessed 2017 Nov 19]. https://www .theguardian.com/science/audio/2017/ nov/15/tomorrows-technology-from -asteroid-mining-to-programmable -matter-science-weekly-podcast.
	In-text	(Semple 2017)

The next table shows CSE references using citation-sequence and citation-name formats. The main difference from the previous table is that the date appears later in the reference. I have used the same examples, in case you want to compare formats.

CSE: CITATION-SEQUENCE AND CITATION-NAME SYSTEMS

Journal article	Reference list	Dannemann M, Kelso J. The contribution of Neanderthals to phenotypic variation in modern humans. Am J Hum Genet. 2017;101(4):578–589. Wong KK, deLeeuw RJ, et al. A comprehensive analysis of common copy-number variations in the human genome. Am J Hum Genet. 2007;80(1):91–104. Guerrero-Sanchez VM, et al. Holm oak (*Queras ilex*) transcriptome. *De novo* sequencing and assembly analysis. Front Mol Biosci. 2017 [modified 2017 Oct 6; accessed 2017 Oct 21];4:70. https://doi.org/10.3389/fmolb.2017 .00070.
Book, one author	Reference list	Bickley LS. Bates' guide to physical examination and history taking. Alphen aan de Rijn (Netherlands): Wolters Kluwer; 2016. Vetter RS. The brown recluse spider. Ithaca (NY): Cornell University Press; 2015.

Book, multiple authors	Reference list	Provost JJ, Colabroy KL, Kelly BS, Wallert MA. The science of cooking: Understanding the biology and chemistry behind food and cooking. Hoboken (NJ): John Wiley & Sons; 2016. ▸ In the reference list, name up to ten authors, then add "et al."
Book, online or e-book	Reference list	Schmitz OJ. The new ecology: rethinking a science for the Anthropocene. Princeton (NJ): Princeton University Press; 2016 [accessed 2017 Oct 22]. Google Play Books. ▸ Include a URL or DOI at the end of the reference if the book is read online.
Book, multiple editions	Reference list	Gerard JE. Principles of environmental chemistry. 3rd ed. Burlington (MA): Jones and Bartlett; 2014. Snell RS. Clinical anatomy by regions. 8th ed. Philadelphia: Lippincott Williams & Wilkins; 2007.
Book, multiple editions, no author	Reference list	Publication manual of the American Psychological Association. 6th ed. Washington (DC): American Psychological Association; 2010.
Book, edited	Reference list	Rish, I, Cecchi GA, Lozano A, Niculescu-Mizil A, editors. Practical applications of sparse modeling. Cambridge (MA): MIT Press; 2014.
Chapter in edited book	Reference list	McGrath J. Environmental factors and gene-environment interactions. In: Mitchell KJ, editor. The genetics of neurodevelopmental disorders. Hoboken (NJ): John Wiley and Sons; 2015. p. 111–127.

Preprint	Reference list	Muir CD. Light and growth form interact to shape stomatal ratio among British angiosperms. Preprint. bioRxiv; 2017 [posted 2017 Jul 14, accessed 2017 Oct 22]. https://doi.org/10.1101/163873.
Government document	Reference list	Marinopoulos SS, Dorman T, Ratanawongsa N, Wilson LM, Ashar BH, Magaziner JL, Miller RG, Thomas PA, Prokopowicz GP, Qayyum R, Bass EB. Effectiveness of continuing medical education. Rockville (MD): Agency for Healthcare Research and Quality; 2007. AHRQ Pub. No. 07-E006. [EPA] Environmental Protection Agency (US), Office of Air and Radiation, Indoor Environments Division. A brief guide to mold, moisture, and your home. Washington (DC): EPA; 2012 [modified 2012 Sep 1; accessed 2015 Nov 28]. https://www.epa.gov/nscep.
Video	Reference list	3D human anatomy: Regional edition [DVD-ROM]. London (England): Primal Pictures; 2009. The secret social life of a solitary puma [video]. Scientific American. 2017 Oct 12, 1:43. [accessed 2017 Nov 19]. https://www.scientificamerican.com/video/the-secret-social-live-of-a-solitary-puma.
Database	Reference list	RCSB Protein Data Bank. 1971– [accessed 2017 Aug 1]. http://www.rcsb.org/pdb/home/home.do Swedish Life Sciences Database. Zurich (Switzerland): Venture Valuation. [date unknown]– [accessed 2017 Sep 15]. http://www.swedishlifesciences.com/se/portal/index.php.

Website, webpage, or blog	Reference list	[CSE] Council of Science Editors. Wheat Ridge (CO): Council of Science Editors; c2017 [accessed 2017 Oct 19]. https:// www.councilscienceeditors.org/ resource-library/editorial-policies/cse -policies/. [USDA] US Department of Agriculture, Agricultural Research Service. Washington (DC): USDA; [modified 2017 Feb 2; accessed 2017 Nov 8]. https://www.ars .usda.gov/. Haran M. Active parenting behaviors of the Caribbean spiny lobster. BMC series blog. 2016 Sep 7 [accessed 2017 Jul 29]. https://blogs.biomedcentral.com/ bmcseriesblog/2016/09/07/active -parenting-behaviors-caribbean-spiny -lobster.
Podcast	Reference list	Semple I. Tomorrow's technology: From asteroid mining to programmable matter. The Guardian science weekly podcast. 2017 Nov 15, 30:42 minutes [accessed 2017 Nov 19]. https://www .theguardian.com/science/audio/2017/ nov/15/tomorrows-technology-from -asteroid-mining-to-programmable -matter-science-weekly-podcast.

Although individual references (shown above) are the same for both the citation-sequence and citation-name systems, their full reference lists are compiled in different orders.

Order of items within reference lists:

- Citation-name system: alphabetical by author
- Citation-sequence system: order of first appearance in the text

To illustrate, let's take the opening sentence of an article and show how each style would handle the citations and reference list.

CSE: CITATION-SEQUENCE SYSTEM

(ILLUSTRATION OF REFERENCE LIST ORDER)

Opening sentence   This research deals with the ABC transporter family and builds on prior studies by Nguyen et al.,[1] Sheps et al.,[2] and Kerr.[3]

Reference list
(in order of
appearance in
text)

1. Nguyen VNT, Moon S, Jung, K. Molecular biology: Genome-wide expression analysis of rice ABC transporter family across spatio-temporal samples and in response to abiotic stresses. J Plant Physiol. 2014;171(14):1276–1288.
2. Sheps JA, Ralph S, Zhao Z, Baillie DL, Ling V. The ABC transporter gene family of Caenorhabditis elegans has implications for the evolutionary dynamics of multidrug resistance in eukaryotes. Genome Biol. 2004;5(3):R15.
3. Kerr ID. Sequence analysis of twin ATP binding cassette proteins involved in translational control, antibiotic resistance, and ribonuclease L inhibition. Biochem Biophys Res Commun. 2004;315(1):166–173.

▶ Nguyen's article is listed first because it is the first one mentioned in the text.

CSE: CITATION-NAME SYSTEM

(ILLUSTRATION OF REFERENCE LIST ORDER)

Opening sentence   This research deals with the ABC transporter family and builds on prior studies by Nguyen et al.,[2] Sheps et al.,[3] and Kerr.[1]

Reference list
(alphabetical)

1. Kerr ID. Sequence analysis of twin ATP binding cassette proteins involved in translational control, antibiotic resistance, and ribonuclease L inhibition. Biochem Biophys Res Commun. 2004;315:166–173.
2. Nguyen VNT, Moon S, Jung, K. Molecular biology: Genome-wide expression analysis of rice ABC transporter family across spatio-temporal samples and in response to abiotic stresses. J Plant Physiol. 2014;171(14):1276–1288.
3. Sheps JA, Ralph S, Zhao Z, Baillie DL, Ling V. The ABC transporter gene family of Caenorhabditis elegans has implications for the evolutionary dynamics of multidrug resistance in eukaryotes. Genome Biol. 2004;5:R15.

▶ Nguyen's article is listed second because it is second alphabetically.

The two systems, citation-sequence and citation-name, present *each item* in the reference list the same way. What's different are (1) the *order* of items in the reference list and (2) their *citation numbers* in the text.

There's one more item you may wish to include in your citations: the PMID number. All medical articles have this electronic tag, which identifies them within the comprehensive PubMed database. The PMID appears as the last item in the citation and is *not* followed by a period:

Christakos S. In search of regulatory circuits that control the biological activity of vitamin D. J Biol Chem. 2017 Oct 20;292(42):17559–17560. PMID: 29055009

The PubMed database, covering more than four thousand biomedical journals, was developed at the National Library of Medicine and is available online at http://www.ncbi.nlm.nih.gov/pubmed/.

10

AMA CITATIONS FOR THE BIOMEDICAL SCIENCES, MEDICINE, NURSING, AND DENTISTRY

. . . .

AMA citations are used in biomedical research, medicine, nursing, dentistry, and some related fields of biology. They are based on the *AMA Manual of Style: A Guide for Authors and Editors*, 10th ed. (Oxford: Oxford University Press, 2007), and the *AMA Manual of Style* online (www.amamanualofstyle.com), which is periodically updated.

Citations are numbered (1), (2), (3), in the order they appear in the text. Full references appear at the end of the paper—in the same order. For coauthored books and articles, you should list up to six authors. If there are more, list only the first three, followed by "et al." Rather than using the authors' first names, use their initials (without periods) and do not put spaces between the initials: Lipson CH. Abbreviate the titles of journals. Journal titles along with their standard abbreviations can be found in the PubMed journals database available at http://www.ncbi.nlm.nih.gov/journals.

AMA CITATIONS

Journal article   Neto AS, Schultz MJ. Optimizing the settings on the ventilator: high PEEP for all? *JAMA*. 2017;317(4):1413–1414.

➤ AMA uses sentence style for journal article titles and does *not* capitalize the first letter of a subtitle.

Drinka PJ, Krause PF, Nest LJ, Goodman BM. Determinants of vitamin D levels in nursing home residents. *J Am Med Dir Assoc*. 2007;8(2):76–79.

► Journal titles are abbreviated without periods. (There's a period after *Assoc.* only to separate the journal title from the information about date, volume and issue, and pagination.)

Ho EC, Parker JD, Austin PC, Tu JV, Wang X, Lee DS. Impact of nitrate use on survival in acute heart failure: a propensity-matched analysis. *Am Heart J.* 2016;5(2):e002531. https://doi.org/10.1161/JAHA.115 .002531

Liu J, Xiong E, Zhu H, et al. Efficient induction of Ig gene hypermutation in ex-vivo-activated primary B cells. *J Immunol.* 2017;199(9)3023–3030. http://www.jimmunol .org/content/199/9/3023. Accessed October 5, 2017.

► Digital Object Identifiers (DOIs) are available for many journal articles—in fact, it's becoming hard to find an extant medical journal that doesn't assign them. A URL based on a DOI (appended to https://doi.org/) is preferable to another kind of URL. When you cite a DOI, you do not have to list a URL or an access date. An access date is required, however, if you list a URL.

► For citations of journal articles, AMA recommends copying the URL from the address bar in your browser rather than citing a home page—apparently without regard for length.

► Online journals do not always have page numbers. You may include other identifiers such as an article or e-page number if available.

► Name up to six authors in articles or books. If there are more, name the first three, then use "et al." This article, for example, has fifteen listed authors:

Watson LM, Bamber E, Schnekenberg, et al. Dominant mutations in GRM1 cause spinocerebellar. *Am J Hum Genet.* 2017;101(4):638. https://doi.org/10.1016/j.ajhg .2017.09.006.

► For more than one group of authors—common in medical papers—separate them by a semicolon. Terms such as *for* or *and* are optional:

Singh AK, Szczech L, Tang KL, et al; for CHOIR Investigators. Correction of anemia with epoetin alfa in chronic kidney disease. *N Engl J Med.* 2006;355(20):2085– 2098.

Journal article (*continued*)	▸ AMA's use of period-free abbreviations extends to many terms, including "et al"—in which "et" is a word and "al" is an abbreviation. (Most publications would write it "et al."—with a period.)

Abstract of article	Erkut S, Uckan S. Alveolar distraction osteogenesis and implant placement in a severely resorbed maxilla: a clinical report [abstract]. *J Prosthet Dent*. 2006;95(5): 340–343.
	Erkut S, Uckan S. Alveolar distraction osteogenesis and implant placement in a severely resorbed maxilla: a clinical report [abstract taken from *Dent Abstr*. 2007; 52(1):17–19]. *J Prosthet Dent*. 2006;95(5):340–343.
	▸ The upper reference is to the abstract, as published in the article itself. The lower reference is to the same abstract, published in a different journal.

Preprint or unpublished paper	Song Z. Using Medicare prices—toward equity and affordability in the ACA marketplace. [Epub ahead of print October 18, 2017]. *N Engl J Med*. https://doi.org/10.1056/NEJMp1710020.
	▸ Once the journal has been published, information about issue and pagination should be added to the citation.
	Flynn HW. Management options for vitreomacular traction: use an individualized approach. Paper presented at: Retina Subspecialty Day, Annual Meeting of the American Academy of Ophthalmology; October 14, 2016; Chicago, IL.

Published letter, comment, or editorial	Guazzi M, Reina G. Regarding article, Aspirin use and outcomes in a community-based cohort of 7352 patients discharged after first hospitalization for heart failure [letter]. *Circulation*. 2007;115(4):e54. https://doi.org/10.1161/CIRCULATIONAHA.106.646182.
	Baden LR, Rubin EJ, Morrissey S, Farrar JJ, Drazen JM. We can do better—improving outcomes in the midst of an emergency. [editorial]. *N Engl J Med*. 2017;377:1482–1484.

Book, one author	Basu S. *Modeling Public Health and Healthcare Systems*. New York, NY: Oxford University Press; 2017.
	▸ Book titles use caps for main words. Articles use caps only for the first word in the article title.

Wiggins CE. *A Concise Guide to Orthopaedic and Musculo-skeletal Impairment Ratings*. Philadelphia, PA: Lippincott Williams & Wilkins; 2007.

Lizza JP. *Potentiality: Metaphysical and Bioethical Dimensions*. Baltimore, MD: Johns Hopkins University Press; 2014.

> Note that states are included even after well-known cities.

Book, multiple authors	Schlossberg DL, Samuel R. *Antibiotics Manual: A Guide to Commonly Used Antibiotics*. Hoboken, NJ: John Wiley & Sons; 2017.

Book, multiple editions	Briggs GG, Freeman RK, Towers CV, Forinash AB. *Drugs in Pregnancy and Lactation: A Reference Guide to Fetal and Neonatal Risk*. 11th ed. Philadelphia, PA: Lippincott Williams & Wilkins; 2017. Mazze R, Strock ES, Simonson GD, Bergenstal RM. *Staged Diabetes Management*. 2nd rev ed. Hoboken, NJ: John Wiley & Sons; 2007. > The edition number appears between the book's title and the place of publication. > For an unnumbered revised edition, use "Rev ed" (followed by a period) in place of the specific edition.

Book, multiple volumes	Cone D, Brice JH, Delbridge TR, Myers B. *Emergency Medical Services: Clinical Practice and Systems Oversight*. 2 vols. Hoboken, NJ: John Wiley & Sons; 2015. > To cite only the second volume: Cone D, Brice JH, Delbridge TR, Myers B. *Emergency Medical Services: Clinical Practice and Systems Oversight*. Vol 2. Hoboken, NJ: John Wiley & Sons; 2015. > The abbreviation for "volume" does not have a period. AMA eliminates periods after abbreviations. > If the volumes have individual titles separate from the collective title, you can also cite them using the author (or editor) of that volume, plus its title and publication date, followed by the series name and the volume within the series. You do not need to include the editor of the series. Chorghade MS, ed. *Drug Development*. Hoboken, NJ: John Wiley & Sons; 2007. *Drug Discovery and Development*; vol 2.

Book, multiple editions, no author	*Dorland's Illustrated Medical Dictionary.* 32nd ed. Philadelphia, PA: Saunders; 2011. *Nursing 2018 Drug Handbook.* 38th ed. Philadelphia, PA: Lippincott Williams & Wilkins; 2017.
Book, edited	Hurlemann R, Grinevich V, eds. *Behavioral Pharmacology of Neuropeptides: Oxytocin.* New York, NY: Springer; 2018. Gravlee GP, Davis RF, Stammers AH, Ungerleider RM, eds. *Cardiopulmonary Bypass Principles and Practice.* 3rd ed. Philadelphia, PA: Lippincott Williams & Wilkins; 2007.
Chapter in edited book	Prinz J. Is the moral brain ever dispassionate? In: Decety J, Wheatley T. *The Moral Brain: A Multidisciplinary Perspective.* Cambridge, MA: MIT Press; 2015:51–68.
Book, online or e-book	Dalal AK. *Cultural Psychology of Health in India: Well-Being, Medicine and Traditional Health Care.* New Delhi, India: Sage; 2016. http://web.a.ebscohost.com/ehost/ebookviewer/ebook/bmxlYmtfXzEyNTYzODZfXoFOo?sid=aad89e12-a6e0-494f-a52c-f7a4b4d7a72a@sessionmgr4006&vid=0&format=EB&rid=1. Accessed October 26, 2017. Yefenof E, ed. *Innate and Adaptive Immunity in the Tumor Microenvironment* [Kindle edition]. Vol 1. New York, NY: Springer; 2008.
Government document	Global Task Force on Cholera Control. Ending cholera: a global roadmap to 2030. Geneva, Switzerland: World Health Organization; 2017. US Environmental Protection Agency, Office of Air and Radiation, Indoor Environments Division. *A Brief Guide to Mold, Moisture, and Your Home.* Washington (DC): Environmental Protection Agency; 2012. https://www.epa.gov/nscep. Modified September 2012. Accessed November 4, 2017. ▸ Use journal style for titles of articles, and book style for titles of longer works.

Personal communications	▸ Using AMA style, your reference list cannot include personal communications such as letters, emails, text messages, private discussions, or informal talks. Instead, cite those in the text.

DVD or online video	National Library of Medicine. *Changing the Face of Medicine* [DVD]. Washington, DC: Friends of the National Library of Medicine; 2004.
	Madara JL. Talk presented at: 2017 AMA annual meeting [video]. https://www.youtube.com/watch?v=d6-6UCiH728. Posted June 10, 2017. Accessed October 29, 2017.

Database	RCSB Protein Data Bank. http://www.rcsb.org/pdb/home/home.do. Accessed May 5, 2017.
	National Institutes of Health. Office of Dietary Supplements. Dietary Supplements Subset Database. http://ods.od.nih.gov/Health_Information/IBIDS.aspx. Accessed June 30, 2016.
	National Center for Health Statistics. Tables of summary health statistics for the U.S. population. Atlanta, GA: Centers for Disease Control and Prevention; 2017. https://www.cdc.gov/nchs/nhis/shs/tables.htm. Updated January 24, 2017. Accessed October 26, 2017.
	Vital Health Stat 10 (243). DHHS Pub No 2010-1571. Hyattsville, MD: National Center for Health Statistics (US Dept of Health and Human Services); 2009.

Website, webpage, or blog	Zika cases in the United States: Cumulative Zika virus disease case counts in the United States, 2015–2017. Centers for Disease Control and Prevention website. https://www.cdc.gov/zika/reporting/case-counts.html. Updated October 26, 2017. Accessed November 22, 2017.
	Sun R, Karaca Z, Wong HS. Characteristics of homeless individuals using emergency department services in 2014. US Department of Health and Human Services website. https://www.hcup-us.ahrq.gov/reports/statbriefs/sb229-Homeless-ED-Visits-2014.jsp. Updated October 2017. Accessed November 3, 2017.

Website, webpage, or blog (*continued*)	Lamberts R. There will be patients like this. Musings of a Distractible Mind. http://more-distractible.org/musings/2017/10/3/there-will-be-patients-like-this. Published October 2, 2017. Accessed October 21, 2017.
Podcast	Whitaker R. Muscle groups in the thigh [podcast]. Instant Anatomy. October 13, 2017. https://www.instantanatomy.net/podcasts/IA009.mp3. Accessed December 1, 2017.

To illustrate how these citations appear in the text, let's take the opening sentence of an article.

AMA: ILLUSTRATION OF REFERENCE LIST ORDER

Opening sentence	This research deals with the ABC transporter family and builds on prior studies by Nguyen et al,[1] Sheps et al,[2] and Kerr.[3]
Reference list (in order of appearance in text)	1. Nguyen VNT, Moon S, Jung, K. Molecular biology: Genome-wide expression analysis of rice ABC transporter family across spatio-temporal samples and in response to abiotic stresses. *J Plant Physiol.* 2014;171(14):1276–1288. 2. Sheps JA, Ralph S, Zhao Z, Baillie DL, Ling V. The ABC transporter gene family of *Caenorhabditis elegans* has implications for the evolutionary dynamics of multidrug resistance in eukaryotes. *Genome Biol.* 2004;5(3):R15. 3. Kerr ID. Sequence analysis of twin ATP binding cassette proteins involved in translational control, antibiotic resistance, and ribonuclease L inhibition. *Biochem Biophys Res Commun.* 2004;315(1):166–173. ► Nguyen's article is listed first because it is the first one mentioned in the text. Notice that "et al" does not include a period when it is used in sentences, according to AMA style.

Finally, all medical articles have an electronic identification number, known as a PMID. You are not required to include it, but it often helps your readers. It will help you, too, if you need to return to the article. If you include a PMID, you do not need to include a DOI or URL. The PMID appears as the last item in the citation and is followed by a period:

Christakos S. In search of regulatory circuits that control the biological activity of vitamin D. *J Biol Chem.* 2017;292(42):17559–17560. PMID: 29055009.

The PMID identifies the document within the PubMed database, which includes virtually all biomedical journals. This database was developed at the National Library of Medicine, and it is available online at http://www .ncbi.nlm.nih.gov/pubmed/.

11

ACS CITATIONS
FOR CHEMISTRY

. . . .

The American Chemical Society (ACS) has its own style guide, *The ACS Style Guide: Effective Communication of Scientific Information*, 3rd ed. (Washington, DC: American Chemical Society, 2006). The guidelines for citations, which are also available online at the ACS's website, give you a choice of citation formats:

- In-text citations with name and year, similar to APA or CSE. The reference list is alphabetized and appears at the end of the paper.
- Numbered citations, with a reference list at the end of the paper. End references are numbered in the order they appear in the text. These numbered citations, as they appear in the text itself, are either
  - superscript, such as[23], or
  - parentheses with the number in italics, such as (*23*).

Each format is used by scores of chemistry journals. Your lab, instructor, or journal may prefer one over the other. Whichever one you choose, use it consistently throughout each paper.

Fortunately, you collect the same information for either format. In fact, the items in the reference list are presented exactly the same way whether the list is numbered or alphabetized. And both types of reference lists use hanging indents. That is, the first line of each reference is full length; all subsequent lines are indented.

As you'll see below, there are some format differences particularly between citations for journal articles and books. For example, publication dates are boldface in journal citations but not in book citations. There is no explanation for these mysterious details. My guess: the chemists were overcome by fumes many years ago, and the odd results are now beloved traditions.

ACS (CHEMISTRY): REFERENCE LIST AND IN-TEXT CITATIONS

| Journal article | Reference list | Schoepff, L.; Kocher, L.; Durot S.; Heitz, V. Chemically Induced Breathing of Flexible Porphyrinic Covalent Cages. *J. Org. Chem.* **2017,** *82,* 5845–5851. |

> or

Schoepff, L.; Kocher, L.; Durot S.; Heitz, V. *J. Org. Chem.* **2017,** *82,* 5845–5851.

Xing, Y.; Lin, H.; Wang, F.; Lu, P. An Efficient D-A Dyad for Solvent Polarity Sensor. *Sens. Actuators, B* **2006,** *114,* 28–31.

> or

Xing, Y.; Lin, H.; Wang, F.; Lu, P. *Sens. Actuators, B* **2006,** *114,* 28–31.

> Authors' names are separated by semi-colons.

> Articles title may be included or omitted. Just be consistent, of course. (Until recently, article titles were always omitted. Now the *ACS Style Guide* considers it "desirable" to include the title, both to indicate the subject matter and to help readers find it.) Words in the article title are capitalized as they would be in a book title.

> Journal titles are italicized and abbreviated according to the *Chemical Abstracts Service Source Index* (CASSI).

> Year of publication is in boldface; volume number is italicized; complete pagination is in regular type. Do not put "pp" before page numbers.

Fadaei, E.; Martin-Arroyo, M.; Tafazzoli M.; Gonzalez-Rodriguez, D. Thermodynamic and Kinetic Stabilities of G-Quadruplexes in Apolar Solvents. *Org. Lett.* [Online] **2017,** *19,* 460–463. https://doi.org/10.1021/acs.orglett.6b03606 (accessed October 27, 2017).

> A URL based on a DOI (appended to https://doi.org/) is preferable to another kind of URL.

Journal article (*continued*)	In-text	(Schoepff et al., 2017) (Xing et al., 2006) (Fadaei, 2017)

Chemical abstract	Reference list	Taneda, A.; Shimizu, T.; Kawazoe, Y. *J. Phys.: Condens. Matter* **2001**, *13* (16), L305–312 (Eng.); *Chem. Abstr.* **2001**, *134*, 372018a.

▶ This article by Taneda et al. was published in a journal and referenced in *Chemical Abstracts*. This citation shows a reference to both the full article and the abstract. The abstract always comes second and is separated from the article by a semicolon.

Taneda, A.; Shimizu, T.; Kawazoe, Y. *Chem. Abstr.* **2001**, *134*, 372018a.

▶ Same article but shown only as mentioned in *Chemical Abstracts*. It is better to refer to the full published article than to the abstract, but that requires you actually examine the full article.

Chem. Abstr. **2001**, *134*, 372018a.

▶ This is the same article, referred to solely by its *Chemical Abstract* number. That number—*134*, 372018a—is the CAS accession number. The number *134* is the volume, and 372018a is the abstract number in the print version of *Chemical Abstracts*. These numbers also work with the CAS databases that have recently taken the place of the printed *Abstracts*.

▶ In editions of *Chemical Abstracts* prior to 1967, abstracts did not carry unique numbers. Instead they must be identified by column number and their position on the page. Abstract f, column 1167, can be cited as 1167f (or 1167*f*).

▶ It is usually better to include the authors, as in the previous references to Taneda et al.

	In-text	(Taneda et al., 2001) (*Chem. Abstr.*, 2001)

Book, one author	Reference list	Bahadori, A. *Waste Management in the Chemical and Petroleum Industries*; John Wiley & Sons: Chichester, UK, 2014; pp 23–42.

- ▸ Always include and italicize book titles.
- ▸ Put the publisher's name before its location.
- ▸ Do not use boldface for the year of publication.
- ▸ Do include "pp" before the page numbers. Or, if you're citing a whole chapter, you can list Chapter 3 instead of the page range.

	In-text	(Bahadori, 2014)

Book, multiple authors	Reference list	Theodore, L.; Dupont, R. R.; Ganesan, K. *Unit Operations in Environmental Engineering*; John Wiley & Sons: Chichester, UK., 2017.

- ▸ What if there are many authors? The *ACS Style Guide* says to name them all. It also notes that some chemistry journals list only the first ten, followed by a semicolon and "et al."

	In-text	(Theodore et al., 2017)

- ▸ Include up to two names for in-text citations; for three or more use "et al." If there are two authors, use this form: (Theodore and Dupont, 2017)

Book, online	Reference list	Olovsson, I. *Wonders of Water: The Hydrogen Bond in Action* [Online]; World Scientific: Hackensack, NJ, 2017. http://www.worldscientific.com/worldscibooks/10.1142/10684#t=toc (accessed November 10, 2017).
	In-text	(Olovsson, 2017)

Book, multiple editions	Reference list	Tro, N. J.; Vincent, J. J.; Livingston, E. J. *Laboratory Manual for Chemistry: A Molecular Approach*, 4th ed.; Pearson Education: Columbus, OH, 2017.

Book, multiple editions (*continued*)		▸ For a revised edition, use "Rev. ed." instead of "4th ed."
	In-text	(Tro et al., 2017)

Book multiple editions, no author	Reference list	*Reagent Chemicals: Specifications and Procedures*, 11th ed.; American Chemical Society: Washington, DC, 2016. *McGraw-Hill Encyclopedia of Science and Technology*, 11th ed.; McGraw-Hill: New York, 2012; 20 vols.
	In-text	(*Reagent Chemicals*, 2016). (*McGraw-Hill*, 2012) ▸ To cite a particular volume: (*McGraw-Hill*, Vol. 6, 2012)

Book, multivolume	Reference list	*The Encyclopedia of Mass Spectrometry*; Gross, M. L.; Caprioli, R., Eds.; Elsevier Science: Oxford, 2007; Vol. 6. *Hyphenated Methods*; Niessen, W., Ed. Vol. 8. In *The Encyclopedia of Mass Spectrometry*; Gross, M. L.; Caprioli, R., Eds.; Elsevier Science: Oxford, 2007.
	In-text	(Gross and Caprioli, Vol. 6, 2007) (Niessen, Vol. 8, 2007)

Book, edited	Reference list	*Applications of Molecular Modeling to Challenges in Clean Energy*; Fitzgerald, G.; Govind, N., Eds.; American Chemical Society: Washington, DC, 2017. ▸ or Fitzgerald, G.; Govind, N., Eds.; *Applications of Molecular Modeling to Challenges in Clean Energy*; American Chemical Society: Washington, DC, 2017. ▸ If there are only editors and no authors, the editors' names can go either after or before the title. Putting them before the title will make it easier if you are using an alphabetized reference list.

	In-text	(Fitzgerald and Govind, 2017)
		▸ For in-text references, editors' names are treated the same as authors'.

Chapter in edited book	Reference list	Kolosa, A.; Maciejowska, I. In *Chemistry Education and Sustainability in the Global Age*; Chiu, MH., et al., Eds.; Springer: New York, NY, 2013; pp 15–26.
		▸ or
		Kolosa, A.; Maciejowska, I. Polish Education Reform and Resulting Change in the Process of Chemical Education. In *Chemistry Education and Sustainability in the Global Age*; Chiu, MH., et al., Eds.; Springer: New York, NY, 2013; pp 15–26.
		▸ You may include or omit the chapter title (which would be styled like the title of a journal article); just be consistent.
	In-text	(Kolosa and Maciejowska, 2013)

Conference paper	Reference list	Fleming, L. Ecological Public Health, Harmful Algal Blooms and Climate Change. Presented at the 17th International Conference on Harmful Algae, Santa Catarina, Brazil, October 2016; Keynote speech.
	In-text	(Fleming, 2016)

Reference work or encyclopedia	Reference list	*Ullman's Encyclopedia of Industrial Chemistry*, 7th ed. [Online]; John Wiley & Sons: Hoboken, NJ, 2014. https://doi.org/10.1002/14356007 (accessed September 16, 2017).
		Vaidya, R.; López, G.; Lopez, J. A. Nanotechnology (Molecular). *Van Nostrand's Encyclopedia of Chemistry* [Online]; John Wiley & Sons: Hoboken, NJ, 2005. http://www3.interscience.wiley.com/cgi-bin/mrwhome/110498369/HOME (accessed May 5, 2010).
	In-text	(*Ullman's Encyclopedia*, 2014)

Government document	Reference list	US Consumer Product Safety Commission. *School Chemistry Laboratory Safety Guide (October 2006)*; DHHS (NIOSH) Publication No. 2007-107; National Institute for Occupational Safety and Health: Cincinnati, OH, 2007.
		Energy Department. Meeting of the Biomass Research and Development Technical Advisory Committee. *Fed. Regist* [Online] **2017**, *82* (205), 49538. https://www.gpo.gov/fdsys/pkg/FR-2017-10-25/pdf/2017-23156.pdf (accessed October 2, 2017).
		National Emission Standards for Hazardous Air Pollutants for Source Categories from Oil and Natural Gas Production Facilities. *Fed. Regist.* 2007, *72* (1), 26–43.
		▸ The *Federal Register* is treated like a journal.
	In-text	(US Consumer Product Safety Commission, 2007)
		(Energy Department, 2017)
Patent	Reference list	Adams, G. W.; Mullaney, J. S.; Oar, M. A. Hybrid Thermoplastic Gels and Their Methods of Making. US Patent 9,736,957, July 12, 2017.
		▸ It is also acceptable to omit the name of the patent.
	In-text	(Adams et al., 2017)
Video	Reference list	Luceigh, B. A. *Chem TV: Organic Chemistry 3.0* [CD-ROM]; Jones and Bartlett: Sudbury, MA, 2004.
		Davis, R. B. *Foundations of Organic Chemistry* [DVD]; The Great Courses: Chantilly, VA, 2014.

Szydlo, A. *The Magic of Chemistry* [Online
video]; The Royal Institution: London, UK,
June 4, 2014. https://www.youtube.com/
watch?v=og8lANs6zpQ (accessed June 15,
2017).

In-text
(Luceigh, 2004)
(Davis, 2014)
(Szydlo, 2014)

Website or webpage	Reference list	Biochemical Periodic Tables. http://eawag -bbd.ethz.ch/periodic/ (accessed August 10, 2017).

▸ If the page has an author, his or her name
and initial appear before the title of the
page:

Oxtoby, J. Biochemical Periodic Tables.
http:// . . .

In-text
(Biochemical Periodic Tables, 2017)

▸ If no date of publication is included with a
document on a website, use the access date
for the in-text citation.

12

PHYSICS, ASTROPHYSICS, AND ASTRONOMY CITATIONS

• • • • • • • • • • • • • •

AIP CITATIONS IN PHYSICS

Physics citations are based on the *AIP Style Manual*, 4th ed. (New York: American Institute of Physics, 1990), and the more recent *AIP Physics Desk Reference*, 3rd ed. (New York: Springer-Verlag, 2003). Most physics journals use numbered citations in the text and the reference list. Items appear in the numbered reference list in the order they appear in the text.

The citations may be numbered either in superscript or in brackets, that is, as [99] or [99]. The *AIP Style Manual* uses superscripts, as do AIP's official journals, such as *Chaos* and *Low Temperature Physics*. On the other hand, the organization's own *AIP Physics Desk Reference* uses brackets, as do journals from the American Physical Society (APS), such as *Physical Review E*. Either approach is fine. Just be sure you use the same style for the text and reference list. (A few physics journals use the author-year style instead. It has an alphabetized reference list with hanging indents.)

Whichever format is used, individual items in the reference list look the same, at least for articles and preprints (which are the way researchers in this field communicate). References are brief: authors' names as they appear on the title page of the work (M. Shochet and S. Nagel), abbreviated journal title, **boldface number for the journal volume**, first page number of the article, and, finally, the year in parentheses.

AIP (PHYSICS): REFERENCE LIST

| Journal article | [1] O. Budriga and V. Florescu, Euro. Phys. J. D **41**, 205 (2007). |
| | [2] G. Battimelli, Nucl. Phys. B **256–257**, 74 (2014). |

▸ The article's title is always omitted. Journal titles are abbreviated and not italicized.

➤ The publication volume (or issue number) and series are in boldface. For example, if a reference is to an article in *Physical Letters B*, issue number 466, page 415, then it appears as Phys. Lett. B **466**, 415 (1999).

[3] B. P. Williams and P. Lougovski, New J. Phys. **19**, 043003 (2017). <https://doi.org/10.1088/1367-2630/aa65de>.

➤ This is an online-only journal; instead of page numbers, it assigns article numbers (in the case of the Williams and Lougovski article, 043003).

➤ The citation may also include a Digital Object Identifier (DOI); for the Williams and Lougovski article, it is 10.1088/1367-2630/aa65de. A URL based on a DOI (appended to https://doi.org/) is preferable to another kind of URL.

Preprint

[1] B. Schuetrumpf, W. Nazarewicz, preprint, arXiv:1710.00579 [nucl-th] (2017). <https://arxiv.org/pdf/1710.00579.pdf>.

[2] F. Dai, et al., preprint, arXiv:1710.00076 [astro-ph] (2017). <https://arxiv.org/pdf/1710.00076.pdf>. To be published in AJ.

[3] A. J. M. Medved, preprint, arXiv:hep-th/0301010v2 (2003). <http://arxiv.org/PS_cache/hep-th/pdf/0301/0301010v2.pdf>. Published in High Energy Phys. **5**, 008 (2003). <https://doi.org/10.1088/1126-6708/2003/05/008>.

➤ A URL based on a DOI (appended to https://doi.org/) is preferable to another kind of URL.

➤ nucl-th = nuclear theory; astro-ph = astrophysics.

Book, one author

[1] Alexander Piel, *Plasma Physics: An Introduction to Laboratory, Space, and Fusion Plasmas* (Springer, Berlin, 2017).

Book, multiple authors

[1] Laurent Baulieu, John Iliopoulos, and Roland Seneor, *From Classical to Quantum Fields* (Oxford University Press, Oxford, 2017).

➤ The *AIP Style Manual* says to list up to three authors. If there are more authors, name only the first and add "*et al.*" in italics. Example: Laurent Baulieu, *et al., From Classical to Quantum . . .*

Book, multiple editions	[1] J. J. Sakurai and Jim Napolitano, *Modern Quantum Mechanics*, 2nd ed. (Cambridge University Press, New York, 2017).
Book, multivolume	[1] J.-P. Françoise, G. L. Naber, and T. S. Tsun, editors, *Encyclopedia of Mathematical Physics*, 5 vols. (Academic Press / Elsevier, San Diego, CA, 2006).
Book, edited	[1] Yatendra S. Chaudhary, editor, *Solar Fuel Generation* (CRC Press / Taylor & Francis, Boca Raton, FL, 2017).
Chapter in book	[1] Heinz Georg Schuster, in *Collective Dynamics of Nonlinear and Disordered Systems*, edited by G. Radons, W. Just, and P. Häussler (Springer, Berlin, 2005).
Database	[1] National Institutes of Standards and Technology, Physics Laboratory, Physical Reference Data. <http://physics.nist.gov/PhysRefData/>.

CITATION IN ASTROPHYSICS AND ASTRONOMY

Astronomy and astrophysics don't use the AIP/physics citation style or, for that matter, any single format. But most leading journals are fairly similar. They generally use (author-year) citations in the text, followed by an alphabetical reference list. The reference list follows some fairly common rules. It generally

- uses hanging indents
- contains no bold or italics
- uses authors' initials rather than their first names
- joins coauthors' names with an ampersand, &
- puts the publication date immediately after the author's name (with no comma between the name and date)
- omits the titles of articles
- includes titles for books and gives publisher information
- abbreviates journal names, often reducing them to a couple of initials

- lists only the first page of an article
- ends references without a period

Because there's no published style manual for astronomy and astrophysics, citation formats vary. I've standardized them based on the most common forms in the leading journals. Here are some illustrations, based on *Astronomy and Astrophysics* and the *Astrophysical Journal*, with a little tweaking for consistency.

ASTRONOMY AND ASTROPHYSICS REFERENCE LISTS

Journal article	Saffe, C., et al. 2017, A&A, 604, L4
	Koepferil, C. M., & Robitaille, T. P. 2017, 849, 4
	Stroman, T., Pohl, M., & Niemiec, J. 2009, ApJ, 706, 38
	Khomenko, E., & Collados, M. 2009, A&A 506, L5, https://doi.org/10.1051/0004-6361/200913030
	▸ *All* astronomy, astrophysics, and physics articles are online and available through standard scientific databases. Adding the Digital Object Identifier (DOI) or other search information may help your readers find them more easily. A URL based on a DOI (appended to https://doi.org/) is preferable to another type of URL.
Journal article, several by same authors	Panaitescu, A. 2005a, MNRAS, 363, 1409
	Panaitescu, A. 2005b, MNRAS, 362, 921
	Pe'er, A., Long, K., & Piergiorgio, C. 2017, ApJ, 846, 54
	Pe'er, A., & Ryde, F. 2017, IJMPD, 26, 1730018-296. 2006, ApJ, 653, 454
	▸ The two articles by Panaitescu are listed as 2005a and 2005b because they have the same author.
	▸ The two articles by Pe'er are *not* listed as 2017a and 2017b because they do not have identical coauthors.
Preprint	Kuruvilla, J., & Porciani, C. 2017, preprint, arXiv:1710.09379 [astro-ph]
Book, one author	Hoyle, F. 2015, Home Is Where the Wind Blows: Chapters from a Cosmologist's Life (Sausalito, CA: University Science Books)
	Harwit, M. 2006, Astrophysical Concepts (New York: Springer Science)

Book, multiple authors	Mathur, R. B., Singh, B. P., Pande, S. 2017, Carbon Nanomaterials: Synthesis, Structure, Properties and Applications (Boca Raton, FL: CRC Press / Taylor & Francis)
Chapter in edited book	Thomas, J. 2012, in Solar and Astrophysical Magnetohydrodynamic Flows, ed. K. Tsinganos (Dordrecht, Netherlands: Kluwer Academic), 39
Book in a series	Branch, D., Wheeler, J.C. 2017, Supernova Explosions (Berlin: Springer), Astronomy and Astrophysics Library Series
Chapter in a book in a series	Daly, P. N. 2006, in Astronomical Data Analysis Software Systems XV, ed. C. Gabriel, C. Arviset, D. Ponz, & E. Solano (San Francisco: ASP), ASP Conf. Ser. 351, 4
Unpublished paper or dissertation	Kilbourne, H, et al. 2017, US CLIVAR Workshop Report, Rep. 2017-3, https://doi.org/10.5065/D6KP8oKR Fiore, F., Guainazzi, M., & Grandi, P. 1999, Cookbook for BeppoSAX NFI Spectral Analysis, available from https://heasarc.gsfc.nasa.gov/docs/sax/abc/saxabc/saxabc.html Lee, E. J. 2017, Ph.D. Diss, University of California, Berkeley
Website	SkyView, the Internet's Virtual Telescope <http://skyview.gsfc.nasa.gov/>

Researchers in the physical sciences often cite unpublished research, usually conference papers or works in progress that will be published later. Known as preprints (or e-prints), these papers are at the cutting edge of the field and are collected in electronic document archives. Besides collections at major research institutions, there's a huge collection at arXiv.org (http://arxiv.org/), with mirror sites around the world. Papers are readily accessible and easy to download. What's hard—unless you are on the cutting edge of physics—is actually understanding their content!

Preprints in the arXiv collection are classified by field (physics, astrophysics, mathematics, quantitative biology, and so forth) and, within each field, by major subfields. Papers are submitted to the subfield archives and are numbered by their date of arrival. As with journal articles, the titles of preprints are omitted from citations. Here are some examples:

Biswarup, P. 2017, preprint, arXiv:1710.09634 [nucl-ex] <https://arxiv
.org/abs/1710.09634>
Brax, P., Cespedes, S., Davis, A. 2017, preprint, arXiv:1710.09818
[astro-ph.CO]

or

Brax, P., Cespedes, S., Davis, A., 2017, preprint (arXiv:1710.09818
[astro-ph.CO])

The classification system is as simple as the papers are complex. Take the Brax et al. paper. It's in the astrophysics archive (astro-ph), under the subject category of cosmology and nongalactic astrophysics (CO), was submitted in 2017 (17), in October (10), and is the 9,818th paper submitted in its category that month. Hence 1710.09818 [astro-ph.CO].

For the Biswarup article I included the URL for the PDF version, but that's not essential. Professionals in the field know where to find arXiv preprints, either at the main archive or on mirror sites. It's sufficient to list the ID.

Preprints like these should be cited and included in your reference list, just like journal articles. Unpublished does not mean uncited.

13

MATHEMATICS, COMPUTER SCIENCE, AND ENGINEERING CITATIONS

• • • • • • • • • • • • •

MATHEMATICS AND COMPUTER SCIENCE

Papers in mathematics and computer science use a variety of citation styles. References in mathematics are usually generated by a document typesetting system called LaTeX, which can churn out a number of different styles. As the writer of a paper, you may not create your own references by hand, but you will still want to check them for accuracy.

In most cases, references in the text are given by bracketed numbers. They may be listed sequentially, beginning with [1], with a corresponding sequential reference list at the end of the paper. Or if the reference list is organized alphabetically by the author's last name, the first reference might be [23], referring to the twenty-third item in an alphabetical list at the end of the paper (for an author named Simpson), while the last reference in the article might be [2] (author named Biel). Specific pages are rarely mentioned, but if you need to, use this form: [23, p. 14].

A less common style uses abbreviations based on the author's last name and date of publication rather than bracketed numbers. So an article by Hirano and Porter, published in *Econometrica*, volume 77 (2009), would be cited in the text as something like [HiP009] or perhaps [HP09] or maybe just [HP]. It's your choice. This abbreviation also appears in the reference list, identifying the entry for Hirano and Porter's article.

Most books and articles are classified by subfield and uniquely identified in the Mathematical Reviews (MR) Database. Whichever citation system you use, you can include this MR number as the last item in each reference, after the date or page numbers. The MR Database is searchable

through the American Mathematical Society's website at http://www.ams
.org/mr-database.

If the article you are citing is available online, mention the DOI (Digital
Object Identifier) just before the MR number. If there is no MR number,
the DOI appears last. Style the DOI as a URL, appended to https://doi.org/;
for example, if the DOI is 10.1515/jgth-2014-0041, use https://doi.org/10
.1515/jgth-2014-0041.

In the following tables I show a standardized mathematical citation
form. Many math journals don't stick to one format. Some use numerical
citations for one article and alphabetical for the next. To add to the fun,
they'll use the same style differently in different articles. One might list the
author as R. Zimmer. The very next article (using the same style) lists the
author as Zimmer, R. If I kept looking, I'd probably find one that calls him
Bob Zimmer. One article puts the publication date in parentheses; the next
one doesn't. In one, the reference list uses italics for every article title and
regular type for journal names. The next one does exactly the opposite.
Some use boldface for journal numbers, and others don't. Frankly, I don't
think any of this matters very much, as long as you are consistent and your
professor or publisher is okay with it.

I've swept away these variations and idiosyncrasies. The tables below use
consistent rules, based on recent editions of major journals in mathematics
and computer science.

MATHEMATICS: NUMBERED REFERENCE LIST (ALPHABETICAL ORDER)

Journal article	[1] A. Obus, *The local lifting problem for A4*, Algebra Number Theory **10** (2016), pp. 1683–1693.
	[2] D. W. Smith and R. G. Sanfelice, *A hybrid feedback control strategy for autonomous waypoint transitioning and loitering of unmanned aerial vehicles*, Nonlinear Anal. Hybrid Syst. **26** (2017), pp. 115–136.
	[3] N. P. Strickland, *Gross-Hopkins duality*, Topology **39** (2000), pp. 1021–1033.
	[4] ——, *Common subbundles and intersections of divisors*, Algebr. Geom. Topol. **2** (2002), pp. 1061–1118.
	▸ Bracketed numbers go in the left margin. References are listed in numerical order, or in alphabetical order, by author's name. For each author in an alphabetical list, the articles or books are listed in their order of publication, with the earliest ones first.

Journal article
(*continued*)

➤ If an author's name is repeated (and there are no new coauthors), then use three em dashes, followed by a comma.
(Em dashes are simply long dashes, about the length of the
letter *m*. If for some reason you can't find these em dashes,
just use three hyphens.)

➤ Journal titles are abbreviated but not italicized. A full
list of journal abbreviations compiled by the American
Mathematical Society is available at http://www.ams.org/
msnhtml/serials.pdf.

[#] C. Banks, M. Elder, and G. A. Willis, *Simple groups of
automorphisms of trees determined by their actions
on finite subtrees*, J. Group Theory **18** (2015), 235–261.
https://doi.org/10.1515/jgth-2014-0041. MR 3318536.

[#] M. Leonelli, E. Riccomagno, and J. Q. Smith, *A symbolic
algebra for the computation of expected utilities in mul-
tiplicative influence diagrams*, Ann. Math Artif. Intell. **81**
(2017), 273–313. https://doi.org/10.1007/s10472-017
-9553-y.

Preprint

[#] J. Glänzel and R. Unger, *Clustering by optimal subsets
to describe environment interdependences*, Technische
Universität Chemnitz, Fakultät für Mathematik (Ger-
many), preprint (2017-3). Available at https://www.tu
-chemnitz.de/mathematik/preprint/2017/PREPRINT_03
.pdf.

[#] S. Dasgupta and J. Voight, *Sylvester's Problem and
Mock Heegner Points*, preprint (2017), submitted for
publication. Available at https://people.ucsc.edu/
~sdasgup2/Sylvester.pdf.

[#] L. Chen, *Algorithms for deforming and contracting
simply connected discrete closed manifolds (III)*,
preprint (2017). Available at https://arxiv.org/pdf/1710
.09819.pdf.

[#] A. Hoque and K. Chakraborty, *Pell-type equations and
class number of the maximal real subfield of a cyclo-
tomic field*, preprint (2017), to appear in Ramanujan J.
ArXiv:1710.09760 [math.NT].

[#] G. Lyubeznik, *On Switala's Matlis duality*, preprint
(2017). arXiv: 1705.00021v1 [math.AC].

▸ In mathematics, as in physics, there's a large, easily accessible electronic archive of preprints available at arXiv. The
math collection is at http://arxiv.org/archive/math. Either
you can cite the entire URL for a preprint, as the reference
above for Chen does, or you can simply list the arXiv archival number, as the references for Hogue and Lyubeznik do.

[#] X. Sun, *Singular structure of harmonic maps to trees*,
preprint (2001), published as *Regularity of harmonic
maps to trees*, Amer. J. Math. 125 (2003), pp. 737–771.
MR1993740 (2004j:58014).

Other unpublished papers	[#] A. Iserles and S. P. Nørsett, *From high oscillation to rapid approximation II: Expansions in polyharmonic eigenfunctions*, DAMTP Tech. Rep. 2006/NA07. Department of Applied Mathematics and Theoretical Physics, University of Cambridge, Cambridge, UK, 2006. Available at http://www.damtp.cam.ac.uk/user/na/NA _papers/NA2006_07.pdf.
	[#] M. Fang, *Data enabled algorithms and analytics of material structural change informatics*, PhD diss, University of Memphis, 2017.
	[#] R. Viator, *Analysis of Maxwell's equations in passive layered media*, IMA postdoc seminar, Minneapolis, MN, 2017.
Book, one author	[#] D. Eisenbud, *The Geometry of Syzygies: A Second Course in Commutative Algebra and Algebraic Geometry*, e-book, Springer, New York, 2005.
	[#] D. Kondrashov, *Quantifying Life: A Symbiosis of Computation, Mathematics, and Biology*, e-book, University of Chicago Press, Chicago, 2016.
	[#] M. A. Parthasarathy, *Practical Software Estimation: Function Point Methods for Insourced and Outsourced Projects*, Addison-Wesley Professional, Upper Saddle River, NJ, 2007.
	▸ Book titles, unlike article or chapter titles, are capitalized headline-style.
Book, multiple authors	[#] A. M. Mathai and H. J. Haubold, *Linear Algebra: A Course for Physicists and Engineers*, Birkhäuser, Boston, 2017.

Book, multiple authors (*continued*)	▸ If there are many authors, then name only the first and add "et al." Example: A. M. Mathai et al., *Linear Algebra* . . .

Book, multiple editions	[#] D. Hughes-Hallett et al., *Calculus: Single and Multivariable*, enhanced e-text, 7th ed., John Wiley & Sons, Hoboken, NJ, 2017. [#] B. Korte and J. Vygen, *Combinatorial Optimization: Theory and Algorithms*, 3rd ed., Springer-Verlag, Berlin, 2006. MR2171734 (2006d:90001).

Book, multivolume	[#] F. Dillen and L. C. A. Verstraelen (eds.), *Handbook of Differential Geometry*, vol. 2, Elsevier, Amsterdam, 2006. [#] D. Knuth, *The Art of Computer Programming*, 3rd ed., vol. 4, fasc. 3: *Generating All Combinations and Partitions*, Addison-Wesley Professional, Upper Saddle River, NJ, 2005. MR2251472. [#] J. Humpherys, T. J. Jarvis, and E. J. Evans, *Foundations of Applied Mathematics*, vol. 1, SIAM, Philadelphia, PA, 2017.

Book, edited	[#] B. J. Copeland, C. J. Posy, and O. Shagrir (eds.), *Computability: Turning, Gödel, Church, and Beyond*, MIT Press, Cambridge, 2013.

Book, translated	[#] P. G. Darvas, *Symmetry*, trans. by D. R. Evans, Springer, New York, 2007.

Chapter in edited book	[#] I. Boglaev, *Uniform convergent monotone iterates for nonlinear parabolic reaction-diffusion systems*, in *Boundary and Interior Layers, Computational and Asymptotic Methods BAIL*, Z. Huang, M. Stynes, Z. Zhang, eds., Springer, New York, 2017, pp. 35–48. ▸ Notice that the chapter is capitalized like a sentence (i.e., only the first word and any proper nouns are capitalized), but the book title is capitalized headline-style.

Chapter in multivolume edited book	[#] W. E. Hart, *A stationary point convergence theory of evolutionary algorithms*, in *Foundations of Genetic Algorithms 4*, R. K. Belew and M. D. Vose, eds., Morgan Kaufmann, San Francisco, 1997, pp. 127–134.

Software	[#] T. G. Kolda et al., *APPSPACK (Asynchronous Parallel Pattern Search Package)*; ver. 5.0.1, 2007. Available at http://software.sandia.gov/appspack/version5.0/pageDownloads.html.
	[#] *Windows 10 Pro*, Microsoft, Redmond, WA, 2015. Available at https://www.microsoft.com/en-us/store/d/windows-10-pro/df77x4d43rkt/48DN.
	► When there is no author, as with this Microsoft program, alphabetize by its title.

TEXT STYLE IN MATHEMATICS

Finally, all math papers (regardless of their citation format) have special rules governing the way to present standard terms such as theorems and proofs, as well as the way to present the text following these terms.

MATHEMATICAL TERM	PROPER FORMAT FOR THIS TERM	TEXT AFTER THE TERM
THEOREM	THEOREM or **Theorem**	*Italicized*
LEMMA	LEMMA or **Lemma**	*Italicized*
COROLLARY	COROLLARY or **Corollary**	*Italicized*
PROOF	*Proof*	Standard, no italics
DEFINITION	*Definition*	Standard, no italics
NOTE	*Note*	Standard, no italics
REMARK	*Remark*	Standard, no italics
OBSERVATION	*Observation*	Standard, no italics
EXAMPLE	*Example*	Standard, no italics

For more details, see Ellen Swanson, *Mathematics into Type*, updated by Arlene O'Sean and Antoinette Schleyer (Providence, RI: American Mathematical Society, 1999).

COMPUTER SCIENCE: CITING SOURCE CODE IN PROGRAMMING

Besides citing articles and texts, you should cite others' computer code and algorithms whenever you incorporate them in your own programs. Follow the same principles you do in papers: openly acknowledge the work of others, and tell your readers where they can find it. That can be done easily in the comment section. Say who wrote the code segment you are using, the version or date it was written, where to find it, and the date you incorporated it. Be clear about where the borrowed material begins and ends, and explain what changes, if any, you made to it.

There is one exception to this citation requirement. If an algorithm is common knowledge, you don't have to cite it.

IEEE CITATIONS IN ENGINEERING

Engineers use three citation formats. Some use APA, described in chapter 5. Most prefer a format designed by one of two professional associations, the Institute of Electrical and Electronics Engineers (IEEE, pronounced "*I* triple *E*") or the American Society of Civil Engineers. The citations in this section are based on the latest *IEEE Editorial Style Manual*, published online at http://www.ieee.org/. The next section explains ASCE citations.

The IEEE publishes hundreds of journals and conference proceedings, and not just in electrical engineering and electronics. It also publishes in computer science, bioengineering, civil engineering, aerospace engineering, and most of the other engineering disciplines. Still, if you're not sure IEEE is the style you should follow, consult your professor or teaching assistant.

Most IEEE journals use numbered citations in the text and the reference list. This system is similar to the one used in medicine (see chapter 7) and physics (see chapter 9). Items appear in the numbered reference list in the order they appear in the text, *not* in alphabetical order. Numbers in the text and in the reference list use brackets: [99]. The reference list uses a hanging indent to make it easier to find the numbers.

The numbers in text are treated just like any other information in brackets: according to Carmine [18]. To refer to more than one source, use commas or hyphens: in the earlier studies [3], [22]–[24]. Unlike other numbered systems, IEEE allows you to include a page number, a numbered equation, or other item along with the numbered reference: [23, pp. 18–23], [24, Fig. 13]. Equation numbers are usually in parentheses, no matter where they appear: [24, eq. (22)]. You should already know how to abbreviate page (*p.*, pl. *pp.*) and equation (*eq.*, pl. *eqs.*); for everything else, consult a dictionary. If you can't find an abbreviation, spell it out.

In the reference list itself, abbreviate authors' first names. If a reference has many authors, include them all. Capitalize titles of articles, papers, and the like as if they were sentences—only the first word and any proper nouns. Capitalize titles of books and periodicals headline-style. For journal titles, use abbreviations. For IEEE publications, you can find most of these abbreviations in the *IEEE Editorial Style Manual.* For anything else, consult the PubMed journals database available at http://www.ncbi.nlm.nih.gov/journals.

IEEE (ENGINEERING): REFERENCE LIST

Journal article	[1] B. Komarath, J. Sarma, and S. Sawlani. "Pebbling meets coloring: Reversible pebble game on trees," *JCSS*, vol. 91, pp. 33–41, Feb. 2018, https://doi.org/10.1016/j.jcss.2017.07.009.

[2] M. Inui and N. Umezu, "Quad pillars and delta pillars: Algorithms for converting dexel models to polyhedral models," *J. Comput. Inf. Sci. Eng.*, vol. 17, no. 3, 031001, Feb. 2017, https://doi.org/10.1115/1.4034737.

- ▸ Use abbreviations for number, volume, page, and month (except for May, June, and July, which are spelled out).
- ▸ IEEE prefers listing the month of publication rather than the issue number, if possible; you can also drop the issue number for consecutively paginated volumes (i.e., most journals in the sciences). But it's always okay to include it.
- ▸ Some online-only articles will not have page numbers. In the Samper et al. example, 041005 is the "citation identifier" used by the *Journal of Computing and Information Science in Engineering* in place of page numbers.
- ▸ For citing online sources, the IEEE follows APA. If a DOI is available—even if you read the article on paper—include it. If you don't see a DOI, list the URL (usually the address in your browser's location bar) instead.

Unpublished article or paper	[#] J. Yu, "Photonics-assisted millimeter-wave wireless communication," *IEEE J. Quantum Electron.*, to be published. https://doi.org/10.1109/JQE.2017.2765742.

- ▸ If an article has been accepted for publication, use "to be published." If it has been submitted but not yet accepted, omit the name of any journal and say "submitted for publication" following the title of the unpublished article.

Unpublished article or paper (*continued*)	[#] M. Cole, "Advanced nanoengineering towards the electronics for tomorrow," presented at the 12th Int. Conf. on Surfaces, Coatings and Nanostructured Materials (NANOSMAT), Paris, France, Sept. 2017. ‣ Abbreviate *conference* and words like *national* or *international*, but for the most part spell out the name of the event.
Published conference proceedings	[#] L. Xie and Z. Mo, "Decision system of urban rail transit line conference construction sequence," in *Proc. 2nd Int. Conf. Transportation Engineering*, Chengdu, China, July 25–27, 2009, pp. 820–825. ‣ The IEEE manual insists on page numbers. ‣ The manual also lists a few terms to abbreviate, including those above. The full title for the proceedings in the example is *Proceedings of the Second International Conference on Transportation Engineering* (notice that prepositions and articles drop out).
Book, one author	[#] S. W. Ellingson, *Radio Systems Engineering*. Cambridge, UK: Cambridge Univ. Press, 2016, p. 92. ‣ Include page number(s) unless the citation is to the whole book.
Book, multiple authors	[#] L. T. Biegler, I. E. Grossmann, and A. W. Westerberg, *Systematic Methods of Chemical Process Design*. Upper Saddle River, NJ, USA: Prentice Hall, 1997. ‣ IEEE says to list all authors. If this gets to be impractical, list only the first and add "et al." Example: L. T. Biegler et al., *Systematic Methods . . .*
Book, multiple editions	[#] G. Rizzoni and J. Kearns, *Principles and Applications of Electrical Engineering*, 2nd ed. Columbus, OH, USA: McGraw-Hill Education, 2016.
Book, multivolume	[#] M. Muste, et al., Eds., *Experimental Hydraulics: Methods, Instrumentation, Data Processing and Management*, 2 vols. Boca Raton, FL, USA: CRC Press / Taylor & Francis, 2017. ‣ IEEE capitalizes the abbreviations for *editor* (Ed.) and *editors* (Eds). They do seem to like their capital *E*s.

Chapter in book	[#] A. Wada, Y. Huang, and V. Bertero, "Innovative strategies in earthquake engineering," in *Earthquake Engineering: From Engineering Seismology to Performance-Based Engineering*, Y. Bozorgnia and V. Bertero, Eds. Boca Raton, FL, USA: CRC Press, 2004, pp. 637–675.
Book, online or e-book	[#] D. Haskell, A. Pillay, and C. Steinhorn, Eds., *Model Theory, Algebra, and Geometry* (MSRI Publications 39) [Online]. Available: http://www.msri.org/publications/books/Book39/contents.html. [#] D. Keith, *A Case for Climate Engineering*. Cambridge, MA, USA: MIT Press, 2013 [Kindle version]. ▸ For internet sources you might omit "Online," since that's clear from the URL. To cite a Kindle book or other electronic edition, put that in the brackets instead of "Online" (e.g., [Kindle version]).
Patent	[#] C. Entsfellner and H. Heuermann, "Vectorial network analyser," US Patent 9,801,082, October 24, 2017.

ASCE CITATIONS IN ENGINEERING

Unlike the IEEE, the American Society of Civil Engineers prefers the author-date style for its book and journal authors. This style is similar to APA (chapter 5). The differences are (what else?) in the details. A few of these details can be found on the ASCE website.

The author-date style uses an alphabetical reference list. Each entry in the reference list must be mentioned in the text, and vice versa. Let's start with a few examples:

Brenner, B. (2009a). *Bridginess: More of the civil engineering life*, ASCE Press, Reston, Va.

Brenner, B. (2009b). "Infrastructure at the end." *Leadersh. Manage. Eng.* 9(4), 205–206.

Brenner, B. (2015). *Too much information: Living the civil engineering life*, ASCE Press, Reston, Va., 60–64.

Compare these if you'd like with the examples at the beginning of chapter 5 (featuring the eminent author C. Lipson). Like APA, ASCE uses authors' initials and puts the date in parentheses. Titles by the same author are listed in chronological order; two titles by the same author in the same year are alphabetized by title and carry letters after the date.

Unlike APA, ASCE prefers quotation marks around article and chapter titles. And like most science publishers, it uses abbreviations for journal titles. Where to find these? If it's not listed along with the journal article, search the PubMed journals database available at http://www.ncbi.nlm.nih .gov/journals. (Just remember to add periods to the ends of abbreviated elements in the title.)

In text, cite the author and year, with no intervening comma: (Brenner 2009b). If you need to include a page number, use a comma; separate two references with a semicolon: (Brenner 2009a; Brenner 2015, p. 62). ASCE journals often differ in these details. Mainly you need to worry about being consistent. If you happen to be writing for a particular journal, look at a few recent articles in that journal and style your references accordingly. If you can't find a particular type of example and it isn't listed below, look at chapter 5 for a model and adapt that.

For the sake of comparison, the examples in the table that follows cite many of the same sources as those in the IEEE section above.

ASCE (ENGINEERING): REFERENCE LIST

Journal article	Komarath, B., Sarma, J., and Sawlani, S. (2018). "Pebbling meets coloring: Reversible pebble game on trees." *JCSS.* 91, 33–41, 10.1016/j.jcss.2017.07.009.
	Inui, M., and Umezu, N. (2017). "Quad pillars and delta pillars: Algorithms for converting dexel models to polyhedral models." *J. Comput. Inf. Sci. Eng.* 17(3), 031001, 10.1115/1.4034737.

▸ ASCE wants you to list volume and issue number instead of month or season.

▸ Some online-only articles will not have page numbers. In the Inui and Umezu example, 031001 is the "citation identifier" used by the *Journal of Computing and Information Science in Engineering* in place of page numbers.

▸ The ASCE online guide for authors doesn't give much advice for citing online sources. Because its system is close to that of APA, follow APA (unless your professor says otherwise). If a DOI is available—even if you read the article on paper—include it. If you don't see a DOI, list the URL (usually the address in your browser's location bar) instead.

Unpublished article or paper	Yu, J. (2017). "Photonics-assisted millimeter-wave wireless communication." *IEEE J. Quantum Electron.*, in press. https://doi.org/10.1109/JQE.2017.2765742.

▸ In the references, list all authors. In text, if there are three or more, cite only the first, followed by "et al.": (Yu et al. 2017).

▸ The Yu article is an early access article, not yet published in its final form. If you cite the advance version, it's best to say so.

▸ ASCE advises against including unpublished articles, papers, reports, and the like in the reference list. But you can cite them in text: According to A. Stradivari (unpublished manuscript, January 2018) . . .

Published conference proceedings	Xie, L., and Mo, Z. (2009). "Decision system of urban rail transit line construction sequence." *Proc., 2nd Int. Conf. on Transportation Engineering*, Southwest Jiantong University, Chengdu, China, July 25–27, https://doi.org/10.1061/41039 (345)136.

▸ Like IEEE, ASCE abbreviates titles of published proceedings. Unlike IEEE, it substitutes a comma for "of the" and doesn't object to the preposition *on*.

▸ These proceedings were also published as a book. To cite the same paper but from the book, you could list the publisher instead of the conference location—in this case, ASCE, Reston, Va. Then you'd include page numbers instead of a DOI.

Xie, L., and Mo, Z. (2009). "Decision system of urban rail transit line construction sequence." *Proc., 2nd Int. Conf. on Transportation Engineering*, ASCE, Reston, Va., 820–825.

Book, one author	Ellingson, S. W. (2016). *Radio systems engineering*, Cambridge Univ. Press, Cambridge, UK.

Book, multiple authors	Biegler, L. T., Grossmann, I. E., and Westerberg, A. W. (1997). *Systematic methods of chemical process design*, Prentice Hall, Upper Saddle River, N.J. ▸ List all authors in the reference list. In text, if there are three or more, list the first and add "et al.": (Biegler et al. 1997).
Book, multiple editions	Rizzoni, G., and Kearns, J. (2016). *Principles and applications of electrical engineering*, 2nd ed., McGraw-Hill Education, Columbus, Ohio. ▸ ASCE recommends "traditional" state abbreviations rather than postal codes (e.g., Pa. rather than PA). There is no traditional abbreviation for Ohio. To find the right one, use a dictionary or consult *The Chicago Manual of Style*.
Book, multivolume	Muste, M., Aberle, J., Admiraal, D., Ettema, R., Garcia, M. H., Lyn, D., Nikora, V., Rennie, C., eds. (2017). *Experimental hydraulics: Methods, instrumentation, data processing and management*, 2 vols., CRC Press, Boca Raton, Fla.
Chapter in book	Wada, A., Huang, Y., and Bertero, V. (2004). "Innovative strategies in earthquake engineering." *Earthquake engineering: From engineering seismology to performance-based engineering*, Y. Bozorgnia and V. Bertero, eds., CRC Press, Boca Raton, Fla., 637–675.
Book, online or e-book	Haskell, D., Pillay, A., and Steinhorn, C., eds. (2000). *Model theory, algebra, and geometry* (Online), MSRI Publications 39, http://www.msri.org/publications/books/Book39/contents.html. Keith, D. (2013). *A Case for Climate Engineering* (Kindle version), MIT Press, Cambridge, Mass. ▸ For internet sources, you might omit "Online," since that's clear from the URL. To cite a Kindle book or other electronic edition, put that in the parentheses instead of "Online"—e.g., (Kindle version).
Patent	Entsfellner, C. and Heuermann, H. (2017). "Vectorial network analyser," US Patent 9,801,082, October 24.

FAQS ABOUT *ALL* REFERENCE STYLES

. . . .

WHAT SHOULD YOU CITE?

Do I need to cite everything I use in the paper?
Pretty much. Cite anything you rely on for data or authoritative opinions. Cite both quotes and paraphrases. Cite personal communications such as emails, text messages, interviews, or conversations with professors if you rely on them for your paper. If you rely heavily on any single source, make that clear, either with multiple citations or with somewhat fewer citations plus a clear statement that you are relying on a particular source for a particular topic.

There is one exception. Don't cite sources for facts that are well-known to your audience. It's overkill to cite any authorities for the signing of the Declaration of Independence on July 4, 1776. There will be time enough to footnote them when you start discussing the politics of the Continental Congress.

How many citations does a paper have, anyway?
It varies and there is no exact number, but a couple per page is common in well-researched papers. More is fine. If there are no citations for several pages in a row, something's probably wrong. Most likely you just forgot to include them. You need to go back and fix the problem.

How many different sources should I use?
That depends on how complicated your subject is, how intensively you've studied it, and how long your paper is. If it is a complex subject or one that is debated intensely, you'll need to reflect that with multiple sources—some to present facts, some to cover different sides of the issue. On the other hand, if it's a short paper on a straightforward topic, you might need

only a couple of sources. If you are unsure, ask what your professor expects for your topic. While you're talking, you might also ask about the best sources to use.

In any case, don't base longer, more complex papers on two or three sources, even if they are very good ones. Your paper should be more than a gloss on others' work (unless it is specifically an analysis of that scholar's work). It should be an original work that stands on its own. Use a variety of sources and make sure they include a range of opinions on any controversial topic.

You certainly don't need to agree with all sides. You are not made of rubber. But at least for longer papers and hotly debated topics, you need to show that you have read different views, wrestled with varied ideas, and responded to the most important points.

By the way, your notes can be negative citations as well as positive. You are welcome to disagree openly with a source, or you can simply say, "For an alternative view, see . . ."

WHAT GOES IN A CITATION?

Can I include discussion or analysis in notes?

Yes, for most styles, *except in the sciences.* Footnotes or endnotes are fine spots to add brief insights that bear on your paper topic but would distract from your narrative if they were included in the text. Just remember that you still need to edit these discursive notes, just as you do the rest of your writing. And don't let them become a major focus of your writing effort. The text is the main event.

If you use in-text citations such as (Tarcov, 2017) and want to add some explanatory notes, you'll have to add them as a special set of citations. They are usually marked with a superscript number, such as (Tarcov, 2017).[3] In this case, note 3 would be the explanatory text.

If you are writing in the sciences and already using superscripts for the citation-sequence system, you're better off avoiding explanatory notes entirely. If you really need to include one or two, mark them with an asterisk or other symbol. In this system you cannot use numbered citations for anything except references.

Some styles, notably Chicago and MLA, use shortened titles in citations. What's the best way to shorten a title?

One standard way to shorten a title is to drop the initial article and any other needless words, including anything in the subtitle (following the colon). That is, focus on the key terms to identify the subject of the work. These aren't necessarily the first words in the title. And sometimes a title is already short and doesn't need to be shorter. So for example:

Long form	*Guardians of Language: The Grammarian and Society in Late Antiquity*
	How to Write a BA Thesis
	"Situating Kingship within an Embryonic Frame of Masculinity in Early India"
	"Autonomous Pigs"
Short form	*Guardians of Language*
	BA Thesis
	"Situating Kingship" or (depending on the topic of your paper)
	"Embryonic Frame of Masculinity"
	"Autonomous Pigs"

In the new MLA style, the rules are slightly different. To shorten a title in this style, include the first noun with any preceding adjectives. If the title does not begin with a noun phrase, just use the first word, as long as it's clear which item from the Works Cited list you're referencing. So for the examples above you would shorten thus:

Short form (MLA)	*Guardians*
	How
	"Situating"
	"Autonomous Pigs"

In the sciences, I'm supposed to abbreviate journal titles. Where do I find these abbreviations?

The easiest way is to look at the first page of the article you are citing. It usually includes the abbreviation and often the full citation for the article. You can also go to various websites assembled by reference librarians, listing journal abbreviations in many fields. One useful resource is "All That JAS: Journal Abbreviation Sources," compiled by Gerry McKiernan, science and technology librarian and bibliographer at Iowa State, and available at http://www.abbreviations.com/jas.asp. And there's always the

National Library of Medicine's publicly accessible database of tens of thousands of journals, available at http://www.ncbi.nlm.nih.gov/journals—and by no means limited to medical titles.

What about citing a work I've found in someone else's notes? Do I need to cite the place where I discovered the work?
This issue comes up all the time because it's one of the most important ways we learn about other works and other ideas. Reading a book by E. L. Jones, for example, you find an interesting citation to Adam Smith. As it turns out, you are more interested in Smith's point than in Jones's commentary, so you decide to cite Smith. That's fine—you can certainly cite Smith—but how should you handle it?

There's a choice. One way is to follow the paper trail from Jones's note to Adam Smith's text, read the relevant part, and simply cite it, with no reference at all to Jones. That's completely legitimate for books like Smith's that are well known in their field. You are likely to come across such works in your normal research, and you don't need to cite Jones as the guide who sent you there. To do that honestly, though, you have to go to Smith and read the relevant parts.

The rule is simple: *cite only texts you have actually used and would have found in the normal course of your research*, not obscure texts used by someone else or works you know about only secondhand. You don't have to read several hundred pages of Adam Smith. You do have to read the relevant pages in Smith—the ones you cite. Remember the basic principle: *when you say you did the work yourself, you actually did it.*

Alternatively, if you don't have time to read Smith yourself (or if the work is written in a language you cannot read), you can cite the text this way: "Smith, *Wealth of Nations*, 123, as discussed in Jones, *European Miracle*." Normally you don't need to cite the page in Jones, but you can if you wish. An in-text citation would look different but accomplish the same thing: (Smith 123, qtd. in Jones).

This alternative is completely honest too. You are referencing Smith's point but saying you found it in Jones. This follows another equally important principle: *when you rely on someone else's work, you cite it*. In this case you are relying on Jones, not Smith himself, as your source for Smith's point.

Follow the same rule if Jones leads you to a work that is unusual or obscure *to you*, a work you discovered only because Jones did the detailed research, found it, and told you about it. For example, one of Jones's citations is to a 1668 book by Paul Rycaut, titled *The Present State of the Ottoman Empire*. I'm not an expert on the Ottoman Empire and certainly would not have discovered that book myself. Frankly, I'd never even heard of it until Jones mentioned it. So I'd cite it as (Rycaut 54, cited in Jones). I can do that without going to the Rycaut book. On the other hand, if I were a student of Ottoman history and Jones had simply reminded me of Rycaut's work, I could cite it directly. To do that honestly, however, I would need to go to the Rycaut volume and read the relevant passage.

Some scholars, unfortunately, sneak around this practice. They don't give credit where credit is due. They simply cite Rycaut even if they've never heard of him before, or they cite Smith even if they haven't read the passage. One result (and it really happens!) could be that Jones made a mistake in his citation and the next scholar repeated the error. It's really a twofold blunder: an incorrect citation and a false assertion that the writer used Smith as a source.

The specific rules here are less important than the basic concepts:

- Cite only texts you found in the normal course of your research and have actually used.
- Cite all your sources openly and honestly.

Follow these and you'll do just fine.

BIBLIOGRAPHY (OR REFERENCE LIST)

Do I need to have a bibliography or reference list?
Yes, for all styles *except* complete Chicago notes. If you use complete Chicago citations, not the short versions, the first note for each item gives readers complete information, including the title and publisher, so you don't need a bibliography. (You are welcome to include a bibliography if you use Chicago style, but you don't have to, unless your professor requires it.)

All other styles require a bibliography or reference list (remember: essentially the same thing) for a simple reason. The notes themselves are too brief to provide full information on the sources.

Should my bibliography include the general background reading I did for the paper?

The answer depends on how much you relied on a particular reading and which reference style you use. MLA, APA, and science bibliographies include only the works you have actually cited. Chicago-style bibliographies are more flexible and can include works you haven't cited in a note.

My advice is this: If a work was really useful to you, then check to make sure you have acknowledged that debt somewhere with a citation. After you've cited it once, the work will appear in your bibliography regardless of which style you use. If a particular background reading wasn't important in your research, don't worry about citing it.

Does the bibliography raise any questions about my work?

Yes, readers will scan your bibliography to see what kinds of sources you used and whether they are the best ones. There are five problems to watch out for:

- old, out-of-date works
- bias in the overall bibliography
- omission of major works in your subject
- reliance on poor or weak sources
- excessive reliance on one or two sources

These are not really problems with the bibliography as such. They are problems with the text that become apparent when someone looks at the bibliography.

Old sources are great for some purposes but antiquated for others. Many consider Gibbon's *Decline and Fall of the Roman Empire* the greatest historical work ever written. But no one today would use it as a major secondary source on Rome or Byzantium. Too much impressive research has been completed in the two centuries since Gibbon wrote. So if you were writing about current views of Byzantium or ancient Rome, *Decline and Fall* would be out of date. Relying on it would cast a shadow on your research. On the other hand, if you were writing about great historical works, eighteenth-century perspectives, or changing views about Byzantium, using Gibbon would be perfectly appropriate, perhaps essential.

"Old" means different things in different fields. A work published ten or fifteen years ago might be reasonably current in history, literature, and some areas of mathematics, depending on how fast those fields are changing. For a discipline moving at warp speed like genetics, an article might be out of date within a year. A paper in molecular genetics filled with citations from 2010 or even 2015 would cast serious doubt on the entire project. Whatever your field, you should rely on the best works and make sure they have not been superseded by newer, better research.

Bias, omission of key works, and overreliance on a few sources reveal other problems.[1] Bias means you have looked at only one side of a multifaceted issue. Your bibliography might indicate bias if it lists readings on only one side of a contested issue. Omitting an authoritative work not only impoverishes your work but leaves readers wondering if you studied the topic carefully.

The remedy for all these problems is the same. For longer, more complex papers at least, you need to read a variety of major works in your subject and indicate that with citations.

However long (or short!) your paper, make sure your sources are considered solid and reliable. Your professors and teaching assistants can really help here. They know the literature and should be valuable guides.

QUOTATIONS

I am using a quotation that contains a second quote within it. How do I handle the citation?

Let's say your paper includes the following sentence:

> As Michael Mandelbaum observes, "the English writer G. K. Chesterton once said America is 'a country with the soul of a church.'"[99]

Of course you'll cite Mandelbaum, but do you need to cite *his* source for the Chesterton quote? No. It's not required. In some cases, however, your readers will benefit from a little extra information about the quote within a quote. You can easily do that in your footnote or endnote:

[99] Michael Mandelbaum, *Mission Failure: America and the World, 1993–2014* (Oxford: Oxford University Press, 2016), 9. The quote is a para-

---

1. Ralph Berry, *The Research Project: How to Write It* (London: Routledge, 2000), 108–9.

phrase from Chesterton's *What I Saw in America* (New York: Dodd, Mead, 1922).

I am quoting from some Spanish and French books and doing the translations myself. How should I handle the citations?
Just include the words "my translation" immediately after the quote or in the citation. You don't need to do this each time. After the first quotation, you can tell your readers that you are translating all quotes yourself. Then cite the foreign-language text you are using.

In some papers you might want to include quotes in both the original and translation. That's fine. Either the translation or the original can come first; the other follows in parentheses or brackets. For instance:

In Madame Pompadour's famous phrase, "Après nous, le déluge" (After us, the flood). As it turned out, she was right.

ONLINE SOURCES

I was reading a blog and found some information I want to cite. But the blog is not the original source. It links to some website for the information. Which one should I cite?
It's best to cite the location where the information originated. In this case, that's the website rather than the blog. To cite the webpage honestly, however, you actually need to go there and check it out.

Unfortunately, you can't always find the original source. One blog links to another, which links to a third, and you can't figure out who in this daisy chain originated the information. What should you do then? First, if you cannot find the original source, cite the best source you have and note that it says the information originates elsewhere (or does not indicate its source for the information). "Blog A, based on information from website B." Second, if you cannot find the original source, be very careful about using the information at all. You don't have a good way to tell fact from urban legend.

These rules are similar to those for print sources: Cite the source that originates the information, not a secondary source, if you can. And remember that to cite any source directly, you *must* go there and check out the information firsthand. You cannot just copy a citation from someone else.

For online sources, do I need to include the date I accessed the material in my citation?

It depends. Some citation styles require an access date, but most do not. However, it's always a good idea to record the date you accessed the material in case you do need it. For example, if a website does not have an official date stating when it was published, posted, or most recently modified, you might need to include an access date to help establish at least some timeframe for when the material on the site was viewable. Check the examples in the relevant chapter. Some instructors might also require access dates even if the official style does not. It never hurts to ask.

I know what a URL is, but what is a DOI? How do I know which one to include? Do I ever include both?

A DOI is a Digital Object Identifier, part of an international system for identifying and exchanging intellectual property online. It is usually a string of numbers, such as 10.1086/681095. It should appear at or near the top of sources, like journal articles, that are part of this system.

The correct way to include a DOI in a citation is by adding https://doi .org/ before the number. So for the DOI above, the citation should say: https://doi.org/10.1086/681095. This effectively makes the DOI into a URL. (This is a relatively new requirement, so some of the style guides do not yet include it, but I have added it in all the chapters here.) If you paste or type that full string into your browser, you will be taken immediately to the source—try it!

DOIs are generally preferable to other types of URLs in citations because they never change. That means anyone who wants to look at the source you're citing will be able to find it. As you've probably discovered, URLs can sometimes change or disappear, which makes your citations less useful. But most general websites, like Wikipedia or nytimes.com or YouTube, don't have (or don't list) DOIs, so you have to cite the URL.

If both are available, most citation styles now either recommend or at least allow DOIs in place of URLs. You don't need to include both in your citations. Check the relevant chapter for guidelines.

What about other online identifiers, like PMIDs?

PMIDs appear in many medical and biological journals. The abbreviation stands for PubMed Identifier. The PubMed database includes virtually all biomedical journals plus some preprints. It is available online at http://

www.ncbi.nlm.nih.gov/pubmed/ and has a tutorial for new users. This invaluable database was developed by the National Center for Biotechnology Information at the National Library of Medicine.

Other specialized fields have their own electronic identifiers. Physics, for example, has arXiv, an extensive online archive with identifying numbers for preprints (prepublication articles), which classify them by subfield.

You are not required to list any of these electronic identifiers in your citations, but doing so may help you and your readers.

Tip on citing online sources: as you take notes, write down the

- URL or DOI for the website or webpage (copy and paste to avoid errors)
- name or description of the page or site
- date you accessed it

I've just explained the difference between URLs and DOIs (and other types of online identifiers). I also covered why it's a good idea to record access dates, even if you don't need to include them in your citations.

Writing the name or description of a website is useful because then if the URL changes (as they sometimes do), you still can find it by searching.

If sites are particularly useful, bookmark them. If you add several sites for a paper, create a new folder named for the paper and drop the URLs into that. A folder will gather the sites in a single location and keep them from getting lost in your long list of favorites.

Finally, whenever you cite something that looks as if it is likely to change or disappear from the internet sometime tomorrow or even next year, it is a good idea to print it out and save a copy of it. This holds for such things as blog posts, comments on social networking sites, articles in wikis, and even online news stories: anything that might be redesigned, deleted, discontinued, or subtly (or not so subtly) altered without notice. If you're citing something like the online version of an article in a scholarly journal, however, you probably don't need to save a copy. Most journals have pretty strict rules about making and posting revisions, and they usually do a good job of archiving past issues.

Aren't there citation management programs that can handle all these issues for me?

Yes and no. There are some well-known programs that can capture information from library catalogs and other online databases and format it for you in most of the citation styles covered in this book.

It sounds easy, but these programs have significant limitations. They work best with books and recent journal articles, where the source information is usually standardized and available for download. They are less helpful when you want to cite a source that's older or more unusual—perhaps a letter in a physical archive, a video on YouTube, a painting in a gallery, a text message, or an article in a long-defunct newspaper. There simply isn't a database with full information about these items.

These differences in source materials mean that citation software is most useful if you are mostly citing books and recent journals or if you're in the physical and biological sciences or the quantitative social sciences. It is less useful if your sources are more diverse and therefore less likely to be encoded in standard databases, as in the humanities and interpretative social sciences.

Let me fill in some details. Programs like EndNote, RefWorks, and Zotero allow you to build libraries of source citations and plug them directly into your papers. You can pick from a variety of citation styles, and you can easily change from one style to another. The programs are designed to work with standardized databases, although you can type in the information if it's not available online.

The good news is that these databases are increasingly common. Most library catalogs and other bibliographic databases are designed so you can download citations directly into the software, and more and more publishers are following suit with their online catalogs. But as with any new program, you'll need to spend some time learning the ins and outs.

This learning process may take longer in the humanities and social sciences, where the range of sources means you'll need to do some extra work. Instead of just pushing a button and downloading your data, you'll often need to pull up a blank record and enter the data from scratch. These records have a specific structure for entering data. You'll need to follow that structure, enter the information carefully, avoid typos, and use any punctuation required by the program. In one program I use, for instance, multiple authors must be separated by semicolons. Not commas. Semicolons.

Later, when you insert citations into your papers, it's wise to double-check the output and make sure it's accurate. That applies to the materials you've downloaded from databases too. If the original material was encoded incorrectly, the citations will show it. I know. I once printed out a citation for a recent edition of Plato's work. It said the editor was Plato's coauthor. Actually Plato did not have coauthors, and if he did, he would have had to wait twenty-five hundred years for this one. I returned to the software and restored Plato to his rightful place as a single (and singular) author.

Before you start using the software, it helps to know which citation style you'll be using for your papers. It's not essential, but it helps. You'll know what to enter for each type of source, and you'll know what you can skip (each record will have spaces for countless details). You might even be able to catch what the software has missed and fix it.

One final point. If you are using your university's citation software and plan to continue your studies, perhaps at another university, you should check with your university and learn about exporting your citation library. If your citation data is stored on the university's servers, you'll need to make arrangements to move it. After you spent all that time building your library, you'll want to keep it with you as you continue your education.

Over time, the software is sure to get better and better and the databases more comprehensive. But right now it's still a mixed bag.

THANKS

Since this book covers citations and academic honesty across the university, it was essential to speak with specialists from different fields. I have done so for each edition of the book.

I was fortunate to receive advice on science labs from Tom Christianson, Nancy Schwartz, and Paul Streileman (biological sciences), Vera Dragisich (chemistry), and Stuart Gazes (physics). All have headed lab programs at the University of Chicago. Diane Herrmann, who headed the mathematics major for many years, offered a number of valuable comments about study groups. So did biologist Michael LaBarbera, who reviewed the chapter on academic honesty. For language learning I spoke with Vincent Bertolini, Helma Dik, and Peter White, all at Chicago, and Robert Kaster at Princeton. For honor codes I spoke with Susan Pratt Rosato of Notre Dame and Keir Lieber of Georgetown. William S. Strong and Perry Cartwright offered wise counsel on plagiarism, grounded in their work on copyrights and contractual issues for the University of Chicago Press. James Marquardt, of Lake Forest College, added helpful ideas about class participation. Physicist Thomas Rosenbaum, formerly provost at Chicago and now president of Cal Tech, provided valuable comments on several chapters. George Gavrilis's suggestion prompted the addition of a chapter on taking notes.

On all these issues I spoke with students from colleges across the country. I particularly wish to thank Erik Cameron, John Schuessler, Jonathan Grossberg, and Jennifer London for their reflections on student experiences.

On general issues of academic honesty, I spoke with advisers, counselors, and deans who handle these issues every day. Many of these issues go through the dean of students' office. I was fortunate to receive help from two longtime professionals in that office. Susan Art was the University of Chicago's dean of students for many years; Jean Treese was associate dean and head of the college's Orientation Program. They know the importance of doing honest work and have seen the practical difficulties students face. I learned from their experience.

For the citation chapters, special thanks in this edition go to Susannah

Engstrom for her painstaking research on updates to the styles and new source types and examples. Thanks as well to Russell David Harper, chief reviser of the *Chicago Manual of Style* and the citation chapters of Turabian, for his insights. From previous editions, I remain grateful to Jenni Fry, Gerald Rosenberg, Janet Dodd, Karen J. Patrias, Peggy Robinson, Sharon Jennings, and Peggy Perkins for their advice on specific citation styles or issues.

Thanks to the University of Chicago Press, I have worked with outstanding editors. Linda Halvorson solicited the first edition, improved every aspect of it, and offered encouragement at every turn. Paul Schellinger handled the second edition with his usual professionalism. Mary Laur, who edited the latest volume, deserves special thanks for helping with all three editions. As senior editor for this one, she supervised every detail and offered valuable suggestions to improve the text.

Those I have thanked hold very different jobs on campus, from academic publishing to science labs to dean's offices. Yet they share a common purpose. All are working to foster genuine learning and honest accomplishments, the heart of a college education. Their generous help made this book possible.

INDEX